THE NEW
DIGITAL
SHORELINE

How Web 2.0 and Millennials Are Revolutionizing Higher Education

ROGER McHANEY

Foreword by Sir John Daniel

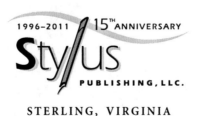

1996–2011 15TH ANNIVERSARY

Stylus
PUBLISHING, LLC.

STERLING, VIRGINIA

COPYRIGHT © 2011 BY
STYLUS PUBLISHING, LLC.

Published by Stylus Publishing, LLC
22883 Quicksilver Drive
Sterling, Virginia 20166-2102

Library of Congress Cataloging-in-Publication-Data
McHaney, Roger.
    The new digital shoreline : how Web 2.0 and millennials are revolutionizing higher education / Roger McHaney.
        p.   cm.
    Includes bibliographical references and index.
    ISBN 978-1-57922-459-2 (cloth : alk. paper)
    ISBN 978-1-57922-460-8 (pbk. : alk. paper)
    ISBN 978-1-57922-601-5 (library networkable e-edition)
    ISBN 978-1-57922-602-2 (consumer e-edition)
    1. Internet in higher education.   2. Web 2.0.
3. Educational change.   4. Generation Y.
I. Title.
LB1044.87.M34   2011
378.1′7344678—dc22
                                        2010043057

13-digit ISBN: 978-1-57922-459-2 (cloth)
13-digit ISBN: 978-1-57922-460-8 (paper)
13-digit ISBN: 978-1-57922-601-5 (library networkable e-edition)
13-digit ISBN: 978-1-57922-602-2 (consumer e-edition)

Printed in the United States of America

All first editions printed on acid free paper
that meets the American National Standards Institute
Z39-48 Standard.

Bulk Purchases

Quantity discounts are available for use in workshops and for staff development.
Call 1-800-232-0223

First Edition, 2011

10   9   8   7   6   5   4   3   2   1

To Mark, Matthew, Megan, and Stacy McHaney,
four tech-savvy millennials
who provided incredible insight
and inspiration for this book

CONTENTS

ACKNOWLEDGMENTS

THE RESEARCH CONDUCTED for this project was supported by Kansas State University's Office of the Provost and the Coffman Chair for University Distinguished Teaching Scholars. Additional support was provided by Kansas State University's College of Business Administration and Dean Yar Ebadi. K-State's Center for the Advancement of Teaching and Learning and Dr. Victoria Clegg provided excellent resources for this project, as did K-State's Division of Continuing Education. Shalin Hai-Jew gave expert help transforming the screen captures into publishable images for this book. The New Boston Creative Group developed several high-quality figures for this project. My gratitude goes to the family of Daniel D. Burke and their generous gift that helped support the research needed to complete this book.

Thanks to Chris Anderson for permission to use *The Long Tail*.

Heartfelt thanks go to John von Knorring. His ideas and guidance transformed a hodgepodge of musings into a book.

Special thanks: Annette McHaney offered countless hours of proofreading and thought-provoking help to make this project possible.

FOREWORD

TWENTY YEARS AGO no less a guru than Peter Drucker forecast that large campus universities, like Roger McHaney's Kansas State, would not survive long into the 21st century. Until recently, however, it seemed that traditional universities could retort, with Mark Twain, that reports of their death were greatly exaggerated. The 2009 recession has changed that. Cuts in public funding to universities across the western world have been described as fiscal carnage, while for-profit institutions are moving resolutely to poach students from public institutions with online programs that are more tightly focused and may offer better value for money.

Furthermore, today's young people, the millennials that the author describes with the empathy of an insider, face an uncertain future. The 20th century assumption that each generation would have higher living standards than its parents no longer seems valid. Middle-class incomes are static in real terms and some of the knowledge-based service employment to which American graduates aspire seems destined to follow an earlier wave of manufacturing jobs to the developing countries of Africa and Asia.

The New Digital Shoreline proposes antidotes to these dispiriting trends with verve and optimism. By embracing contemporary information and communication technologies, faculty can sustain the traditional model of the professor and the class instead of becoming exchangeable nodes in large learning systems. By bringing the rich technologies of their everyday lives to their studies in college, young adults can acquire the flexibility of mind, the creativity of spirit, and the networks of contacts that will ensure their success in a fiercely competitive world.

It is an appealing scenario, persuasively presented. Since he underestimates neither the scope nor the scale of the transformations required, Roger McHaney begins with a compelling analysis of the individual and organizational psychology of change, enlivened by the personal allusions and experiences that recur through the entire book. This is followed by an informed and sympathetic presentation of the habits and attitudes of what he calls the tech-savvy millennials, the term digital natives having now fallen into disfavor.

McHaney then gives us a masterly and authoritative presentation of the topography of the new digital shoreline that will be invaluable to his fellow faculty. Beginning with the more orthodox and established technologies, the platforms for learning, he moves on to explore the characteristics of Web 2.0 and social learning in general before zeroing in on content, applications, and emergent behavior. The analysis is wisely critical. Some technologies are more promising or more acceptable than others. For example, most students seem not to want to meet their professors on their personal Facebook pages, whereas the Internet has more to contribute to academic work than the mobile phone—except as a vehicle for taking the Internet with you. He notes that the formal processes of virtual learning environments—or learning management systems—are less necessary in the Web 2.0 world where students can construct their own digital spaces. However, in order not to spend more time managing those learning spaces than working on content, students do like some continuity of formats from course to course.

Against this backdrop, chapter 6 examines students' expectations of college, reminding us that they are purposeful people who seek relevant skills and knowledge that are taught efficiently while giving them a meaningful experience. Caricatures of four types of instructor, Professors Luddite, Emulate, Digital, and Overenthusiastic show how it is possible to miss the target of student expectations in different ways.

Chapter 7 is the heart of the book and is a brilliant example of what Ernest Boyer identified in 1990 as the scholarship of teaching. The author shows how an instructor's pedagogy can be built on learning theory in various ways. After summarizing the theories of behaviorism, cognitivism, constructivism, and connectivism McHaney argues that the good teacher must have several arrows in his quiver. Depending on the topic, instructivism, constructivism, or connectivism may be the most appropriate style. The versatile teacher should know which to use when and the author gives worked examples to guide the choice.

All this is distilled into simple precepts in a final chapter that encourages teachers to "just start" engaging with the sea of futures that lies beyond the digital shoreline. The presentation is enthusiastic without being starry eyed. Yes, digital technologies make it easier for weak or lazy students to get by. Yes, there is the danger, thoroughly explored in Nicholas Carr's, *The Shallows,* that too much reliance on the "interruption technologies" of the digital age can prevent deep learning. However, the clock will not be turned back and higher education must exploit the fact that today's students bathe in a much richer environment of informal learning than their predecessors.

Martin Bean, an Australian-American who moved from Microsoft HQ to head the UK Open University in 2010, argues that the task of universities today is to provide paths from this informal cloud of learning toward more formal study for those who wish to take them. Good paths will provide continuity of technology. Many millions of people around the world first encounter the Open University through iTunes, its TV broadcasts, or the resources on its OpenLearn website. The thousands who then elect to enroll as students will find themselves studying in similar digital environments.

The Open University is a large and successful teaching-learning system with a worldwide reach. Roger McHaney's concern in this book is primarily for the future of the public universities that constitute the bedrock of higher education in the United States. He has provided us with a lively yet scholarly guide to the changes that these institutions must make if they are to attract today's tech-savvy millennials to their campuses and offer them engaging programs. There is no time to waste. As McHaney recalls, we tend to overestimate the importance of new trends in the short term while underestimating their longer-term impact. It is already later than we think.

Sir John Daniel
President
Commonwealth of Learning

PREFACE

IGHER EDUCATION is facing a new digital shoreline largely shaped by forces outside its control. Two of these forces, Web 2.0 and the arrival of tech-savvy millennials, demand that educators reconsider learning theories, pedagogies, and interactions with students and peers. It is higher education's job to engage new learners without sacrificing good pedagogy and to somehow teach and learn at the same time.

To do this, educators must explore how today's student is different from yesterday's and understand how she or he learns. These students aren't necessarily smarter or technologically superior, but they do have different expectations. Many of them have spent their formative years using a wide array of technology. According to research conducted by the Pew Research Center and others, important attributes characterize tech-savvy millennials and distinguish them from past generations.

First, this group has been empowered by social networking and other forms of convenient, computer-enabled, and mobile communication capabilities to try on various identities and personas. Second, this group has incorporated time-shifting into its lifestyle. For millenials, waiting is undesirable at best and intolerable under most circumstances. Third, members of this group have been endowed with the ability to personalize and customize their world to a degree never before possible. Finally, the tech-savvy millennial has a variety of delightful and promising characteristics. For instance, many are creative, innovative beings. They have the capability to filter, timeslice, commoditize their attention, and synthesize information. They are forging the boundaries of the new digital frontier in ways that never could have been foreseen just five years ago. On the darker side, these same individuals have little regard for their own or other's online privacy, they have developed mechanisms for creating a social order on the Web, and they may behave in ways that prior generations find questionable.

Where do teachers fit on the new shoreline? For a start, tech-savvy millennials don't always recognize they are living in an interesting transition period. In Arthur C. Clarke's third law of prediction, he states: "Any sufficiently advanced technology is indistinguishable from magic" (Clarke, 1962). Today's teachers can learn from this magic to develop fuller pedagogical experiences for students. A number of important technologies have converged to enable this transition. Among these are networked computer systems, interaction devices, content development tools, video game systems, and mobile smart devices. Added to the mix are virtual learning environments (VLEs) meant to leverage the power of the Web within the safety of a controlled classroom.

These platforms converge by virtue of Web 2.0 ideas and technologies. The concept behind Web 2.0 as a new way of using Internet technologies comprises five major, interrelated components: social computing, social media, content sharing, filtering/recommendations, and Web applications. These components can be integrated into classroom pedagogy to provide richer knowledge delivery to the tech-savvy millennial.

For instance, vast free-information resources have reshaped how knowledge is stored and communicated. Information nodes form the basis for personal learning networks and change the way people work and interact. In order to effectively use this emerging information, tools have been created to filter, find, and sort what is needed. Among these, social bookmarking and tagging have become indispensable. With abundant information comes a variety of applications for personal computers and mobile devices. This puts the tech-savvy millennial in the middle of an emerging world filled with new possibilities and behaviors.

Like many business transformations enabled by the Internet and mobile devices, changes in education partially are fueled by a bottom-up dynamic. For higher education, this means our students want to see new media reflected in the delivery of learning material on platforms of their choosing. Is this reason enough to enact fundamental changes to teaching and learning? Does it have to be a choice between new technology and sound pedagogy? The answer to both questions, of course, is no. We educators, however, do need to anticipate change and reinvent ourselves while preserving good pedagogical practices. Achieving this will take more than adding technology to our teaching practices. It means stepping back and learning about opportunities for improving learning theory and then developing smart approaches that rebuild our practice in ways more suitable for the emerging world.

In chapter 1 we define the new shoreline. In chapter 2, we look at characteristics of the tech-savvy millennial to develop an understanding of our future students' mind-sets. In chapters 3 through 5 we explore the technological underpinnings of higher education's new digital shoreline from both platform and application standpoints, together with impacts technology is having on teaching and learning. Chapters 6 and 7 provide holistic views of pedagogy on the new shoreline and encourage rethinking learning theory in ways that consider characteristics of the tech-savvy millennial and good teaching practices. Chapter 8 summarizes and offers future musings.

The forces of change encroaching on today's universities are a summons to action. Higher education must face its new reality head-on and be progressive.

CHAPTER ONE

DISCOVERING A NEW SHORELINE

The forces of technological change are having a major impact on higher education. The spread of social media, the ubiquity of smart phones and new devices like tablet computers, and the growth of wireless communications are changing student expectations. It is higher education's job to engage learners without sacrificing good pedagogy, and to somehow teach them and learn from them at the same time.

Obsessions

IMAGINE FOR A MOMENT you encounter something amazing, power-ful, and perhaps even seductive. Initially you think about it at odd moments while engaged in other activities. But this phenomenon exerts an obsessive force that affects you and everyone who encounters it. Over time, the impact is overwhelming, as you perceive less and less reality and focus more on the entity—until it becomes all you think about. Soon, you have a new reality: a captive life.

Many things can be described in this way. For some people the result might be healthy. They may obsess about diet or exercise. For others, it may be unhealthy. They might become heavy drug users, alcoholics, or Internet addicts. There is a fine line between a controlled obsession and one that spirals out of control and becomes a hazard to physical or mental health.

Educational Tipping Point

Just like people, institutions can have obsessions. Some institutions are obsessed with public image. For many, it is profit. For others it is growth.

1

Sometimes the obsession results in positive change. Other times, it ends in disaster.[1]

In his book, *The Tipping Point*, Malcolm Gladwell talks about the nature of these obsessions from a less personal perspective focusing on societal fads (Gladwell, 2000). His main interests revolve around how local trends can trigger obsessions among the masses. He provides an explanatory framework and relates the causes to social archetypes and key individuals. Although Gladwell's book doesn't report anything new, it does illuminate the process nicely.[2]

For centuries, people have been fascinated by examples of widespread obsession and potentially dire consequences. For instance, the ancient tale of the Zahir is a well-known story of obsession brought to life in the short story "The Zahir" by critically acclaimed Argentine writer Jorge Luis Borges. He describes the insidious effects of obsession through this tale based on seventeenth-century Islamic folklore (Borges, 2004). According to legend, the Zahir is an object that ensnares anyone who so much as looks at it. In past societies, the Zahir has been described as a tiger, an astrolabe, the bottom of a well, a vein in a column of marble in a mosque, and other things. In fact, Borges says anything has the capability of becoming a Zahir, but there can only be a single Zahir at any given time.

In the story, a coin representing freewill becomes a Zahir. It fills the main character's dreams and eventually his waking moments, too. He decides to break the obsession and free himself. He has to get rid of the coin even though, at some level, he loves it. In the end, he carefully avoids looking at street signs and numbers, and uses the Zahir to buy a drink in a nameless bar. If he doesn't break the Zahir's grip, he will lose his ability to perceive external reality. In that state, he would discover that to "live and to dream [would be] synonymous." At that point, he also would know that he isn't the only one obsessed. In the story he says, "When every man on earth thinks, day and night, of the Zahir, which one will be dream and which reality, the earth or the Zahir?" (Borges, 2004, pp. 87–88).

This inspires the question: *What might be a Zahir in our world today?*

Our Zahir

Our Zahir, of course, is information technology and the new global, mobile interconnectedness we share. This is the change poised to strike higher education and the ways we teach our students. In Gladwell's book *The Tipping Point*, he calls societal obsessions "epidemics" and hypothesizes about why some become fads and disappear and others permanently change society. I believe the university community is rapidly approaching a tipping point after which teaching and learning will never be the same again. Those who embrace the new technologies will thrive and excel. Those who choose not to see it will fade away.

In essence, a tipping point is that magic moment when an idea, trend, or social behavior crosses a threshold and spreads like wildfire. And, according to Gladwell, three agents of change—the *law of the few*, the *stickiness factor*, and the *power of context*—precipitate these changes. I examined Gladwell's ideas and their relevance to teaching and learning by conducting face-to-face interviews with about 50 excellent teachers and hundreds of students, and although they may not have been obsessed to the extent of Borges's character in *The Zahir*, they were all aware of the changes impacting all of us.

The Law of the Few

Gladwell uses the Pareto principle to explain a source of societal obsession. The Pareto principle states that 80 percent of the "work" of any enterprise will be done by 20 percent of the participants. Disease may spread in the same way: 80 percent of the cases spread from 20 percent of the population. Social epidemics work in a similar mode: The efforts of a handful of exceptional people with vision and the ability to make things happen start the wave. Their impact comes from attributes such as being sociable, energetic, knowledgeable, and influential among their peers. These same ideas can be extended into higher education. When a critical mass of 20 percent of teachers uses the new technologies favored by tech-savvy millennials, an irreversible tipping point will occur.

The Players: Mavens, Connectors, and Advocates

According to Gladwell, in order for a fad to become an epidemic, several key players must be in place. He identifies three critical archetypes: *mavens, connectors,* and *salesmen* (for education, I call this last group *advocates*) (Gladwell, 2000).

Mavens Prior to a tipping point, it is not unusual to detect the appearance of mavens, who are intense gatherers of information, ideas, and impressions. It is their nature to detect promising trends. Because of their sensitivity to subtle changes in their environment, mavens are often the first to know when something is afoot. Throughout my interviews with excellent teachers, I detected strong mavenlike tendencies.

Many of these teachers offered suggestions, shared ideas they had read about, described their own experiences, and explained how certain teaching approaches resonate with tech-savvy millennials. They discussed using virtual learning environments to create a sense of community for students and teachers. They talked about using chats, discussion boards, and voice management software such as Wimba. They described how RSS feeds, Web 2.0, and podcasting as well as other innovations have transformed their practices. They discussed mobile devices, simulations, and social video games. Many had foreseen these trends and had enthusiastically begun their own explorations and experiments. Now they were ready and excited to pass on their knowledge to others.

I call this new phenomenon in higher education the advent of the *digital maven*. These individuals gather information and are socially motivated to help others. They are obsessive about the details of using technology. Like Gladwell's mavens, they find ways to solve problems and then meet their emotional needs by helping others in turn.

Digital mavens are natural teachers. In my own distance classes, I find that certain students take on maven roles. We, as facilitators, have to nurture this tendency by providing forums for sharing information about the classroom environment and the use of technology to enable learning. E-learning instructors recognize this and often seek to create a community of practice within their classes that embraces the contributions of the student maven. I discovered the most successful online classes empower their mavens and embrace their contributions.

Larry Jackson is an example of a consummate academic digital maven. For several years at Kansas State University, Larry has extolled the possibilities of using *Second Life* as a teaching tool. He was using it, exploring it, and dreaming about it long before most institutions and teachers had even considered 3-D virtual worlds as having a place in education. Of his own accord, Larry continued to explore, acquire virtual land, build educational facilities, train his staff, and send out reminders to K-State faculty about the ways *Second Life* could be used to enhance our students' educational experiences. After several administrative dead ends and fighting a number of battles, Larry convinced a critical mass of faculty members this was an area that needed exploration. Over time, his voice was heard over the red-tape and above the bureaucratic chatter, and a *Second Life* user group developed. With Larry's support several classes began using the technology, including an online hospitality management class that utilized *Second Life* to practice staging events.

Connectors According to Gladwell, the impact of mavens is amplified when they collaborate with a connector. Connectors are charismatic people with an extensive network of social acquaintances. They cut across economic, professional, and class boundaries and belong to numerous groups. Connectors typically introduce people who share interests but are unlikely to otherwise meet. They effectively distribute a maven's insight and expand his or her impact to wider circles of people. They continually reinvent themselves to span new worlds. Connectors gain prominence by transcending weak social connections and cultivating relationships most people don't have or understand.

Teachers expecting to be effective in the future must become connectors between the world of the tech-savvy millennial, the world of higher education, and the ever changing world of technology. Many faculty members I interviewed provided great examples of their connector activities, moving continually between academic resources, people in industry, online resources, traditional academic information, and digital mavens. New media tools make this possible in ways that didn't exist a short time ago.

Digital connectors tap into the power of online social networks as do tech-savvy millennials, who already have networks of friends linked via websites such as Facebook. Student often wonder why higher education classes don't look more like their world. Why are there walls between different disciplines? Why are we always separating and compartmentalizing rather than integrating and synthesizing? Why do learning management systems cut students off from the real world and sever the connections that power their world? We academics need to respond.

Advocates The advocate is another key person instrumental to a tipping point. Although Gladwell uses the term *salesman*, I prefer to say *advocate* when speaking about higher education. Although modern salesmanship is more about matching customers' needs to solutions, to me, *salesman* evokes the image of a failed Willy Loman (Miller, 1949). On the other hand, the term *advocate* connotes a person who extols benefits and spreads the word of new opportunities. Semantics aside, the role of the salesman/advocate is to help create mass appeal.

People in this role transform a local trend into a widespread phenomenon. Web 2.0 and all its communication channels (mobile and otherwise) have enabled the digital advocate to become an even more powerful force than he or she was a scant five years ago. In the world of higher education, with its conferences, accreditation agencies, blogs, websites, and other vectors of communication, the advocate can have a powerful voice. Advocates may be administrators or even evangelical professors that hit the speaking circuit to provide their view of how learning must evolve.

The Stickiness Factor

Sticky Roles?

Of course, a tipping point needs more than the efforts of mavens, connectors, and advocates. Gladwell further suggests something he calls *stickiness*. Lasting impact requires stickiness. The entity with ultimate stickiness is the Zahir of legend. It is the root of an obsession. As Borges suggests, the Zahir ensnares anyone who so much as looks at it, leaving them in an obsessive state that eventually becomes their reality. Information technology, the platform for education in the tech-savvy millennial's world, has already proven its stickiness. But are our classes moving in this direction? Are they sticky?

Sticky Classes?

Gladwell's use of the term *stickiness* implies that a fad can become a lasting cultural element. Stickiness has also been used to describe the lasting impact of learning acquired during a classroom experience. The potential stickiness of future class material (with its technology components) can be investigated using online learning as a surrogate. In many ways, online classes are pilot studies for classes of the future. Empirical evidence is beginning to emerge regarding the effectiveness of online courses, and it looks promising. In a study of over 18,000 course offerings, Benton et al. (2010) of The IDEA Center[3] indicated that student progress on relevant learning objectives and global ratings of instructor/course effectiveness were similar in online and traditional environments (Benton, Webster, Gross, & Pallette, 2010). My own research is consistent with this finding. For instance, in my series of interviews, online learning faculty, in general, seemed reasonably convinced that their courses are sticky. I heard comments like:

Students can listen to the lectures over and over again until they really get it.

[Students] provide way more comments on the discussion board than I ever get in class.

My students are more motivated because they are taking the class at times that suit their personality and schedule.

International students appreciate being able to regulate the class pace.

Because I teach online classes each semester, I began to wonder about the stickiness factor of the material. Do my online students retain and digest the material to the extent that my classroom students do? To test this, I devised and carried out a very small experiment. I was able to teach both an online and in-class version of the same course during the same semester. I used exactly the same material, presenting one class in person and the other via digitized lectures using Microsoft's Presenter for Power-Point and other online tools. The results are presented in Table 1.1.

Did the exercise show that the students in the two classes retained the material in a similar manner? A statistician would tell you that there is insufficient data to provide an accurate answer to that question: The power is low, there is no generalizability, and so forth. However, a cursory look says that, yes, students who experienced both delivery methods seemed to learn the material. Later, I would like to do a study that is more complete and longitudinal to provide a more definitive answer, but for now, this pilot study suggests that digitally mediated class delivery can work for certain class topics and areas. And the strengths of distance classes can be used to augment on-campus classes.

Other Stickiness Lessons

During my interviews of excellent teachers, many emphasized how they employ asynchronous techniques to increase the impact of their courses (both the online and classroom versions). By being allowed to access material at their own discretion, students are better able to digest and internalize it. Also, the ability to think out responses to questions on discussion boards, to refine answers, and to see what peers and teachers say in response add to the stickiness of any course.

Table 1.1   Stickiness Study

Factor	In-Class	Distance
Student Number	27	12
TEVAL[1]: Teacher Effectiveness (0–5)	4.7	4.9
TEVAL: Increased Desire to Learn About Subject	4.1	4.2
TEVAL: Amount Learned	4.2	4.0
TEVAL: Effort to Learn	4.1	3.9
TEVAL: Realized When Students Did Not Understand	4.4	3.9
Grade Distribution	A—35% B—47% C & below—18%	A—25% B—42% C & below—33%
Final Exam Average Score	83%	85%

1. TEVAL is the K-State Teaching Evaluation Score

These sorts of stickiness-makers are interesting because many of these techniques and tools resemble the leisure-time social activities tech-savvy millennials engage in every day. We are learning how they learn and what they know and then applying this information to their education. As educators, we have an opportunity to create stickier educational experiences by adding lifelong learning opportunities and digital conversations to our students' university experiences.

The Power of Context

Gladwell's final determinant of a tipping point is the *power of context*. Without a doubt, the context for change is here and incredibly evident. Social networks, mobile devices, YouTube, video games, virtual reality, Web 2.0, e-learning and other innovations are transforming life. There is no going back. If the tech-savvy millennial doesn't see value in what we educators provide, no matter how sacred we believe our institutions to be, our systems will be disrupted in unexpected ways.

Technology has already completely changed industries and businesses where content can be digitized by eliminating the middle layer, called *disintermediation.* Here are several quick examples that should already be familiar: the way music is sold and distributed; changes in the real estate business; substitution of online services for traditional stock broker services; the disruption of the newspaper industry; and more recently, the revolution in how books are sold and distributed, with Amazon's Kindle e-book reader and other platforms.

Most of these industries share this characteristic: Digital technologies have the capacity to streamline their distribution system. Whether this means getting content to the consumer more quickly, providing additional information, enhancing data consolidation, or disrupting cumbersome channels of distribution, the Web has made its presence felt in both economic and social ways.

So could professors and teaching be vulnerable? If we merely reiterate what a textbook says, then yes, we could be replaced by a more efficient system. High-quality recorded lectures, e-learning games, and online classes offered by top universities could eliminate expensive professorial labor pools. If academic research is deemed irrelevant or low-impact, society may decide to stop supporting our efforts (Donoghue, 2008).

Educators will be expected to deliver specialized, quality lectures that not only synthesize and integrate cutting-edge material but also interface effectively to the real world and its new social connectedness. What balances this duality of greater access to top professors with a greater demand for specialization? Chris Anderson calls this double-edged sword *The Long Tail* (Anderson, 2006). The very thing that can give higher education a long, healthy life could potentially make it struggle. Additionally, future competition in higher education might not be just between universities. Enabled by Internet connectivity, new knowledge and training may come from many sources.

Briefly, a Long Tale

I grew up in the sparsely populated eastern end of Michigan's Upper Peninsula, specifically in a tiny hamlet called Pickford, which at the time boasted a population of around 600 people. My high school graduating class was fewer than 30 students. For much of my early life, I didn't realize the extent to which I was insulated from the rest of the world. Growing up there would have been much easier with Amazon and the multitude of retailers that have emerged on the Web. But at the time, I was blissfully unaware and happy to consume whatever books, music, television shows, and comic books that publishers, producers, and media moguls made available to my community.

In recent years, of course, the Web has provided virtually unlimited choice in a vast array of areas including music, video, books, and news media. The phenomenon has been described by Chris Anderson in *The Long Tail* (Anderson, 2006). In the past couple years *The Long Tail* has become the pop cultural name for a well-known feature of statistical distributions, also called "heavy tails" (see Figure 1.1). In some cases, less frequent events (found in the tail) can cumulatively outweigh the central (or most frequently occurring items) displayed in the graph. This is happening with regard to music and other digital commodities. Best sellers (i.e., top 100 hits) no longer sell as many copies as they did when centralized control and distribution were in force. Many sales now occur in numerous specialty areas which account for fewer items individually but cumulatively, may exceed best seller sales units.

Researchers Brynjolfsson, Hu, and Smith (Brynjolfsson, 2003) found that a large proportion of Amazon's book sales come from obscure books not available in brick-and-mortar stores. The long tail effect

Figure 1.1   Long Tails

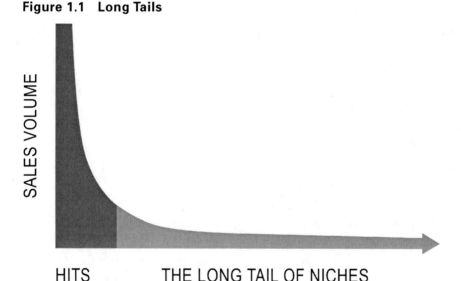

Note: From *The Long Tail* (p. 56), by C. Anderson, 2006, New York: Hyperion. Copyright 2006 by Hyperion. Reprinted with permission.

enables businesses to tap into specialty markets successfully. This means the ability to offer niche courses by leveraging digital technologies is becoming a possibility.

Another example is Netflix, which has built a viable business model stocking a wide range of movies—far more than a traditional brick-and-mortar movie rental store could ever hope to stock. The economics of online storage and rapid distribution enable the exploitation of the long tail: Netflix finds that, in aggregate, its individually low-renting movies are sent out more often than popular movies. Television provides another example. Because the networks have limited time slots for programs and advertisements, the opportunity cost of each is high. This forces station managers to choose programs with high, broad-base appeal. As the number of cable channels has increased and television has begun to merge with the Internet, the long tail effect is having an impact (Stolarczyk, 2008). Wikipedia's entry on the long tail summarizes this nicely:

> Often presented as a phenomenon of interest primarily to mass market retailers and Web-based businesses, the Long Tail also has implications for the producers of content, especially those whose products could not—for economic reasons—find a place in pre-Internet information distribution channels controlled by book publishers, record companies, movie studios, and television networks. [Viewed] from the producers' side, the Long Tail has made possible a flowering of creativity across all fields of human endeavor. (Wikipedia, 2010e)

So what does this mean to higher education? It might mean that low-demand classes can collectively make up a market share that exceeds the relatively few best-selling classes. Universities could be forced down the same path that the music industry and others have already trodden. So what are we to do? Are we ready to embrace something new and ride the technology obsession that offers most of the benefits and fewer of the drawbacks of today's teaching and learning environments?

Musing on Our Zahir

So what do these musings tell us? Some illumination may come from considering the conclusion of the Zahir story. The good news is that not all obsessions have to end in tragedy. In the short story "The Aleph," Borges says the Aleph,[4] one possible Zahir, is a point in space containing all other points. In essence it is infinity. Anyone gazing into it can see everything in the universe from every angle simultaneously, without distortion or confusion. When the story's main character encounters the Aleph, he describes it as such:

> I saw a small iridescent sphere of almost unbearable brightness. At first I thought it was spinning; then I realized that the movement was an illusion produced by the dizzying spectacles inside it. The Aleph was probably two or three centimeters in diameter, but universal space was contained inside it, with no diminution in size. Each thing (the glass surface of a mirror, let us say) was infinite things, because I could clearly see it from every point in the cosmos. I saw the populous sea, saw dawn and dusk, saw the multitudes of the Americas, saw a silvery spider-web at the center of a black pyramid, saw a broken labyrinth (it was London), saw endless eyes, all very close, studying themselves in me as though in a mirror, saw all the mirrors on the planet (and none of them reflecting me). . . . (Borges, 2004, pp. 129–130)

If we apply this to our world today, it quickly becomes evident that "The Aleph" and "The Zahir" have converged. We are obsessed with a single thing, and this single thing can encompass everything. William Gibson, the inventor of the term *cyberspace*, in his sci-fi novel *Mona Lisa Overdrive* (1988), writes of a device called an *aleph*, which he describes as an approximation of all cyberspace. And our job in higher education is to ensure that our Zahir becomes an Aleph. In the next chapters, we will explore ways of making sure this happens under the watchful eyes of the tech-savvy millennials and others well versed in the new media that are transforming society.

Notes

1. As seen in October of 2008 with the economic collapse in the United States and around the globe.

2. Gladwell's website for this book is www.gladwell.com/tippingpoint/index.html

3. The IDEA Center is a nonprofit organization whose mission is to serve colleges and universities committed to improving learning, teaching, and leadership performance. The IDEA Center was established in 1975, and the IDEA student ratings system was made available to other colleges and universities. For more about its widely used evaluation systems, see www.theideacenter.org. The author, Roger McHaney, is on the Board of Directors for this company.

4. Aleph can mean many things. For instance Aleph, Alef, or à, is the first letter of the Hebrew alphabet and the number 1 in Hebrew, and its esoteric meaning can be denoted as the "primordial one that contains all numbers." Aleph numbers exist in mathematics as a sequence of numbers used to represent the size of infinite sets. And remember, the Aleph causes the observer to see all things. Viewing the Zahir causes the observer eventually to see only the Zahir. So what happens if they converge?

CHAPTER TWO

INDIGENOUS POPULATIONS ON THE SHORELINE

If I meet a hundred-year-old man and I have something to teach him, I will teach; if I meet an eight-year-old boy and he has something to teach me, I will learn.

—Chao-Chou

My daughter, Megan, face bathed in a bluish glow, sits at a computer with ear buds connecting her to a Microsoft Zune. An ice cube slowly melts in a glass next to her. The faint rhythm of Ke$ha is just audible over the annoying voice track coming from a "Fred" video streaming from YouTube. At the same time, a dozen Facebook chat windows chirp out their messages and clamor for a position on the screen. Although its window is minimized at the moment, data is downloading from Microsoft's music website into the computer's media library. "Textsfromlastnight" is also running, as is her Flickr account, and although it seems she isn't paying attention to them, every now and again her fingers brush the keyboard to send a few snippets of text to her friends. Across the room, her television is tuned to a home improvement show, and at her feet, her pug, Otis, sits patiently. A second passes, and after typing something into her Blackberry, she pulls out an ear bud and sticks the phone against her head. A new, "Introduction to Pre-Calc" window flashes onto the computer screen and a definition of rays takes center stage. She impatiently asks, "How am I supposed to know what a ray is?" into the phone before giving me a stare that says "you're intruding into

14

my world." I back off and let her continue with her homework. She is an A student. She is a tech-savvy millennial. And I'm not about to unplug her.[1]

New Population

I OFTEN HEAR ACADEMICS fight over whether or not higher education is in the throes of major change. Is it crazy to assume the new generation, tagged "digital natives" by some (Bennet, Maton, & Kervin, 2008; Prensky, 2001) and "millennials" by others (Oblinger, 2003), could be a contributing force? In my opinion, it's certainly the case that an amazing mix of early-adopter millennials, tech-savvy Gen Xers, and curious baby boomers are populating higher education's new shoreline. These groups, in many cases pushed by their technology expectations, are altering the basic fabric of teaching and learning. This chapter explores the beginnings of these changes and emphasizes why it is important to pay close attention to something that surrounds every academic so intimately: his or her students.

Tech-Savvy Hordes

In the spring of 2007 I was honored to be invited as Kansas State University's College of Business commencement ceremony speaker. Like many graduation speakers, I wanted to convey a sense of each student's accomplishments but also provide them all with something to reflect on as they started the next leg of life's journey. I began the address by moving out from the podium and peering at them intently through a small set of binoculars. I told them I needed to check my facts before starting my speech. It was interesting as I looked at the class of students closely. Some were bewildered, some bored, others amused, several rolled their eyes with the bleary look any parent would recognize if they have a teenage daughter, and others shot a "get the crazy guy off stage now" look at me.

After a moment, I remarked to the Dean that this was a fine-looking group, but that they weren't significantly different in appearance from many of the others I'd seen during my tenure at K-State. I then dropped into my professorial mode and gave them something all students hate and didn't expect, particularly during their graduation ceremony—a quiz. I told them to think of it as the final quiz of their academic career. I used the moment to make a point: Most of them had been born in the mid-1980s—mostly in 1984 and 1985—and that placed them among the first generation of millennials. As part of that group, many possessed characteristics that qualified them to be tagged "digital natives."[2]

I have heard many takes on the idea of millennials being different from baby boomers and Gen Xers (Oblinger & Oblinger, 2005). My own experience, having been involved in technology all my adult life—starting as a CNC (computer numerical control) programmer at Olofsson Fabrication and later working as a simulation developer and software engineer at Control Engineering Company and finally as a professor in information systems—is that many in the new generation are different.

I don't mean they are smarter nor have the ability to learn faster or in more depth than I do. Nor do I mean they are more technically savvy than members of my generation. However, collectively, millennials have advantages making them capable of using technology in ways that might slip by the "older" generations' attention. For instance, they aren't encumbered by remembering the way things used to be or used to work. Their starting point is the here and now. For example, our grandparents (or perhaps great-grandparents) invented automobiles and highways, allowing us to take those inventions to the next level without being encumbered by remembering the old road systems or how horse and buggies were designed and constructed. This doesn't mean they are worse drivers or are incapable of coming up with a revolutionary new idea. I do believe each generation both builds on the prior and develops disruptive new ideas. And I have also heard counterarguments that this advantage is actually a disadvantage (e.g., repeating mistakes of the former generation). But rather than debate whether millennials are in some way superior beings (Bennet et al., 2008), I operate from the perspective that many millennials' expectations about and propensity to develop uses for technology are high (Palfrey & Gasser, 2008).

I witness this phenomenon every day with my own kids. They grew up with video games, computers, and other devices that weren't yet invented when I was young. And I can say without a doubt that having grown up from their earliest days with access to technology has given them insight, skills, and talents I don't possess and never will.

So why should higher education pay special attention to this complex mix of millennials, Gen Xers, and baby boomers and their aptitudes, attitudes, and perspectives? First, they are the people sitting in our classrooms, hearing our lectures (or not), filling out our teaching evaluations, and ultimately, paying our salaries (albeit indirectly in many cases). Second, technologically savvy individuals will increasingly become our colleagues and will bring their unique perspectives, new skills, and ideas into higher education. As colleagues, their tool kits, social-network-enabled work habits, and expectations will be dramatically different.

And, whether or not you believe a generation of digital natives is emerging, our youngest constituents have grown up in different times. Perhaps the best way to view the consumers of higher education, which include the smartest individuals with the highest potential on this planet, is to think of them as early adopters *en masse*.

Early Adopters

Early adopters have been studied by technology, marketing, social, and other researchers and are thought to comprise about 13 to 14 percent of the population. As the name implies, early adopters embrace new technology before most others. They often are optimistic and see potential others might consider marginal. Early adopters like to tinker, explore, and enjoy experimentation without self-doubt or fear. If a "discovery" meets or exceeds their expectations, they are more than happy to share their experiences with others (Rogers, 1995). Although most early adopters are not risk takers in all areas of their lives, they are willing to enthusiastically plunge into new technologies and share their experiences with friends and peers, as depicted in Gladwell's description of the maven (Gladwell, 2000).

Taking this idea a step further, it becomes apparent that early adopters may be willing to embrace new technologies and ideas because often they don't have much to lose. For instance, they might use new technology primarily in their hobbies, rather than their job duties. If an individual works in an organization and has invested time, training, and expensive organizational resources on an information system, she will be less willing to continue investigating alternatives, trying new software, and jumping to new technologies. However, such reluctance doesn't automatically qualify a person as a Luddite, the counterpart to the early adopter who has no interest in new technology and no willingness to change "the way we've always done things." Luddites take an extreme view of change as a threat to their jobs, their social status, their power structures, or the systems they've used to bring success about in their own lives.

So what does a discussion of early adopters have to do with higher education's constituency, specifically the millennials? The millennial has the potential to be the ultimate early adopter of the most recent technological advances. Being in the formative stage of becoming an adult, he or she is more open to new influences and ideas. That's the first factor that contributes to making the millennial a natural and super-charged early adopter.

There are other factors, too. Many middle-class (and higher) millennials don't have to worry about sustaining their own livelihood. Many are under the care of their parents and are free to experiment with the new and different technologies appearing as if by magic from all parts of the world. Millennials often have more free time than their Gen X and baby boomer counterparts. Many are encouraged by their schools, friends, parents, and what they read online to explore, learn, and try new things. Additionally, like many early adopters, the millennial has the freedom to experiment and, in most cases, just stop using technology that is no longer appealing. Most of what they use is free for them, so they have little time or money invested in any particular technology.

Another reason many millennials are a turbo-charged group of early adopters relates to the nature of their technology. This very technology is designed to facilitate communication in many ways, and Web 2.0 ideas have transformed the Internet into a gigantic computer-mediated communication system (Chilton & McHaney, 2010). According to Rogers (1995), early adopters spread the word about the items they are using. By putting the means to more effectively communicate into the hands of the millennial early adopters, word spreads even faster.

Millennials are also able to help determine what features should be introduced into the technology they are using. Marketing departments and product developers are eager to collect data regarding the positive and negative aspects of a new product. Early adopters want to provide this information as long as their feedback is considered and used for improvements. If the pleas of the early adopter are ignored, they may turn their backs on an innovation and move to the next promising thing, particularly if they perceive it might address the weak points of the first. Their emotional investment often is minimal, and switching does not disturb or worry them. With current technology and the rapidly changing landscape of the Web, technology adoption and switching can be extremely fast. One week's "cool" application can rapidly become next week's castaway (Gary, 2008). For example, prior to Facebook, the social networking site, MySpace was the rage. Razor phones quickly gave way to iPhones and other smart devices. Netbooks have lost sales as Apple's iPad gains in popularity. Product lifecycles grow increasingly shorter.

More Than Just Early Adopters

Simply classifying many millennials (and some Gen Xers and baby boomers) as early adopters misrepresents a complex group. A few other important features characterize and differentiate these individuals from those of past generations.

Tech-savvy millennials and their expectations are altering the basic fabric of teaching and learning. Higher education must explore how students today are different from students of the past and understand the way they learn. While these students aren't necessarily smarter or somehow technologically superior, they do have different expectations, and many have spent their formative years using a wide array of technology. These and other important features characterize and differentiate them from past generations. First, this group has been empowered by social networking and other forms of convenient, computer-enabled and mobile communication capabilities to "try out" various identities and social personas. Second, this group has incorporated time shifting into their lifestyle. For them, waiting is undesirable at best and intolerable under most circumstances. Third, this group has been endowed with the ability to personalize and customize their world to a degree never before possible. Fourth, unlike any other generation, this group has incorporated ubiquitous mobile communication into their daily lives. Finally, the tech-savvy millennial has a variety of delightful and promising characteristics. For instance, many are creative, innovative beings. They have the capability to filter, timeslice, commoditize their attention, and synthesize information. They are forging the boundaries of the new digital frontier in ways that never could have been foreseen just five years ago. On the darker side, these same individuals have little regard for their own or others' online privacy, they have developed social structures on the Web that can be used to the detriment of their peers (e.g., cyberbullying), and they may behave in ways that prior generations find questionable.

For now, let's examine how tech-savvy millennials are using these online social structures to experiment and redefine themselves until an acceptable social construction of their person emerges. I believe that the current generation could become the first group in which it is socially acceptable and perhaps even expected to assume a multitude of identities.

Who Was That Guy (or Gal)? Shape Shifters

I recently received a completed assignment via email from one of my university students. As a way to warm up the introductory technology class and engage their interest, I assign them a relatively simple business blog project. I ask them to show ways blogging technology might be used to further the mission of an organization. And I ask them to create a blog on a topic of personal interest. Of course, I always receive submissions that revolve around beer, favorite sports teams, student clubs, hobbies, or pets. But this time, I received a unique submission that marked a trend in new business models.

What struck me immediately about this submission was that I had no idea who completed it. This wasn't like a student forgetting to put his or her name on a research paper. This person had a clear identity: Orc-Chik.[3] And she had branded her blog professionally with self-developed graphics and text to ensure you knew exactly who she was (or at least the image she was projecting for herself) and what her blog was all about. She said something to this effect in the author profile:

> I began playing World of Warcraft 4 years ago. To date I have 3 level 70 toons, and three 60 + level toons close to that point, as well as a virtual army of lower level alts ranging from level 1 blank toons to the lovely level 47 Bloodelf [Paltina]. I have logged countless hours as a rogue, my first max level character, a druid, who wishes never to heal another Kara, and on the very lovely [OrcChik], who is my most played alter ego, in the game.

She proceeded to show a picture of OrcChik and give several example pieces of poetry that have value in her online world and that could conceivably be sold or traded on World of Warcraft (WoW). Her blog promotes this "Orc Poetry," which she develops within the virtual reality world and video game, WoW.

You may be asking yourself, "Why is this so significant?" First, the definition of *business* is challenged. Can business be transacted in a virtual world? The question would be met by a tech-savvy millennial with incredulity. Of course it can. Does poetry have value in the real world? Of course. It may have even more value in a creative and highly interactive world like WoW. Second, here's a business student writing poetry for fun. Take a moment to get your head around that. This poetry is something she developed for her own amusement and that is valued by her peers. Third, she openly alluded to her multiple identities in this online world: She had three level-70 toons[4], three level-60 + toons, and a whole cast of toons ranging from level 1 to level 47.

Each of OrcChik's identities has acquired different resources, different social contacts, and different sets of attributes. Her blog was submitted using the identity of one of these toons. Although it took me a while to decipher it, I determined the owner of the identity, using the process of elimination.

This seemingly insignificant event is a sign of changes to come. In past generations, identity was difficult to control or alter. Identity was closely tied to your physical person and to where you lived, your family, your income level, the school you attended, your clothes, and so forth. To the tech-savvy millennial, identity has become much more complex and malleable.

For my generation, one of the few ways to achieve a new identity was to leave your former life behind. For instance, you could move to a new town and paint the picture you wished to portray. Your new world might still intersect with your old one in limited ways. For instance, if you had a police record, your new friends might learn about it. Or if someone from your "previous life" moved nearby, your old identity might become known again. In most cases, your past was veiled by geographic distance and initial anonymity.

With the advent of the digital age, a paradox of sorts has arisen. It is easier to both develop a new identity and leave behind traces of your former ones. As far as creating new identities, the tech-savvy millennial can do this on a whim. Different identities can be acquired within the same social network (like OrcChik's being only one of my student's multiple WoW identities) or by joining a variety of social networks and projecting different personalities in each. Depending on her or his purpose, the tech-savvy millennial feels varying degrees of freedom to develop, experiment with, alter, and abandon identities.

I have been speaking with groups of high school students recently as part of the Kansas State University Presidential Lecture Series, and after each lecture, I have the opportunity to interact with students and collect their opinions regarding various aspects of being a tech-savvy millennial. What I have discovered, and not unexpectedly, is that most have a dichotomous existence (over 80 percent): A typical high school student has at least one or two profiles on Facebook, MySpace, or Bebo that mirror their self-constructed image rooted in reality. These profiles include comments from acquaintances, posted pictures, and selected representations of their actual lives. People from different generations might feel uncomfortable providing the details they do. This becomes even more uncomfortable when one realizes that information is persistent and accessible into the foreseeable future via search engines that pull information from archived versions of the Web. An example of one such Internet archive, WayBack-Machine on Archive.org (WayBackMachine, 2008), is shown in Figure 2.1.

The tech-savvy millennials' own friends keep them somewhat honest about their pictures and profiles via comments on both their site and on their friends' sites, which are out of their friends' control. By allowing users to tag pictures with names, identities rooted in the physical world can be verified to some extent, and for at least that reason, the tech-savvy millennial represents herself or himself in a reasonably accurate way (Thomas, 2007).

Generally, the tech-savvy millennial's public persona is an intersection between digital representation and physical reality that can be mostly verified by one's closest friends. But it can get more complicated. Based on my student focus group discussions, I learned the accuracy of the tech-savvy millennials' identity construction hinges on whether they expect to meet with their online friends in physical reality. For instance, a totally anonymous identity allows exploration in potentially embarrassing situations. Social network developers have responded and created websites

Figure 2.1　Part of WayBackMachine's Archive of Kansas State University's Website

INTERNET ARCHIVE
WayBackMachine

Enter Web Address: http://　　All ▾　Take Me Back　Adv. Search Compare Archive Pages

Searched for http://www.ksu.edu

Note some duplicates are not shown. See all.
* denotes when site was updated.
Material typically becomes available here 6 months or more after collection, with some exceptions See FAQ.

Archived Results from Jan 01, 1996 - latest

1996	1997	1998	1999	2000	2001	2002	2003	2004	2005	2006
0 pages	3 pages	2 pages	10 pages	26 pages	92 pages	28 pages	33 pages	136 pages	230 pages	108 pages
	Jun 06, 1997 *	Feb 04, 1998	Jan 25, 1999	Mar 01, 2000 *	Jan 18, 2001	Jan 04, 2002	Feb 05, 2003 *	Feb 04, 2004 *	Jan 06, 2005 *	Jan 01, 2006
	Jun 07, 1997	Dec 12, 1998 *	Jan 25, 1999 *	Mar 02, 2000 *	Jan 30, 2001	Jan 24, 2002	Feb 08, 2003 *	Feb 07, 2004 *	Jan 07, 2005	Jan 02, 2006
	Dec 11, 1997 *		Jan 27, 1999 *	Mar 04, 2000 *	Feb 02, 2001	Apr 01, 2002 *	Feb 10, 2003	Feb 18, 2004	Jan 09, 2005	Jan 03, 2006 *
			Feb 08, 1999 *	Mar 04, 2000 *	Feb 07, 2001 *	Feb 02, 2002 *	Feb 11, 2003	Mar 04, 2004	Jan 11, 2005	Jan 06, 2006 *
			Feb 08, 1999 *	Mar 05, 2000 *	Feb 24, 2001	May 24, 2002 *	Feb 18, 2003 *	Mar 17, 2004 *	Jan 12, 2005	Jan 07, 2006
			Feb 18, 1999 *	Apr 07, 2000 *	Feb 26, 2001 *	May 25, 2002 *	Mar 24, 2003	Apr 04, 2004 *	Jan 13, 2005	Jan 08, 2006
			Apr 22, 1999 *	May 10, 2000 *	Feb 28, 2001 *	Jun 05, 2002 *	Mar 31, 2003	Apr 23, 2004	Jan 14, 2005	Jan 12, 2006 *
			Apr 22, 1999 *	May 11, 2000 *	Jun 06, 2001 *	Jun 06, 2002 *	Apr 02, 2003 *	May 10, 2004 *	Jan 15, 2005	Jan 17, 2006
			Oct 04, 1999 *	May 20, 2000 *	Mar 01, 2001 *	Jul 21, 2002	Apr 09, 2003	May 19, 2004	Jan 16, 2005	Jan 18, 2006 *
			Nov 04, 1999 *	May 20, 2000 *	Mar 02, 2001 *	Jul 22, 2002 *	Apr 19, 2003	May 20, 2004 *	Jan 17, 2005	Jan 25, 2006
				Jun 20, 2000 *	Mar 06, 2001 *	Aug 13, 2002 *	Apr 20, 2003 *	Jun 09, 2004	Jan 18, 2005	Jan 27, 2006
				Jun 20, 2000 *	Mar 30, 2001 *	Aug 27, 2002 *	Apr 20, 2003 *	Jun 10, 2004	Jan 19, 2005	Feb 01, 2006
				Jun 22, 2000 *	Apr 04, 2001 *	Sep 18, 2002	Jun 10, 2003 *	Jun 12, 2004 *	Jan 20, 2005	Feb 02, 2006 *
				Jul 07, 2000 *	Apr 05, 2001	Sep 22, 2002 *	Jun 19, 2003 *	Jun 12, 2004	Jan 21, 2005	Feb 03, 2006
				Jul 07, 2000 *	Apr 07, 2001 *	Sep 25, 2002	Jun 23, 2003	Jun 15, 2004 *	Jan 22, 2005	Feb 05, 2006
				Aug 15, 2000 *	Apr 10, 2001 *	Sep 27, 2002 *	Jun 23, 2003 *	Jun 15, 2004	Jan 22, 2005 *	Feb 08, 2006 *
				Aug 24, 2000 *	Apr 12, 2001 *	Sep 29, 2002	Jul 21, 2003	Jun 16, 2004	Jan 24, 2005 *	Feb 09, 2006 *
				Sep 29, 2000	Apr 13, 2001	Oct 03, 2002	Jul 27, 2003 *	Jun 18, 2004 *	Jan 25, 2005	Feb 16, 2006
				Oct 04, 2000	Apr 14, 2001 *	Oct 07, 2002	Aug 02, 2003	Jun 19, 2004 *	Jan 26, 2005	
					Apr 17, 2001 *	Oct 14, 2002				

Note. From http://web.archive.org/web/*/www.ksu.edu

intended to be completely anonymous, such as experienceproject.com (Experience Project, 2010) and 43things.com (43 Things, 2010). The Experience Project website (see Figure 2.2) also provides a confessions section where users can unburden themselves of secrets without revealing personal, real-world details. Other uses for anonymous identities include experimenting with gender, race, age, authority, and sex. This seems particularly true in virtual worlds like Second Life (http://secondlife.com) and World of Warcraft (www.worldofwarcraft.com).

Myriad sites exist between these extremes. For instance, message boards may allow posting of opinions and encourage debate without revealing the author's identity. Gaming sites such as Everquest (Sony Online Entertainment, 2010) and virtual worlds such as ActiveWorlds (ActiveWorlds Inc., 2010) allow for varying degrees of anonymity. Often a tech-savvy millennial says she or he starts out intending to be anonymous but, after making friends with particular site users, may reveal more about themselves including links to their primary digital identity on Facebook. Frequently, tech-savvy millennials' created identities are used for a while and then abandoned. If they acquire too much baggage, they leave the identity behind and form a new one. Some have said they create multiple anonymous identities and use these to leave favorable comments regarding their own anonymous primary identity on a game site or message board. As you can see, digital identities can get very convoluted and complex.

Figure 2.2 Experience Project Website

www.experienceproject.com

As far as education goes, an identity created in a virtual learning environment (VLE) such as Blackboard or Axio Learning might be viewed by the tech-savvy millennial as no more than a temporary representation of her- or himself that can be manipulated to achieve a goal, such as passing a course, getting an "A," or hopefully, actually learning something about the subject. Some call this use of different personalities *online dissociative behavior* (Hayes, 2008, p. 115).

What, Me Wait? Time Shifters

Another hallmark of the tech-savvy millennial is time shifting. This became very apparent to me during a discussion with Kevin Stocks, professor of accounting from Brigham Young University. He was visiting Kansas State University as part of a reaccreditation team and was reviewing distance learning with a small group of faculty members. After the required formalities, he recounted how learning has changed in the past few years, particularly regarding student expectations and their time management habits. He told us how several distance learning students paid a live visit to a professor friend of his they had previously only interacted with online through digital lectures. The first thing they noted was that his voice sounded so different. I wondered about this until he said the technology they used allowed lectures to be played at faster rates, and these students had used this feature to speed through the lectures. Until that day, they had always heard a squeaky, Mickey Mouse voice coming from his talking head. To the tech-savvy millennial, time is at a premium, and their attention is a commodity. Anything perceived as too slow results in *latency intolerance* and produces stress (Hayes, 2008, p. 99).

The tech-savvy millennial has a different sense of time than previous generations. This movement, at least in part, can be traced to the advent of VCRs and the ability to tape a television program to view it at a more convenient time and fast-forward through the commercials. The tech-savvy millennial takes this even further with TiVo and other video-recording services, and with the ability to digitally capture television broadcasts and post the result on peer-to-peer networks like Bit Torrent. Many shows even end up on video-sharing sites such as YouTube, often with the blessing of the broadcasters. It seems inevitable that all television-style content will be decoupled from broadcast times and be consumed at the viewer's leisure, with the only time-related factor being original release date.

This mindset is closely related to the mass customization movement that has begun to unseat established systems. Broadcasters will find it difficult to ensure a captive audience sits through commercials. The heyday of time-based programming has come and gone.[5] The current generation has decided to flex their muscle and shift the power from the top to the grassroots.

So what are the long-term ramifications of time shifting? Some would say it is rewiring the tech-savvy millennials' brains. The need for speed is addictive and rapidly becoming an expectation. The ability instantly to obtain digital content including music, photos, movies, artwork, documents, assignments, books, news, lectures, and myriad other things has altered the expectations of the current generation. I remember the frustration of my tech-savvy millennial son, Mark, when he had to wait for a bass guitar to arrive via UPS. The three-day shipping time was difficult to bear when most things he ordered arrived within seconds via the Internet. Back in my day (Ugh! he would say), three-day shipping would have been viewed as a miracle.

This same phenomenon is becoming particularly true in the digital classroom. Take the case of email. A colleague and friend of mine, Dr. Sue Williams, a renowned sociologist who participated in my study of successful distance learning methodologies, surprised me one morning when at 3:00 A.M. I sent out an email regarding interview times and a few other things. Seconds later, I received a rather lengthy reply. Later she told me she likes to surprise her students with extremely prompt answers to their questions, and she just happened to be up doing that at the time.

If that story sounds surprising, rest assured you are not a tech-savvy millennial. With their mobile devices linked to email and instant messaging (IM) software, they are in nearly constant communication with a variety of people. Lifting geographic constraints is part of the reason. Acquaintances from social networks, business colleagues, friends, and relatives may be located at different points across the globe in various time zones. Frequently, my son, Matthew, is online with friends in Greece, Germany, or Japan. After a while, communication at all times seems natural. Dr. Williams uses this to her advantage and as a way to connect with tech-savvy millennials on their level, using their rules.

In my interactions with students, I have noticed this 24/7 connectedness can be both a blessing and a curse. I understand the freedom it provides. Knowledge workers are no longer tied to a desk, location, or time. Professors have enjoyed that secret for some time with their flexible schedules (the one exception being scheduled classroom teaching time!).

The tech-savvy millennial does not view time as being as constraining as prior generations might. I have fewer visits during my scheduled office hours, and so I have fewer physical office hours and more virtual office hours (when I am available via email, phone, or Instant Messenger). The net effect has been positive. I have more student interaction with less effort, resulting in more efficient use of both my time and my students' time. Of course, more complex issues can require face-to-face interaction, and I am not advocating a complete abdication of student meetings in person.

I also have noticed a change in student expectations. If I don't send a response to an email quickly, I may get follow-up messages. Some students experience "email lag anxiety." This seems to happen to students who use IM technology. I have gotten as many as ten emails in an hour from the same person wondering why I hadn't responded to their initial inquiry. That is a little extreme, but indicative of new thinking and reveals that tech-savvy millennials often see email as old-fashioned and slow.

To combat the expectation of instant responses, 24/7, I generally manage my classes by explaining my email habits. I check my messages first thing in the morning and again in late afternoon. On days before exams and project deadlines, I try to check more often. Although I frequently check more often than that, I have to manage my time to create blocks where productive, deep-thinking work can be accomplished without constant interruption. I can't be effective when continuously switching rapidly from task to task, a mode of behavior I call timeslicing. Instead, I need longer time spans for deep thinking!

Persistent and Accessible: Piracy and Storage

When I was a college student, I remember the tattered, nearly illegible copies of old exams that had been salvaged by enterprising frat guys. The old exams were great for studying, and if you got lucky, some of the questions might even be repeated on the current semester's exams. The quality of copies was poor at best (an early-stage photocopy of a blue, ditto-machine carbon copy, but still a fun forbidden fruit waiting to be picked).

The tech-savvy millennial today doesn't just seek out forbidden fruit—he or she cultivates it scientifically. The ability to digitally store and reproduce material is alarming. Forget the ethics for a moment: The reality is that unheard-of cheating activities are possible and in many cases practiced by small percentage of students.[6]

A recent event highlighted state-of-the-art cheating. I received a frantic email from a student at Boston University. He had been accused of cheating by turning in work that I had done. He claimed he had never heard of me nor knew anything about me. He had found me via Google, learned that I was a professor at K-State, and obtained my email address. He wanted to clear his name. I asked him to elaborate. He said his teacher (a graduate teaching assistant [GTA]) claimed he had stolen my work for a computer-programming project. This GTA had noticed that, under the student's document properties in Microsoft Word, "Author Name" was set to my name. The accused student had no idea how the document's author field came to have my name in it, so he started his search for answers with me.

I thought about the problem for a while then asked the student to send me a copy of the assignment in contention. He attached and emailed it. I looked it over and immediately realized what had occurred. A couple of years earlier, I had authored the *assignment* and posted it to my unprotected K-State website. This was before I started using a virtual learning environment in which all assignments are password protected. The GTA who alleged the plagiarism had actually copied that assignment from me without permission. He had changed the course title, due date, and a few other things but never asked for permission. The student had downloaded the assignment document from the GTA's website and used the downloaded MS Word document as a starting point to write his report. My name remained set as the author. In the end I emailed the GTA and told him how I believed my name came to be in place as the document's author. He was embarrassed but eventually agreed the student didn't plagiarize and apologized. I asked that he not use any of my material without first contacting me. I never heard from him again, but the student thanked me for helping him clear his name and said he was passing on the information to the honors council at BU. Whether he did, I don't know.

Another startling observation is how some publishing companies have lost control of test banks and supplemental teaching material. By chance, I discovered a plethora of these items available on eBay. I was helping a student locate a textbook for an online class of mine and instead found copies of test bank CDs for sale. This piqued my interest, and I searched for several other test banks relevant to my classes and located available copies of them as well. Several test banks were ones I had authored. I was a bit disturbed because I realized the day of using test banks to quickly generate exams had ended. In all fairness, several book publishers now place their test banks in online secure sites. This makes it more difficult, though not impossible, for the content to leak out.

In the not-too-distant past, a given teacher at a university could decide whether to allow students to take exams home after marking. As students became more sophisticated, fraternities, sororities, and other campus clubs collected copies of these exams and made them available to future and present members as study guides and practice exams. Most professors were aware of this and turned a blind eye to the practice, changing the questions enough to ensure students would have to understand the material and not simply memorize answers.

Now, with social networks, sophisticated distribution tools, and unlimited storage, if one professor allows an exam based on a test bank to be taken home after marking, that exam could find its way into nearly any student's hands, regardless of whether he or she is in the United States, Canada, Europe, China, or anywhere else. And once it hits cyberspace, it will probably be around in one form or another for the foreseeable future. In fact, because of mobile devices, the paper exam doesn't even have to leave the classroom. A quick picture of each page can be taken in mere seconds and rapidly sent to peers. *Persistent and accessible*—that is reality.

Many tech-savvy millennials don't regard this as a problem, moral dilemma, or questionable behavior. They have "cut their teeth" on free information and free exchange of information, and have a sort of rebel desire to "buck the system" and democratize information. I sympathize in many ways. In my interviews with tech-savvy millennials, particularly ones from developing countries, I hear a number of stories about why it is okay to pirate information, violate copyright laws, and not worry about paying.

A Chinese student once told me he wasn't very worried about Tom Cruise's not being paid a royalty on the movie the student had pirated to his laptop because Mr. Cruise already was paid $20 million to play the leading role. "The extra money he would receive in royalties is more than my father earns in a week," the student said. "Where is the morality in that? Why should he live in a mansion, fly around in a jet, and eat food that costs more per meal than a month's worth of food for my entire family?"

But that takes us to a different point. The purpose of this book is not to debate the ethics of privilege, nor the morality of the stories we tell ourselves to justify our behaviors, but rather to lay out what is happening in the world and then push the academic community to make the right choices to coexist with this new world. The simple fact is this: Free information exchange is going to continue to spread and proliferate. There are too many countries, legal systems, and smart rebels out there for it not to happen.

In fact, many activists, professors, professionals, students, and everyday Internet users advocate the complete freedom of creative content. They want to see revenue generated in other ways, such as through selling embedded advertising or using other mechanisms to fund viewer attention. This free culture idea

> is a social movement that promotes the freedom to distribute and modify creative works, using the Internet as well as other media. The movement objects to overly restrictive copyright laws, or completely rejects the concepts of copyright and intellectual property, which many members of the movement also argue hinder creativity. They call this system "permission culture." (Wikipedia, 2010d)

Test bank exchange and sharing is not the only way information technology has impacted class-material sharing by tech-savvy millennials. For instance, take a closer look at writing term papers. I know the value of writing papers and creating new, deep content. But the tech-savvy millennial may decide this is not a good use of his or her time. Instead, he or she may employ an online service to provide ideas, a citation library for references, a base paper for structure, or a completely finished paper. And all this can be done easily (see Figure 2.3).

A primary example is WriteWork, formerly called CheatHouse (WriteWork, 2010). As of July 5, 2010, this site had 115,249 essays and over 376,000 members (mostly students), 56 of which were searching for essays at the time I looked (CheatHouse, 2010). Figure 2.4 provides an example paper for sale from the business essays area (I almost selected an example called "AICPA Code of Ethics"—that would be ironic, buying an ethics paper from an essay writing and exchange service). Figure 2.5

Figure 2.3   WriteWork Website

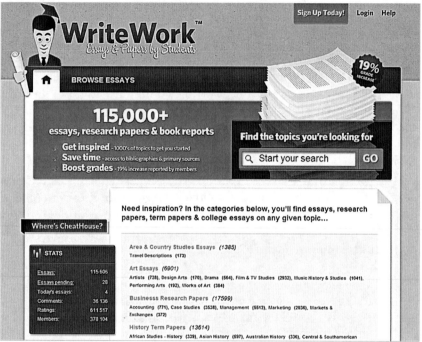

www.writework.com

shows how easy it is to gain access to material on the site. Figure 2.6 provides examples of similar sites.

Similarly, exam sharing is booming (Guess, 2008). Websites like Post-YourTest.com give students (and faculty, some sites claim) the ability to share examinations that cut across institutions. So if a professor at any school anywhere in the world passes back an exam, those items may enter the student's public domain. There is no practical way to effectively police these services. Instead, it is important to design courses and assignments in ways that make these paper mills worthless.

Are You Paying [for] Attention?

The tech-savvy millennial is deluged from all sides with information of all sorts—audio, video, text, pictures, and multimedia. Former Microsoft

Figure 2.4   Paper for Sale From WriteWork

Home Depot Incorporated and Lowe's Market Report

Subject > Businesss Research Papers > Accounting

View This Essay

66 Home Depot Incorporated and Lowe□s Market ReportThere are many competitors in the home improvement industry today and competition is at an all time high. There are two very strong leaders in the industry today and they are The Home Depot and Lowe□s. An industry of competition, and tight margins these two companies still at it. Both of these companies stand now as the industry standard for the home improvement sector, and have extremely strong financial positions and a long future in the home improvement industry. This paper will cover each company□s strengths and limitations, Home Depot□s and Lowe□s focus for the next year and next five years. This paper will also discuss the companies□ strongest competitors, and their geographical ... 99

essay sample (first 120 out of 2976 words)

ESSAY DETAILS

Date: March 22, 2008

Level: University, Bachelor's

Grade: A

Length: 12 pages (2976 words)

Essay rating:
☆ ☆ ☆ ☆ ☆

Keywords:
home improvement industry, home improvement sector, tight margins, flooring stores, retail flooring, lowe s, …

executive Linda Stone describes the necessary coping mechanism as continuous partial attention (Stone, 2008). On her website, she further clarifies what this means:

> Continuous partial attention describes how many of us use our attention today. It is different from multi-tasking. The two are differentiated by the impulse that motivates them. When we multi-task, we are motivated by a desire to be more productive and more efficient. We're often doing things that are automatic, that require very little cognitive processing. We give the same priority to much of what we do when we multi-task—we file and copy papers, talk on the phone, eat lunch—we get as many things done at one time as we possibly can in order to make more time for ourselves and in order to be more efficient and more productive. To pay continuous partial attention is to pay partial attention—CONTINUOUSLY. It is motivated by a desire to be a LIVE node on the network. Another way of saying this is that we want to connect and be connected. We want to effectively scan for opportunity and optimize for the best opportunities, activities, and contacts, in any given

Figure 2.5   How to Get a Paper on WriteWork

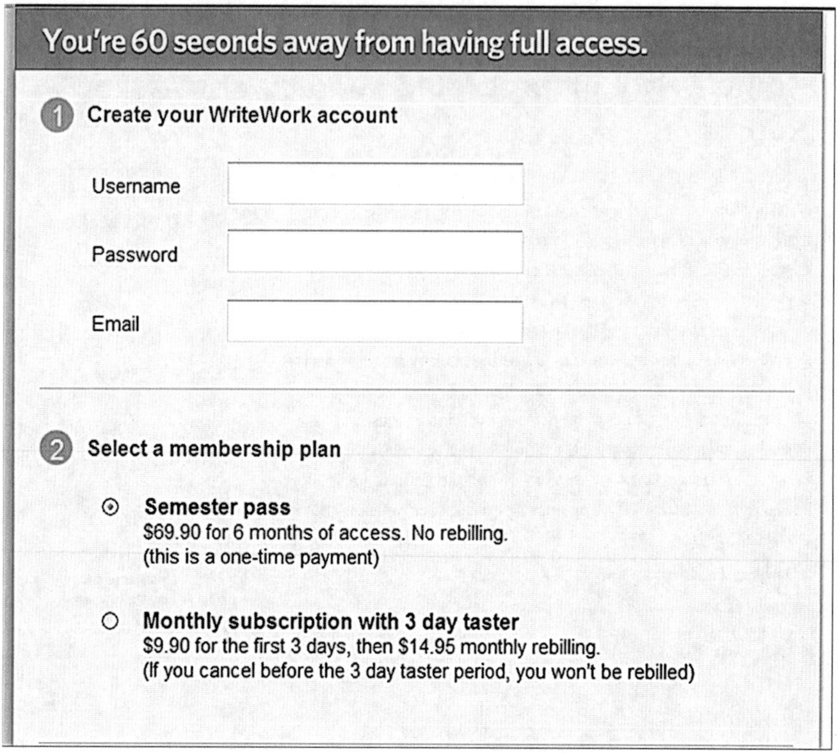

> ### You're 60 seconds away from having full access.
>
> **1** Create your WriteWork account
>
> Username   [   ]
>
> Password   [   ]
>
> Email   [   ]
>
> ---
>
> **2** Select a membership plan
>
> ⊙ **Semester pass**
> $69.90 for 6 months of access. No rebilling.
>   (this is a one-time payment)
>
> ○ **Monthly subscription with 3 day taster**
> $9.90 for the first 3 days, then $14.95 monthly rebilling.
>   (If you cancel before the 3 day taster period, you won't be rebilled)

Figure 2.6   Other Websites That Sell Academic Papers

> Http://www.123helpme.com
> http://www.universityessays.com/
> http://custom-writing.org/university-essay-writing
> http://www.planetpapers.com

moment. To be busy, to be connected, is to be alive, to be recognized, and to matter. We pay continuous partial attention in an effort NOT TO MISS ANYTHING. It is an always-on, anywhere, anytime, anyplace behavior that involves an artificial sense of constant crisis. We are always in high alert when we pay continuous partial attention. This artificial sense of constant crisis is more typical of continuous partial attention than it is of multi-tasking. (Stone, 2008)

So in other words, Stone believes tech-savvy millennials become information-monitoring specialists and connected nodes on the Web. When a particularly interesting item comes *across the wire*, tech-savvy millennials focus with a greater degree of attention. I've noticed this phenomenon with my students and my children. They are continually receiving messages on their cell phones or computers. This information comes in synchronously, but if it isn't of immediate importance, it becomes asynchronous and is placed on the back burner. Over time, if enough of these asynchronous items build up, the recipient may feel stressed and overwhelmed. Hmmm, sounds familiar doesn't it? Have you checked your email inbox lately? Continuous partial attention is a temporary fix that prevents short-term information overload but does little for the long-term ability to control one's accessibility and demands for attention. Linda Stone calls this communication mode "semi-sync." It falls into the crack between asynchronous or synchronous.

Recognition of this situation allows a teacher to provide tools and techniques that mitigate this situation. Course information, deadlines, and other important material will help the tech-savvy millennial in the classroom. They are naturally in the mode of filtering. By prefiltering and organizing material, teachers can ensure students will have greater success. Their world has moved from memorization to connecting, searching, and filtering. The tech-savvy millennial allows "the machine" to remember and expects to access and apply the information they know is there.

As teachers, we should be glad. After all, for years we have argued against memorization and instead have suggested deeper learning needs to take place. Why not replace memorization with techniques for obtaining the correct, reliable information using the "toys-now-tools" that form the backbone of the digital world today? We need to emphasize using information in creative ways: developing it further, adding to it, extending it, and linking it to other information in synergistic networks. This makes sense in the tech-savvy millennials' world. And that is already happening naturally outside the classrooms with wikis, blogs, and discussion forums.

The information coming to the tech-savvy millennial arrives from a variety of places. Much of it is from their social network of friends. Other information comes from the media, content providers, and creative peers. But more and more, information is coming from businesses that recognize the true economic and dollar value of potential consumers' attention. What this means to the teacher and those in higher education is that the tech-savvy millennial's attention can't be taken for granted. In other words, their time is money. And their attention can be leveraged in ways that might fund their education without directly paying the skyrocketing tuition bills. Marketing firms would love to sponsor online education with sidebar ads to siphon off even a tiny portion of this important demographics' coveted attention. Could this become the "free" education academics have long dreamed of providing?

Not Now, I'm Busy Vs. Of Course Now, I'm Busy: Timeslicing

So, are tech-savvy millennials natural multitaskers? Although there is no doubt they engage in multiple activities at one time, it is questionable whether this is a good thing, whether it provides benefits, and whether it even can be called *true* multitasking. In recent discussions[7] I had with Dr. Robert Savoy, a well-regarded experimental psychologist and radiology instructor at Harvard Medical School, he described his experiences in this area (R. Savoy, personal communication, June 30, 2010). Savoy suggested millennials are able to perform simplistic tasks somewhat simultaneously, but once complex decision making enters the equation, severe degradation of outcomes almost always occurs. For instance, it is possible to walk and talk on a cell phone at the same time, but it is not possible to effectively demonstrate a complex dance routine while talking on the phone. It is possible to watch television and text but not to watch television and take the ACT test effectively. Recent studies support this premise, showing that high levels of multitasking result in degraded task performance (J. Hamilton, 2008; Ophir, Nass, & Wagner, 2010).

So why does anecdotal evidence seem to indicate something different? In my opinion, it results from the tools available to high-tech millennials.

In a 2007 study by Laxmisan et al., it was shown that multitasking creates a higher memory load, which in turn contributes to medical error. This was particularly evident in the emergency department (Laxmisan, Hakimzada, & Sayan, 2007). Introducing technology to alleviate higher memory loads was suggested by the authors as a potential solution. By offloading short-term information to a computer, emergency room doctors would be more able to manage decision making.

It seems the tech-savvy millennial has already stumbled upon this solution in his or her personal life and uses technology to become more efficient at a variety of tasks. Communication by mobile device, texting, leaving short messages on Facebook, running multiple applications simultaneously, and so forth all provide the illusion of multitasking. MRI (i.e., magnetic resonance imaging) studies by Daniel Weissman at the University of Michigan indicate the brain has to process a single task at a time. Weissman found the brain pauses and dumps previously collected information in order to focus on the current task. This dumped information might be recovered and processed later (J. Hamilton, 2008).

This phenomenon reminds me of 1970s and 1980s mainframe computers that "multitasked" by virtue of time sharing, or what my colleagues and I called *timeslicing*. In my early days as a computer simulation analyst, I had to run models of manufacturing systems that required substantial processing time on the corporate mainframe computer. When I ran my models, the accountants complained that their software slowed to a crawl. As a result, the mainframe administrator assigned my programs a low priority so they would get CPU time only when the accountants were not using the system. This frustrated me until I discovered that the highest priority for the system was related to user input. As long as I continued to hit the return key, my simulations ran. I was able to sneak CPU time away from the accountants using this technique. The administrator could not figure out why the priority scheme didn't work and became frustrated. I, on the other hand, got my work done faster and more efficiently.

Computers that ran that way were classified as preemptive multitasking, or time-sharing, devices (Wikipedia, 2010b). However, only one instruction ran at any given moment. The software sliced the CPU's time up and allocated it to the various programs vying for resources. I suspect the tech-savvy millennial is operating in much the same way. They are timeslicing between various demands that have become more efficient through technology. This gives the illusion of multitasking. It becomes our job as educators to help them realize when timeslicing tendencies degrade performance and when it can be an asset. Certain tasks can be timesliced and others should receive undivided attention. Continuous partial attention is not always the best strategy.

Timeslicing in the Classroom

The classroom is going through a time of extreme change and transformation. It is interesting to observe the habits of the students during lectures. Many, particularly returning or older students, still take notes with pencil and paper. Others have preprinted PowerPoint slides downloaded from virtual learning environments and are highlighting those in class. Still others are using their laptops or, as in some of my classrooms, the university-owned desktop computers to annotate the slides during the lecture. Then there are the truly digitally inclined students. Several of them type notes directly into their email, instant messenger or Facebook account. One student even told me he was Twittering my lecture on a mobile device so he and his friends could review the notes later. I've asked my students who Facebook, Twitter, or IM the lectures about their habits. Some say they send the material to classmates they know. Others say they post the material to websites or social networking walls that have been created for the class. One student uses a virtual flashcard software package to take that day's lecture material and transform it into a study aid. He makes it available to anyone who wants to see it and says students from other universities using the same textbook have worked with him to create decks of flashcards and other study material of their own initiative.

The tech-savvy millennials have begun to bring their "toys" to the classroom as tools. Currently, I experiment with permitting cell phones and smart devices in my classes. I ask students not to talk/social network on personal matters but to use the technology as a data input device for notes or recording class information. Some students take photos of images projected on the screen in class. My goal is to instill appropriate mobile-technology behaviors because they will be using these devices in their professional careers. As a teacher, should I be alarmed about their desire to stay connected? Quite the opposite, I believe. Information used to be my own private asset. That is no longer true. I knew the material, where to get it, and how to parcel it out to enable a fair and equitable exam that would motivate students to read, study, and hopefully learn. Now, instead, information is available to anyone that cares to use it. This is a good thing. No—a great thing! It will ultimately free everyone to make better use of their time and progress more rapidly. In addition to the methods of taking notes I've already mentioned, I've also observed the following in my classroom:

Video Recording   Students use cell phone cameras, digital cameras, webcams on their laptops, and even small video recorders to capture the lecture and post it on the Web or email it to a classmate who is not in class. Some students ask permission, and others just turn on their video-recording device and do it. This practice makes a professor want to be sure the lecture is accurate and articulate. That recording could be around for a long time. Some professors have posted policies about video recording to describe what is appropriate and what is not. Although none of my lectures (to my knowledge) have been posted to YouTube or another video-sharing site, I have heard from colleagues that this is happening.

Audio Recordings and Podcasts   It is much easier to create an audio track of a lecture than a video. Although this may not be too effective in some courses, in others it works fine. The idea of audio recording has been around for a long time. I remember in my undergraduate years receiving a tiny tape recorder from my parents as a gift and then using it to record complicated lectures for which note-taking was difficult. I would listen to certain parts of the lecture a couple of times until it made more sense. That same technique is being used today with one major difference: Once a digital recording is made it can be copied, emailed, posted, distributed, podcasted, and so forth. I am not so vain as to believe that's what happens to my lectures, but once in existence, the digital artifact takes on an existence of its own completely out of the professor's control.

A variety of Web 2.0 tools are being used by students for note taking and classroom enhancement. Details of these technologies and ideas for formalizing their use in teaching will be covered in chapters 4 and 5. Brief examples of student-initiated uses follow.

Wikis   I have noticed two types of student-initiated wikis emerging recently. One is a space made available by teachers. Students are invited to contribute their notes as shared content in productive ways. Generally, these wikis are "reset" at the end of a semester so the next group of students can enjoy the same learning benefits as the previous one. A few wikis using this model are more persistent, and subsequent classes start with the existing material and continue upgrading and improving it. Students add to the wiki during or after class using laptops, mobile devices, or other computing platforms.

The second type of wiki is fully student created. It usually persists beyond the semester. These wikis are often oriented toward important information for exams and may provide answers for chapter end questions. Wikis such as these often are maintained by student organizations (e.g., sororities or fraternities). In my opinion, these wikis will eventually become larger and more interconnected. Students from all around the world can add material based on class subject, textbook, or other attribute to engage in global learning and information-exchange experiences.

Blogs   Several students blog their classroom notes, but this lacks the power of community development. The students who blog report they use it as a tool of convenience and to avoid losing notes if their computer crashes or they misplace their USB drive.

Twitter (Microblogging)   When smart mobile devices are permitted in class, Twitter and microblogging becomes a viable tool. Students can text small messages about class content, important concepts, reminders, and other material to themselves. Twitter can also permit students to organize and interact with classmates who share their tweets with one another. A historical record of their tweets becomes available on the Web and can be used as a basis for studying or creating a more detailed set of notes later. Several of my students tell me that Twittering during class has improved their ability to recall important concepts and gives them a huge advantage when it comes to studying.

Social Networking   It almost goes without saying that today's tech-savvy millennial uses social networking as an education enhancement tool. I have students Facebooking in class every day. Once during my lecture, I used my laptop to send messages to a couple of students I knew were on Facebook. I watched their expressions change and sheepish smiles creep across their faces. Did they stop Facebooking? Of course not. They were using it to jointly take notes and create a record of the class lecture. At the same time they were chatting. In the true timeslicing sense of a tech-savvy millennial, they were also posting comments, humorous in their minds I'm sure, and browsing through a couple of websites, reading up on the upcoming K-State football game.

I frequently see my daughter doing homework while communicating with her friends who are logged in to Facebook. Is this bad? Something we should stop? Of course not. They are learning in teams in a cooperative way. This is what we've been trying to teach, but without such a useful tool. Leave it to them to learn on their own, especially because networking has become truly useful, beneficial, and fun.

Cell Phones and Smart Mobile Devices   In the survey I hand out to tech-savvy millennials during my high school talks, one finding remains constant: the universal love of cell phones and smart mobile devices. One question asks which technology they would be unable to survive without. In my youth, it was television. Then, over time, video games (like Nintendo 64) gained favor, giving way to computers with Internet access. Now, overwhelmingly, 90+ percent of student respondents cite smart mobile devices as the technology that makes their lives worth living! They are the ultimate timeslicer's tool. Many tech-savvy millennials consider text messaging, Internet, music, digital imaging, voice, and video all as integral and natural parts of their mobile devices.

After giving the survey, I often ask the students why they can't live without smart mobile devices but can live without the Internet. One student in the back yelled out: "My phone is the Internet so I don't need it separately." The others murmured in agreement. It wasn't the point I was trying to make, but it illuminated the topic. The tech-savvy millennial doesn't necessarily see a dividing point between their mobile phone, digital networks, and themselves. The student feels part of the system, a node on the network. So for a timeslicer, a mobile device provides the ability to walk, talk, listen to music, snap photos, and text a friend at nearly the same time. This tool, which I still fumble with, has become the symbol of a generation, and anytime a teacher takes them "offline" and makes them shut off their mobile devices, these students feel stressed. Mobile devices are data-entry tools for the tech-savvy millennial and are the key interface point that makes them a node on the Web.

Instant Messaging and Texting   A quick and dirty, less persistent social networking application, students often use IM as a computer-mediated communication technique that enables classroom note taking. IM uses laptops and computers as a platform. Texting is the same thing done with mobile devices. You can imagine all the possibilities this technology enables. On the simplest level, answers to in-class problems can be exchanged. This, of course, is not how a teacher hopes students will use their capabilities. Taking it one step further, if homework or in-class assignments are being completed, students may compare their results and explore why certain answers differ. In a sense, this helps them understand where they went wrong and how to fix their errors. Along these same lines, I have seen students photograph solutions to math problems and then share the documents using IM software. In an ideal world, students would work together to take lecture notes and then cooperatively solve in-class problems to understand concepts.

Live Streaming   One period, I had an international student in class position a small Webcam on her desk and point it toward me as I lectured. Afterward, I approached her, assuming she had digitally recorded the lecture for later use. There was no recording, she said. Instead the entire lecture had been streamed out through a website called Stickam.com. A friend of hers was traveling and unable to attend class that day but had watched it remotely through Stickam's live broadcasting capabilities.

Tablet Devices   The release of Apple's iPad tablet device impacted the classroom almost immediately. It makes functions performed on smart mobile devices easier with a larger screen and smoother interface. Wikis, blogs, IM, and social networking all become more manageable. Students use tablets to view class material posted in VLEs or on websites. Electronic textbooks can be accessed and annotated during class on these devices. Podcasts can be obtained easily from iTunes University. Students are able to take better notes and store, email, or microblog these out to themselves and their friends. In many ways, this class of devices may become the unifying educational platform for our students.

Thinking in Circles? Nonlinear Thinkers

The tech-savvy millennial's inventive way of viewing the world is hastening change in higher education. Many say new ways of interacting, thinking, timeslicing, and discovering information have resulted in strengthened cognitive abilities among today's youth. I realize I am stepping out on a limb by supporting this opinion, but it holds up under my observations.

If I compare my generations' linear access to information to what my sons, daughter, and their peers experience, an amazing difference is evident. Although that difference might not result in physical neurological differences, I suspect it could (but the jury is still out on this matter). Here are some examples.

Let's start with television. During my formative years, I turned a knob through a sequence of channels to find a scheduled program. Even if I knew the channel and time, I still had to move through the options. The tech-savvy millennial watches television using a set with numbered stations too, but instead of flipping sequentially, she or he directly selects the desired station. With dish television and some cable systems, the numbers are giving way to branded station names. Other tech-savvy millennials watch "television" on the Web, where station sequence is meaningless. Search engines and services deliver the programs on demand (e.g., Hulu).

In my formative years, when I searched for library information, I used the Dewey decimal system. Encyclopedias contained items in alphabetical order. Computer storage used sequential tapes. My music was found on sequentially recorded albums and cassette tapes. Later, when eight-track tapes came out, I had four sequences to choose from (even though the sound of one track sometimes bled over into the others). I read books and stories from left to right and flipped through the pages in a newspaper looking for articles of interest.

How about the tech-savvy millennial? He or she has grown up in a world where hyperlinks are the norm. Information is linked logically by various attributes instead of by the first letter in a word. Key words and tags group information, and sophisticated search engines power millennials toward desired information. They are in the constant mode of discovery and commonly find paths to related items of data that are very different than expected. Their research is discovery, exploration, and connections, with many dead ends and redirections but also an ability to recover from them quickly. Our generation planned careful forays into information, but the tech-savvy millennial can leap before looking without much worry. Today's patterns promote trial and error, encourage free association, and engender a greater sense of ambiguity, experimentation, and adventure.

Does this new freedom and ability to navigate in nonlinear ways change worldviews and help develop different cognitive styles, capabilities, and skills? Are peoples' thinking patterns changing and their neurons being retrained? I believe it is possible.

Are We There Yet? Mobility and the
Tech-Savvy Millennial

I've already alluded to the massive change in the "where" of technology use. The vast and rapidly expanding proliferation of mobile devices such as cell phones, notebook computers, MP3 players, e-book readers, GPS systems, smart mobile devices, netbooks, tablets, and digital video cameras, coupled with the increasing availability of Wi-Fi hotspots and open wireless networks, have enabled the tech-savvy millennial and new learners to consume, create, and manipulate information almost everywhere.

Around university campuses, the patterns of student study groups, previously congregating in the library and in computer labs, have been modified by new geographic flexibility. There is a resurgence of students working together on projects and homework, physically alone but in virtual groups sitting behind laptops in coffee shops. Meetings are facilitated by features found in most VLEs or for free on the Web. Students don't have to be in close proximity to communicate or share information.

This same trend has followed many students out into the workplace. In fact, technologies that enhance mobility are favorites among Gen Xers and baby boomers. For the most part, salespersons, project managers, reporters, writers, telecommuters, programmers, and others all enjoy having the ability to alter their work location in countless ways. This book, for instance, has been written in various countries, coffee shops, offices, rooms in my home, and even outside, depending on my mood and other factors. While writing it, I have enjoyed the freedom to wear the clothes I want, snack on various foods, have the TV on or not, and even do laundry or cook something.

This doesn't mean these technologies have precluded people from wanting to be in close physical proximity. In fact, many times I see technology being used to arrange a time and place where people can get together. Those in the workplace have suggested the same thing. Over time, technology falls short of replacing human contact. For instance, a trend has emerged that congregates "digital nomads" in a common area. Most are employed by different organizations or as freelancers. This has resulted in "Jellies." According to Chris Messina,

> Jellies or Juntos are coworking spaces that facilitate the development of a community of café-like collaborative spaces for developers, writers and independents. The social interaction within these Jellies helps to supplement an otherwise digital existence with face-to-face human contact, camaraderie, and all the things that go along with being in the

physical presence of others. This trend is emerging in a number of major cities including New York, Atlanta, Philadelphia, and Austin. (Messina, 2008)

Cesar Torres writes:

In February 2006, New York City roommates Amit Gupta and Luke Crawford invited friends to work out of their living room after missing the social aspect of an office. Word quickly spread about the meetings the duo eventually dubbed Jelly. Now, coworkers—the term given to anyone participating in the coworking movement—meet up in over 20 cities, with more and more Jellies popping up all over the globe. By designating a time, a location and a shared purpose for coming together, Jelly provides a social platform for interactions to occur in places like coffee shops and living rooms, places where interactivity might otherwise be stonewalled by social norms. While business incubators and executive suites are targeted towards startups and freelancers, "coworking spaces" have emerged as one alternative. These environments tend to be more professional than cafés and are great surroundings when you find yourself changing out of your PJs into some "real" clothes for client meetings. Amenities vary from space to space, but you can bet you will find all the normal offerings you would need from a conventional office like conference rooms, whiteboards, fax and copy machines, and Wi-Fi access. If burning the midnight oil is when you find yourself working, some offices even offer 24-hour access—long past closing time at your neighborhood café. Look for drop-in rates if you want to try a space on for size or happen to be traveling for business; some spaces give free access to drop-ins! (Torres, 2008)

Jelly-like study groups have formed on and off campus. Students get together and work on separate homework items, projects, or studies. They socialize physically while being virtually connected to relevant partners. Geographic and time constraints are relaxed in this environment, but the need for physical social interaction is also addressed. Time after time I watched my son, Mark, and his girlfriend (now wife), Stacy, work together physically while interacting with separate virtual academic partners. This curious blend of physical togetherness with virtual separation is another characteristic of the tech-savvy millennial.

If I Can't Find It, I'll Make It: Creators

An amazing thing about the tech-savvy millennial is the creativity of this generation. Never before have so many tools been available for creating what has become a tidal wave of new content. Young people from all over the world are inventing imaginative and incredibly innovative digital artifacts including poetry, art, prose, comic strips, videos, animations, and numerous other things. Most items have nothing to do with their formal educational experience but instead result from their artistic urges and desire to post their creations and receive feedback from their peers.

One example website that encourages this artistic expression is deviantART (www.deviantart.com). DeviantART exemplifies the revolution of artistic sharing and emerging synergy of works being shared on an unprecedented scale. DeviantART has categories for the traditional arts such as painting, ceramics, literature, photography, and nearly any other form of expression imaginable. Typically, artists share digital replications of their nondigital works and directly display all forms of digital art. DeviantART was started in August of 2000 by Scott Jarkoff, Matthew Stephens, Angelo Sotira, and others with the aim of providing a place for any artist to exhibit, discuss, and share her or his work. By October 2009, over 11 million artists, writers, and enthusiasts were members. On average, deviantART has about 100,000 new items posted daily (Wikipedia, 2010c). See Figure 2.7.

Why Are Artistic Expression and Creativity Blooming?

The tech-savvy millennial arguably may form the heart of the most creative generation to walk the face of the earth. Is this because they are

Figure 2.7   deviantART Website

www.deviantart.com

smarter? If you boil the creative wave into its basic components, artistic expression requires several key elements. Among these are time, tools, inspiration, and the ability to transmit the artist's work. All of these elements have received incredible boosts in recent years with the advent of new information and communication technologies. Let's spend a moment looking at these components.

Time   Many tasks now take less time to complete. The ability to use new tools to complete school projects and an inherent bent toward timeslicing gives students time to engage in creative endeavors. Think back to how much time constructing a typed term paper required in the 1970s. Today, there is no comparison. From research right through to final draft construction, less time is required.

Tools   Thousands of creative software development tools and techniques now exist. Tech-savvy millennials (and anyone else) can easily use technology to transform their ideas into art, music, video, and voice products. There is no need to purchase paints, paintbrushes, or instruments or to rent a music studio. Access to a computer in a public library provides almost everything needed. The result of this creative enabling of an entire generation is a growing collection of content—some good and some missing the mark. The tech-savvy millennial is not afraid to experiment and is more than willing to throw away results that don't capture positive attention.

Inspiration   A world of inspiration exists just the click of a button away. Online communities such as deviantART (where art and music can be bought, sold, and displayed), Second Life, Facebook, MySpace, and even online equivalents of national museums provide the fodder and creative spark for an entirely new set of artistic expression. Tech-savvy millennials are exposed to an amazing array and diverse set of material that no generation (especially during their formative years) has collectively had at their disposal. These communities inspire, excite, and provide instruction on how to access, create, and view nearly an infinite set of material.

Transmission   What happens after the art is created? I remember finding a decrepit painting in a storage space of a house once. It was too far gone to preserve but had been an amazing oil painting created by the wife of a local farmer. Had she lived today, it is very likely that at least a digital version of that painting might be enjoyed by numerous people who would view it on deviantART. Perhaps art is no more popular than it ever was—it is just easier to share and view.

Honor Among Thieves or High-Tech Con Artists?

Nearly every tech-savvy millennial I have interviewed (over 90 percent of them), in one way or another, has enjoyed the forbidden fruit of digital content in violation of copyright protection laws. This illegal content ranges from downloading music to swiping software packages (like Microsoft's Office Suite) to copying full-length Hollywood movies. I have heard stories about students "helping" in their small rural high school's computer lab by loading hacked copies of different software packages onto each machine. These aren't bad kids nor are they conniving thieves. In fact, most truly believe what they are doing is okay, or they just haven't thought about legality. I hear justifications like *Well, my friend bought the download from iTunes and doesn't listen to it anymore so I used SoundTaxi to copy it over to my machine. He bought it, so he can do what he wants with it, right?* and *I paid to watch that movie in the theater, so it's okay to get a copy of it now. They already got my money for it.* I asked one student about the copyright agreement that plays at the beginning of the film. *No problem*, he said, smiling, *I edited that part out.* Or in the video game arena: *I own the Nintendo 64 version of the game. I just wanted to be able to run it on my computer, so I used Bit Torrent to download the PC version.* Or more commonly: *Everyone downloads free stuff. Why shouldn't I?*

Further compounding the problem is the culture of creating mash-ups. In general, mashups allow data from a variety of sources to be combined into a single useful application. Sounds perfect for educators, doesn't it? The good news is that mashups are legal in many cases. For instance, several major software vendors offer mashup web development tools (e.g., Yahoo! Pipes). These tools promote creativity and a culture of remixing, customizing, and personalizing digital content, provided the materials' copyrights permit such use. The tech-savvy millennial, however, doesn't always acknowledge copyright nuances. As a result, both Microsoft and Google have discontinued their tools for mashups.

Other mashups include remixing music. A well-known example is *The Grey Album*, released by Danger Mouse in 2004. It uses vocal tracks from rap artist Jay-Z's *The Black Album* and overlays instrumental tracks derived from *The Beatles (The White Album)*. The *Grey Album* was widely downloaded by tech-savvy millennials and others and has gained notoriety because of the flurry of publicity and lawsuits that it spawned.

For some, it has become a game about protection schemes and the thrill of cracking them. However, most tech-savvy millennials I interviewed have no ill intentions. It is easy to obtain content, experiment with different digital objects, and then delete and forget them. Adding to the situation are the mixed messages being sent to the tech-savvy millennial. Some recording artists publish ads against stealing digital material. Others say, *Please download our latest album (but then buy a ticket for our next concert)*. Society has not yet settled this issue decisively.

The emerging cultural networks and sense of linking into online communities have facilitated the idea of sharing. In this world, there is honor among thieves and digital pirates. By opening your hard drive up to the world, you are treated well in return. The issue of scarcity is not there. You are getting copies, and as many copies as are needed can be made.

Although some believe fewer tech-savvy millennials engage in piracy, major studies from the Business Software Alliance (BSA) show a 43 percent increase in software piracy in 2009 (BSA, 2010). Piracy is becoming more sophisticated and harder to track. Much of the sharing is done among friends and members of tightly knit social communities. Darknets are emerging almost daily as alternates to openly available websites. Darknets are private virtual networks that connect only users verified as "safe" or "cool." Most darknets are used for sharing digital content and are careful to block unknown users. Plenty of software exists to enable anyone to create their own darknet. Some examples are Allpeers, anoNet, and Freenet. The amount of digital content being traded and shared on these types of networks is staggering.

That being said, the purpose of this text is not to debate the ethics of digital piracy and who is right or wrong in this regard (although I foster that debate in my online classes). Instead, I am more interested in the reality of the situation. The tech-savvy millennial lives in a world where large-scale sharing exists. That sharing extends to any digital content and will include any educational material that is digitized. This means electronic textbooks, online lectures, term papers, assignments, test banks, and the like will be shared more and more.

Higher Education's Opportunity With Tech-Savvy Millennials

Most of us are not truly prepared to teach tech-savvy millennials on their terms. And perhaps we shouldn't do so without prudence. After all, the world may be changing, but in general, facts are facts, and mastery of a subject is dependent on delivery method only to some extent. Important material still must be presented in a way that makes it understandable. That being said, it is important to face the future and prepare our students for the world they will face. In some ways that is difficult. Looking back only five years, how many of us would have anticipated the current pace of technology, the unexpected innovations, and the realities of today's world?

Chapters 6 and 7 get into specific teaching ideas that will engage the tech-savvy millennial in a variety of ways. But for the moment, consider why today's learner is important to the way we must teach. Besides simply realizing new technologies are emerging continually and those technologies change how students complete assignments, study, and learn, we need to recognize that deeper changes are at hand too. Several issues we will be dealing with include the following:

1. Changing priorities regarding what should be learned and what should be recognized as reference material.
2. Teaching tools for filtering and accessing reliable information on an "as-needed" basis.
3. Understanding that our students are truly different people. They have been shaped by the society around them, and this society is vastly different from what most of us experienced. And it is not going back to the way it was. Ever.
4. Rethinking educational delivery. We may have to take our current system of higher education back to the basics and rethink the very way classes are delivered. Is it best to offer fixed semester courses, meeting at certain locations and at certain times? Is it best to trudge through preselected material in a linear fashion with the instructor/expert as the guide? Are socially networked learning methods a better way to go? Should learning break through the university walls and link together scholars and students from around the world in ways that leverage the incredible strengths of emerging new technologies and social changes? Or should we keep

things relatively the same and let our students be the catalysts of change later, when their generation becomes the primary force in the workplace and in higher education? After all, our students are going to be working in a world dominated by Gen Xers and baby boomers until our generations retire.

Perhaps we can only offer them the best tools and skills of our generation while encouraging them to change the world with the playthings of their youth. We can teach them and they can teach us. We may discover this cooperative approach results in better and higher quality learning for all of us. We professors need to use our judgment to help students understand our subject areas and why it is necessary to take a particular path toward their destination, subject mastery. Then we need to make sure we keep ourselves up-to-date and familiar with all the ways information is being developed, shared, and connected.

Notes

1. Just a few months after writing this, I was informed by Megan how "out of date" this paragraph already had become!

2. The term *digital native* recently has fallen out of favor with many researchers and pundits. The initial image of a cohesive group of young people easily coexisting with rapidly advancing technology is being reevaluated and reconsidered as a much more complex dynamic than the "digital native" characterization provides. It is true that many youth interact with technology in surprisingly sophisticated ways. However, their experience and skill levels are far from uniform. Evidence of their technological superiority has not been documented nor have changes in neurological development or learning styles. Further, many first-generation students may not have enjoyed the same privilege of access to high-tech devices in the home as their middle-class counterparts. This is not to say that teaching and learning are not undergoing changes. To explore these changes, this chapter focuses on a tech-savvy subset of millennials who, in some literature, might be tagged as digital natives. I believe it is important to rigorously investigate the phenomenon taking place while trying to understand the magnitude of any changes. Higher education needs to be vigilant not to be caught off guard as have many industries in the past.

3. I have altered the name to protect her online identity.

4. These are identities or characters that aquire a number of privileges with reaching level 70.

5. Perhaps with the exception of first-run sports events and other live-action events.

6. I hope it's only a small percent but sometimes suspect otherwise.

7. The discussions took place at the 2010 Gmunden NeuroIS Retreat held June 28–30, 2010, in Gmunden, Austria (http://neurois.org).

CHAPTER THREE

THE NEW SHORELINE'S TOPOGRAPHY

Platforms for Learning

Tech-savvy millennials don't always recognize the amazing days in which they live. Transition periods are far more interesting times to be alive. In Arthur C. Clarke's third law of prediction, he states, "Any sufficiently advanced technology is indistinguishable from magic" (Clarke, 1962, p. 36, footnote). Currently, plenty of "magic" is being embraced by tech-savvy millennials. Today's teachers can learn from this to develop more meaningful and fuller pedagogical experiences for students. A number of important technologies have converged to enable this transition. Among these are interaction devices, content development tools, video game systems, and probably the most important, smart mobile devices. Added to the mix are virtual learning environments (VLEs) meant to leverage the power of the Web within the safety of a controlled classroom. But should tech-savvy millennials use VLEs or move directly into the powerful social webs and information resources emerging in cyberspace?

THE TITLE OF THIS CHAPTER, "The New Shoreline's Topography: Platforms for Learning," is meant to convey the reality infusing higher education today. Recently, I attended a talk by a well-known communications professor and she summed up her presentation with a comment to the effect that, as professors, we need to get our students back into the library where they can learn to appreciate books the way we did.

As much as I agree with the premise of her argument, I don't agree with the reasoning behind it. She suggests that the ease with which information of varying quality can be collected on the Web has stunted the ability of students to do meaningful research. Although there may be some truth in this, the changes taking place will not reverse. Having greater access to more information can be only positive in the long run. While there is little doubt that libraries will continue to hold books, new platforms, such as e-book readers, are emerging to augment traditional books with searching, annotating, and note taking.

Students are living in a fundamentally transformed world, restructured by incredible new forces with the potential to reshape the way humans interact. The ease of exchanging information as well as the ability to make complex, meaningful social connections is a new, global reality.

As educators, we have the monumental task of learning to use these new capabilities in ways that enhance and build on what we already have learned to be true and useful. This is not an occasion for despair, because changes have the potential for a transformative synergy of technology, scholarship, and pedagogy. One can add an entire generation of eager, motivated, excited, and engaged young people to the mix. But we must bear in mind that, just because they are ready to accept and use information systems, computers, mobile devices, social networks, and virtual reality games doesn't mean they are experts in understanding how to filter information and determine its value and relevance. They are more willing to dabble and explore, and they have good instincts regarding ways to make better use of the digital world emerging around us, but we still have an incredible responsibility to ensure the continuity of higher education.

Technological Changes and the Future

For centuries or even millennia, men and women have worked hard to understand and predict the future. I tend to view futurists with skepticism but still allow my eyes to peer out ahead. For that reason, I appreciate sci-fi writer Arthur C. Clarke's (1973) three laws of prediction:

1. "When a distinguished but elderly scientist states that something is possible, he is almost certainly right. When he states that something is impossible, he is very probably wrong" (p. 14).
2. "The only way of discovering the limits of the possible is to venture a little way past them into the impossible" (p. 21).

3. "Any sufficiently advanced technology is indistinguishable from magic" (Clarke, 1973, p. 36, footnote).

To rise to the next level, higher education must, to quote Clarke, "venture a little way past [its limits] into the impossible" and use "sufficiently advanced technology [that] is indistinguishable from magic."

Roy Amara of the Institute for the Future once said, "we tend to overestimate the effect of a technology in the short run and underestimate the effect in the long run" (PCMag.com, 2010a). Current computer and communication technologies are not going to change higher education instantly, but 10 years from now, many of our traditional approaches to education will no longer be recognizable.

Is that to say what is here today will be gone? Not gone—it will be changed in some ways and constant in others. We are currently in a transitional state brought about by the convergence of several disruptive technologies including computers and communications networks. Out of this we have the World Wide Web, mobile computing, rich media, and many other examples of the *new magic* sweeping the world. Change accelerates with innovation then levels out when its potential is realized (Hughes, 2004). For example, many everyday items we take for granted still are constructed in tried-and-true ways. Glass is made the same way it was centuries ago. We continue to have windows, vases, jars, and other glass items. Concrete remains a fundamental building block for most construction projects. Older technologies make it possible to advance into new ones. Without electricity, computers and the World Wide Web would not be feasible (Seidensticker, 2006).

Likewise, it is important not to become infatuated with technology just because it exists. In higher education, we should not use technologies just because they are available. Innovation needs to make pedagogical sense and contribute to the learning experience of students.

Many of the most successful advances in teaching and learning are related to technologies that enhance student experiences and mirror their new capabilities in the broader world.

I attended a talk by MIT research scientist Dr. David Cavallo. He told an amusing anecdote about the bane of all grade school children: division of fractions—dividing 13/34 by 7/9 and so forth. He had tried to explain the importance and relevance of mastering this skill to an elementary school student. However, he had a hard time remembering an instance when he was faced with such a problem in real life. After going back and forth on the issue for a while and being given a demonstration by the student of how easy it was to accomplish the task on a computer, he finally said, "Great, but what happens if the electricity goes out and you can't use your computer?" The student paused a moment and then answered, "If our electricity is gone, we've got a lot more to worry about than what 13/34 divided by 7/9 would be." This makes a great deal of sense. Certain levels of drudgery must be ceded to technology (Cavallo, 2007). The questions become where to draw the line today and where to relocate that line tomorrow.

Reducing some skills opens the door to spend time learning the next set of skills (Edgerton, 2007). As teachers, we must learn to gracefully determine which skills are important and which complexities to cede to technology. Our minds need reduced clutter so new problems can be solved.

Albert Einstein was of the same mindset. He attributed much of his success to his ability to stop thinking about "the way things are done" and instead visualize breakthroughs and the big picture (even though his big pictures were at the subatomic level!). Einstein said, "Imagination is more important than knowledge." Extended to the modern day, it makes more sense to focus on extending knowledge that technology can supply rather than relearning and stepping through the details of first principles. Cultivation of obsolete skills must be pushed aside to open the door to new advancements. Imagination and creativity can be enhanced by reducing rote learning and reaching for the next big idea.

Overview of Platforms

Several key technological structures undergird the *magic* elements found on higher education's new shoreline. These structures are both artifacts of the broader changes taking place and enablers of the revolution. Although entire books could be dedicated to the details and uses of these technologies, we will focus on a specific, key subset and its importance to the higher education community.

In order to better understand the use of technology and why these changes are taking place, a quick overview of societal trends is warranted. A general observation about technology is that it has moved from broad, public applications to increasingly personal levels. This trend is impacting higher education in many ways. Traditionally, technology in education has been implemented only on a broad scale for highly visible use in the classroom, usually by the teacher. Examples range from chalkboards to whiteboards to today's interactive smart boards and overhead projectors.

Educational technology began its migration from public systems to more personal ones with the advent of the personal computer in the early 1980s. Linda Stone (2009) maps the progress of these trends, assigning them to several categories (see Table 3.1). First, information, documents, spreadsheets, and various tools became available for personal use on a desktop computer. This is what Stone calls the *personal layer computing* trend. Personal computing has moved into the private sphere in recent years with the advent of cellular phones, smart mobile devices, and tablets: In *private layer computing*, individuals control information flow through mobile devices, apps, and social networking.

Higher education is still trying to understand how these technologies fit into the classroom. Web 2.0 technologies have pulled back the shroud on our private lives and integrated technology into all parts of our social lives. This trend will continue as technologies move again, this time from our private lives into intimate proximity with our physical being. *Intimate*

Table 3.1 Movement of Technology to More Intimate Levels

Public Layer	Mainframe Computers (1945–1965)	Power of information was controlled by a select few individuals such as corporate managers.
Personal Layer	The Personal Computer (1965–1985)	Power of information moved to the desktop so knowledge workers could control data, words, and images.
Private Layer	Mobile Devices (1985–2005)	Power of information moved to the individual so anyone with a network connection and computing platform could control data, words, video, and images.
Intimate Layer	Self Technologies (2005–2025?)	Power of information will be intimately connected to the individual's physical presence and integrated with networked computing platforms.

Note: Adapted from *Why Managing Vulnerability and Reputation is More Important Than Ever Before* by Linda Stone, 2009. Retrieved from http://lindastone.net

layer computing will result in devices that monitor our brain waves, examine our sleep patterns, and clock our heart rates—examples of the wide array of technologies being developed and tested.

Currently, higher education is experimenting with integration of private layer technologies into teaching and learning. This chapter examines a number of these in the following sections and provides insights about and examples of how higher education's mavens are enhancing teaching. Specifically, we look at interaction devices (such as clickers, microphones, and webcams), content development tools (such as digital and video cameras), video game consoles, a range of mobile devices, and course management systems. Software-based Web 2.0 technologies will be explored in much the same way in chapters 4 and 5.

Interaction Devices

The tech-savvy millennial has come of age in an environment that fosters and expects communication in a variety of ways. Websites provide space for comments and suggestions. Online vendors allow products to be rated and ranked. Older paradigms for one-way communication from a central source to the masses are being pushed aside for models that promote interactivity.

These ideas are finding their way into the classroom as well. As technology becomes more prevalent in the private arena, good teachers have searched for mechanisms to foster multichannel communication both in class and beyond. This has resulted in the expansion of classrooms into ClassSpace, a learning environment that uses the best of both traditional classroom and new media/social network augmented teaching practices. Using technology, classrooms can be connected both internally (giving student attendees a bigger voice) and externally (with other classrooms and with online learning systems). Interaction devices such as clickers, microphones, and webcams can help.

Clickers

These input devices, often called student response systems (SRS), permit students in a classroom to express their views anonymously. A public screen displays a cumulative view of the entire class's opinion when questions are asked or opinions solicited. Although responses are publicly anonymous, the instructor has access to a number associated with each device so classroom contributions can be better understood. According to Martyn (2007), clickers help instructors in three major ways:

- ♦ Actively engage students during the entire class period
- ♦ Gauge their level of understanding of the material being presented
- ♦ Provide prompt feedback to student questions

Clickers can help move a class from passive to active learning and allow teachers to assess whether an entire class understands a concept, moving the focus from the most outspoken members of a class to the entire group. Martyn (2007) also says that clickers "follow the principles of game-based learning. Students of the twenty-first century have grown up using computer games for learning and entertainment."

Microphones

Of course, microphones can be used to amplify teachers' or students' voices in the classroom. A variety of high-quality products are available for this purpose. However, as classrooms morph into ClassSpaces, a variety of participants need enhanced voice capabilities both physically and virtually so they can communicate in virtual venues. These participants use technology to provide discussion, feedback, and lectures. One successful technique used by good teachers, particularly in asynchronous class delivery, is recording audio clips for individual students. Free software packages such as Audacity (http://audacity.sourceforge.net) interface with inexpensive microphones to enable teachers to interact with students regarding assignment feedback, grades, and other individual and group communications. Quickly recording and sending an audio clip is often faster than typing an email message, and it enables a richer form of communication. Other interaction paradigms include permitting "outside" speakers to lecture via voice and allowing students to record and post their commentary.

Webcams

Extending voice to include video means richer communication can be accomplished with an inexpensive webcam. Lectures can be posted. Virtual guest speakers can be streamed in live or asynchronously. Student feedback can be recorded and sent easily. Off-campus students can connect to the classroom via webcam and still have their voices and faces seen and heard. Services such as BlogTV and Stickam can be used for streaming webcam video into the classroom. Individual solutions can also be developed with Skype and other communication tools such as Yahoo Messenger.

Teaching Implications of Interaction Devices

A goal of classroom teaching has been to move passive learners into an active mode. Technology has provided innovative ways of attaining this goal with clickers, microphones, webcams, and other devices. While clickers are a step in the right direction, some teachers find the interactivity too limited and instead embrace the idea of more sophisticated solutions. One professor, Perry Sampson, who teaches atmospheric, oceanic, and space sciences at the University of Michigan, has developed a "next generation interaction device" that uses a laptop or other computer to run his open source software application called LectureTools (Sampson, 2010; see Figure 3.1).

LectureTools adds a wide variety of question types to the clicker function including *multiple choice, true/false, reordering, association, free response and image-based questions*. Additionally, classroom learning is enhanced with other features: annotation on PowerPoint slides, sharing

Figure 3.1   LectureTools Application

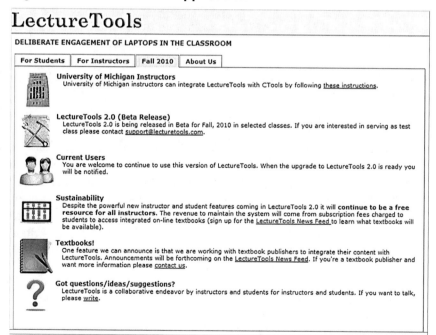

www.lecturetools.org

learning objects, and podcast downloads. LectureTools brings many online learning features into the physical classroom. Some tools in this system are for teacher monitoring and others are for student interaction. Overall, the idea of increasing connectivity in the classroom between teachers and students in all directions is being achieved (Briggs, 2009).

Other interaction methodologies also are being developed. Microsoft released a piece of software that uses computer mouses to interact with a PowerPoint add-on in the classroom. While not intended to be a clicker replacement, it enables students to annotate and interact with teachers in a variety of sophisticated ways (Nagal, 2010).

Higher education has realized the need for active learning. Today's tech-savvy millennials expect and need connections and interactivity for learning. The tools starting to emerge are moving the classroom, and by extension ClassSpaces, in this direction.

Content Development Tools for Students

Tech-savvy millennials have documented their lives with digital pictures and digital video. They regularly post photos of themselves and their friends on social networking websites. They frequently take photos with their mobile devices and share them via texting. They capture funny moments on video for friends. It is no surprise they expect to incorporate photos and videos into their learning experiences. The technology to accomplish this is readily available.

Digital and Video Cameras

In my classes, I often assign projects that require the use of video or photo creation. The resulting digital artifacts are not the focus of the course. However, the content contained in the artifacts is expected to be accurate, meaningful, and relevant to the course like any term paper or other assignment. Five years ago, many students did not have access to video or photography equipment the way they do now. At Kansas State University, students who don't own these devices can borrow them from the library, and so access is no longer an issue.

I generally don't provide instructions regarding how to create, edit, and produce photos or videos. Instead, I provide my students with links to websites that describe how to use a video editor and what file formats should be used to publish videos. I run across the rare student requiring more help, but he or she is the exception to the rule.

Teaching Implications of Content Development Tools

Creating content for learning and as components of projects can have enormous benefits for both students and teachers. Content development can enhance learning, motivate students, foster creativity, and in general empower students as active learners. It can also enhance their visual literacy.[1]

In general, successful teachers I interviewed report using digital cameras and video cameras for projects that involve developing tutorials or training. When events take place in a sequence, such as in an experiment or when constructing an object, photo or video documentation can be very powerful.

Students can share digital content with classmates using a VLE message board or via a website such as Flickr.com or YouTube.com. Karen Schrock's website[2] on Discovery Education provides resources that promote and discuss the use of these technologies in teaching and learning (Schrock, 2010).

Video Game Consoles and Devices

Video games have gained popularity in the education sector at a steady pace. Generally, video games (also called computer games) represent reality as a form of simulation. These games convey realism and permit learners to experience emulated situations requiring decisions and outcomes similar to what they might encounter in the real world. Video games for education encompass business simulations, ethical decision-making scenarios, civilization development, historical situations, city growth, economics, emergency response, stock trading, engineering problems, marketing decisions, and other situations. Video games are generally played on consoles (e.g., Nintendo Wii, Sony PlayStation, and Microsoft Xbox 360) but can also be played on PCs and Macs. Video games were once considered the domain of young adolescent males but now are much more pervasive, with the average game player being 35 years old and about 65 percent of American households including at least one video game player (GrabStats, 2010).

Major Players

In 2009, three main console manufacturers dominated the video game platform marketplace. (As you might guess, the three tech-savvy millennials living in my household ensured we owned all three.) Of these, the

Nintendo Wii held the top slot, with approximately a 47 percent market share. Microsoft's Xbox 360 was second at 35.1 percent, and Sony's PS3 held a 17.9 percent share (Gruener, 2009). In the portable game marketplace, a different picture is emerging. With the advent of the iPhone and iPod Touch as game platforms, Apple has cut into the traditional leaders' market shares. Up from a 5 percent share in 2008, Apple's platforms held a 19 percent share in 2009. The leader, Nintendo's DS, had a 70 percent share and the Sony Portable, 11 percent (Dalrymple, 2010). That trend continued to swing in Apple's favor following the 2010 release of the iPad.

Most analysts don't believe any one of the game consoles is clearly superior in all demographics but instead continue to predict fierce competition among the rival companies. An important feature of all video game consoles and portable game platforms is Internet connectivity. This feature not only provides a mechanism to acquire and update games but, more important, enables users to engage in multiplayer games with rivals located anywhere in the world. This connectivity has added greatly to the surge in video game use.

Teaching Implications of Video Game Consoles

Most tech-savvy millennials have enjoyed access to video game consoles their entire lives. They have learned complex material, practiced actions, and experienced decision making in the context of simulated situations. This is normal in their world and makes sense for their learning. Linguist John Paul Gee supports the idea that various forms of literacy and the learning process are enhanced through the use of video games (Gee, 2003). He points out that in today's world language is not the only communication system available. He believes visual images and symbols have increased in significance and must be included in the learning process. He further suggests that visual literacy is becoming as important as that of the spoken and written word in communication media.

Within this context, games can be used to support teaching and learning in ways familiar to the tech-savvy millennial. Games offer a realistic way to promote content and encourage active learning. They become learning objects useful to both students and teachers. Further, with the features found on most consoles, video games enable students to connect with the world and with each other. Social computing is, in part, a side effect of the gaming environment emerging from the entertainment industry.

Game consoles are not prevalent in academic settings, and this is due in part to the lack of true educational games for these devices. While this area offers great promise, the time required to develop a world-class game is immense, and this has slowed the spread of these tools. Specific applications in this area will be discussed in chapter 4.

Mobile Devices

Mobile devices have redefined daily life for many people (including me!) and have been a primary tool associated with the tech-savvy millennial. Mobile devices range from simple cell phones to full-featured smart devices and laptop computers with large amounts of memory and computing capacity. The advent of the mobile device has required higher education to reevaluate its thinking about what devices should be permitted in the classroom and how these widely varying tools can be used to enhance the learning process. The transition of mobile device from communication tool to comprehensive computing platform has enabled higher education to experiment with integrating private layer technologies into teaching and learning. While some researchers report disappointment with the slow rate at which mobile technologies are permeating the educational landscape, others see a great deal of promise and point to early successes. The latter group foresees the day when education will be defined by mobile technology in what some call "m-learning."

Mobile Phones and Smart Devices

Modern mobile phones, also called cellular phones, were introduced by Motorola in 1973 (Cassavoy, 2007).[3] Initially, these devices were bulky and cumbersome, weighing in at over two kilos, and were priced too high for mass-market use (Heeks, 2008). Between that time and the present day, a steady progression of technological improvements from a variety of competing organizations has resulted in an environment where mobile phones are nearly ubiquitous and offer a wide range of capabilities and services. Most recently, these devices have evolved into mobile-computing platforms.

Most mobile phones offer the same basic features, but competing manufacturers use innovative ideas to differentiate their products and stimulate sales. Basic phones, known as feature phones, offer telephone service and often add music players, cameras, and text messaging. However, these are increasingly rare.

As early as 1996, Nokia introduced the Nokia 9000 Communicator, which combined a personal digital assistant (PDA) with a mobile phone (Nokia, 1996). This class of device, later known as a smartphone, triggered moves by other manufacturers to change from simple telephone devices to mobile-computing platforms, or smart devices, by embedding sophisticated microchips into their phones. Today, most smart mobile devices include features in addition to telephony such as texting, music and video players, GPS navigation, alarms, memo recording, calendaring, video recording, cameras, ringtones, email service, and Internet browsing.

The release of Handspring's Palm OS Treo smartphone in 2002 marked the beginning of the next wave of innovation. The Palm operating system allowed this device to combine prior smartphone features such as Web browsing, email, and calendaring with the ability to run third-party-developed mobile phone applications obtained from the Internet and synched with a desktop or laptop computer. This capability provided a platform for the development of specialty applications suited to a wide variety of mobile users (Wildstrom, 2001).

In 2005, Nokia's press releases rebranded its N-Series of 3G smartphones as multimedia mobile computers. In 2007, Apple countered with the first version of the iPhone. Within a year, Apple revealed its Internet-based App Store modeled after its highly successful online music store, iTunes. The Apple App store immediately began to offer thousands of both free and paid apps (i.e., application programs) for iPhone users. By January 2010, Apple announced that its three billionth app had been downloaded (Apple, Inc., 2010a). During that same time period, Apple's App Store hosted more than 200,000 items for use on iPhones, iPod Touches, and iPads. These items were developed largely by registered third-party software developers and delivered via the Internet. The apps can be synched between computer and mobile device using the iTunes application on a Mac or PC.

A major competitor to Apple's mobile-computing platforms, Android, was released in 2008. It is an open source platform that enables third-party applications to be developed and run on a number of different smartphones. Because it is open source, development on this platform is less controlled than Apple's. Android is backed by a number of powerful organizations that formed the Open Handset Alliance. Included in this effort are Google, Intel, Motorola, and eBay. Google has developed mobile software for the platform based on its free online software tools such as Maps, Calendar, Gmail, and its browser. In July of 2010, Google's Android Market offered nearly 100,000 free and paid apps for smart-phones using the Android operating system (AndroLib, 2010).

E-Book Readers

Without a doubt, one of the most hotly contested markets in the next few years will be for e-book readers. The current market climate reminds me of what was experienced in the MP3 music player market prior to the Apple iPod's becoming the de facto standard and redefining the way music is distributed, played, and shared. In general, e-book readers, or e-readers, are portable devices designed to display digital books, journals, newspapers, magazines, documents, blogs, RSS feeds, and other material. E-readers can either be dedicated devices like the Amazon Kindle or Sony Reader, or they can be a function found on a device that also serves other purposes such as the Apple iPad or an Android OS smart phone. Most e-readers provide a variety of features in addition to interfaces to digital documents. At least four important devices have influenced the early e-book reader market: Amazon's Kindle, Sony Reader, Barnes & Noble Nook, and Apple's iPad.

Amazon's Kindle   In November of 2007, Amazon released its entry in the e-book reader market. The first-generation Kindle was a handheld device that weighed a little over 10 ounces and held over 200 books. Removable memory cards gave it even more storage capacity. It was attached to Sprint's EvDO wireless broadband network (dubbed Whis-pernet by Amazon) giving the Kindle access to hundreds of thousands of books, magazines, blogs, and other documents. Kindle was the first e-book reader to provide high-speed network access without monthly subscription fees. All network costs were built into the price of purchased material. In February of 2009, the Kindle 2 was released, with its lighter, slimmer profile, sharper contrast, ability to hold over 1,500 titles, and longer battery life (Bezos, 2009). In October of 2009, Amazon released an international version of the Kindle 2 that uses AT&T's U.S. mobile net-work and a variety of GSM networks in over 100 countries.

Sony Reader   What is the real name for this reader? It took me a while to figure that out. When I first heard about its release, I scoured the Web expecting to find a device with a catchy, high-tech-sounding, or literary name, but instead of finding something like the "Hemingway," the "Faulkner," or even the "Tolkien," I found instead the underwhelming "Sony PRS-700 BC Reader." Well, in a way the name belies the enthusiasm with which the public has adopted the device. Although the Sony Reader is at least aesthetically attractive, in my opinion, its drawbacks as compared to the Kindle are access to fewer titles through the Sony Reader Store (e-bookstore) and its less-powerful networking capability. Many of this reader's general characteristics are similar to the Kindle. The Sony Reader relies on the same e-Ink electronic paper technology as the Kindle, which means power is consumed only when text changes (Sony, 2009).

Barnes & Noble Nook　　The Nook was developed by Barnes & Noble to mirror Amazon's success with the Kindle. The Nook utilizes Google's mostly open source Android mobile platform and so has the potential to become a broader mobile-computing platform. Like Kindle 2, Nook uses AT&T's 3G network but also works on Wi-Fi. In addition to offering many of Kindle 2's features, Nook recreates various aspects of the traditional paper-based reading experience with features such as book sharing between friends and reading an e-book for an hour for free before purchasing in a Barnes & Noble store. Because the Nook uses an open source platform, third-party software adds to the capabilities of this reading platform and allows integration with other applications and platforms.

iPad From Apple　　April 2010 marked the release of Apple's iPad tablet device. Intended to provide a means for Internet browsing, video, audio, and other media consumption, gaming, personal productivity, and organizational tools, the iPad moved mobile computing and communications to the next level (Apple, Inc., 2010c). Among the 150,000 + applications available following the iPad's release, several related to e-books. Apple's free book reader app, called iBooks, can be downloaded and installed on the iPad (see Figure 3.2). The application starts with an image of a wooden bookshelf that holds a library of books. When a book is selected, it expands to cover the screen and provides a sense of location within the book by showing the depth on edges of the pages and shadowed central spine region. Pages can be turned with a motion that mimics turning a physical book page. The book can be viewed in either portrait or landscape mode with a variety of font types and sizes. The iPad is backlit and provides a color interface. A dictionary, bookmarks, searches, and other

Figure 3.2 Apple's iBooks App

features are available to make it possible to perform computer-enabled tasks related to book reading.

Books can be purchased from the iBooks store, which is concealed "behind" the bookshelf. Purchased books are protected and can be read only on an iPad. However, non-DRM (i.e., non–digital rights management) books in the EPUB file format can be acquired from other sources and read on the iPad.

In response to the iBook app, Amazon quickly provided a Kindle iPad app that makes it possible for Amazon book titles intended for the Kindle to be read on the iPad. New purchases to be read with the iPad's Kindle app must be made through Amazon's website and not through the app itself. Existing books purchased previously or that have been loaded onto a Kindle device using the same account number can be accessed and loaded onto the iPad Kindle app easily, and I have transferred most of my Kindle titles to my iPad. Barnes & Noble quickly followed with a Nook app that offers similar features. Another e-book reader app on the iPad is Kobo. This app serves as a cross-platform e-book client and is promoted by Borders. Kobo clients are also available on other mobile devices including the Blackberry and Google's Android platforms. Kobo makes it possible to purchase books and access a large collection of free public domain books.

The appearance of these e-reader apps—Kindle, Nook, and Kobo—means it is no longer necessary to purchase a separate device to utilize its functionality. In fact, all three also offer free apps for laptop and desktop PCs:

Kindle—https://kindle.amazon.com
Nook—www.barnesandnoble.com/u/nook-for-pc/379002322/
Kobo—www.kobobooks.com/desktops/

Tablets

Some e-readers, particularly the Nook with its Android-based operating system, are essentially multipurpose mobile-computing platforms that belong to the category of tablet PCs. According to *PC Magazine*, a tablet computer is a "complete computer contained in a touch screen. Tablet computers can be specialized for Internet use only or be full-blown, general-purpose PCs. The distinguishing characteristic is the use of the screen as an input device for stylus or finger movement" (PCMag.com, 2010b). Tablet computers have been commercially available since September 1989, when the GridPad was released (Byte, 1990). From 1989 to 2001, a wide variety of tablet-like devices were produced by a variety of manufacturers (Ward, 2010). None of these definitively caught the public's imagination. In 2001, Microsoft announced its Windows XP Tablet PC Edition operating system and demonstrated it on a prototype hardware platform. This encouraged more hardware development, and a variety of new platforms emerged.

It wasn't until April 2010 with the release of Apple's iPad that the public became enamored with the idea of tablet computing. Apple reported sales exceeding 3 million units in less than three months following the iPad's debut in stores (Apple, Inc., 2010b). The iPad's success can be attributed to several factors. First, it was released to a customer base loyal to other popular Apple products such as the iPhone and iPod Touch. Second, it was designed specifically to support private layer application of technology (Stone, 2009), with tools for acquiring and consuming movies, music, books, and magazines. A wide variety of games, entertainment applications, and educational tools were also available for the platform upon release. Specifically, iPad came with the Safari Web browser, email applications, a photo viewer, a video player, iTunes, App Store, iBooks, iPod, calendar, notes, and other tools.

The iPad has an appealing, slim design with a 25-centimeter, backlit liquid crystal display that is meant to be controlled with bare fingers. Sensors enable up to 11 fingers to simultaneously operate the screen. The display moves between portrait and landscape modes depending on the orientation of the device. Versions of the iPad have both Wi-Fi and 3G Internet connectivity and can also be connected to a PC or Mac to synch application data and multimedia libraries. The iPad is not intended to be a mobile phone but can run phone apps such as Skype (Lendino, 2010) when coupled with a Bluetooth headset (Sarno, 2010).

Netbooks and Small Laptops

Netbooks and small laptop computers have gained widespread acceptance since their introduction in 2007 (Bajarin, 2008). Sometimes called ultra-portables, these lightweight, inexpensive computers have found their way into higher education's landscape in a big way. Although for most users these are not their primary computing platforms, they can be used in the classroom for taking notes, for composing papers, and for Internet access. They also are convenient tools to use while traveling or attending meetings.

Typical netbooks weigh between 1.5 and 3 pounds and have 5- to 7-inch screens. Netbooks were initially envisioned as computers with reduced capabilities, but like all mobile-computing platforms have demonstrated that even CPU-intensive applications can be successfully moved to these smaller-footprint machines. The name "netbook" is derived from the original concept that these machines would serve primarily as Internet clients for applications running on servers. As a result, many netbooks come with wireless Internet service packages, and some netbooks are free with the purchase of an extended wireless Internet service contract (Vance & Richtel, 2009).

In 2009, netbooks helped fuel a surge in technology purchases (Fortt, 2008), but by 2010 the sales figures were already being reduced by the release of Apple's iPad tablet computer (Crothers, 2010).

Teaching Implications of Mobile Devices

In 2009, Alan Livingstone, director of research, development, and planning at Weber State University, wrote an article published in *EDUCAUSE Quarterly* titled "The Revolution No One Noticed: Mobile Phones and Multimobile Services in Higher Education." In it he says, "The past decade has witnessed two revolutions in communication technology. The first—the Internet revolution—has changed everything in higher education. The second—the mobile phone revolution—has changed nothing." Although this might not be entirely true, it does make a valid point: Our

students have embraced mobile technology and, in response to my surveys, overwhelmingly named it as the *one technology they can't live without.* Yet the mobile-computing revolution has had very little impact on
the way most of us teach and learn.

I believe those of us working and teaching in higher education can
point to at least two major failings that have contributed to this oversight.
First, our initial impression of mobile technology was to dismiss it as
distracting from our students' education. Second, like hapless frogs swim-
ming in a pot of water slowly brought to a boil, we have failed to realize
that technology is "heating up" in this area. We have largely missed an
unprecedented technological convergence (Jenkins, 2006) that took place
as both devices and software evolved from the personal to the private
layer (Stone, 2009). These changes are driving new developments that
cannot be ignored, because our students have tightly integrated these
capabilities into their daily lives. Let's look at these two points more
closely.

The other day I walked into one of my favorite sandwich shops in
Manhattan, Kansas. I immediately noticed that the large, annoying hand-
written sign announcing "Cell phones not permitted while waiting in
line!" was gone. I casually asked the person taking orders what happened
to their sign. He smiled a little and shrugged before mumbling something
like, "I guess we joined the 21st century." I asked him what he meant,
and he said that their corporate offices send out coupons and specials to
customers' mobile phones. These mobile offers are to be used by customers at the store to get discounts or try new items. Sure, it is annoying to
take an order from someone busy yakking with their friends, but phones
are for more than just talking.

If teachers in higher education (me included!) were to look at their
class syllabi, they would probably see that same annoying sign: *Cell phones
not permitted while learning!* If this does not appear on your syllabus, then
I would guess you tell your class that cell phones are not to be used
during class time. Traditionally, most elementary and high schools limit
or ban the use of mobile phones. Colleges and universities do the same
for obvious reasons. Phones can be used to cheat on tests and in-class
assignments. Phones distract students and encourage texting rather than
paying attention.[4] Other bans on cell phones are meant to protect student
privacy in restrooms and locker rooms, where built-in cameras are a
concern.

Am I advocating cell phone use in the class? Perhaps not "no holds barred" use, but responsible use should be considered. Just as smart mobile devices have become indispensible in the business world, students have to learn how to use their devices in respectful and productive ways. In the words of the sandwich-shop worker, I guess it is time we joined the 21st century and start seeing how the benefits of smart mobile devices can outweigh the disadvantages.

One of the reasons I advocate mobile device use is because of my second point: the fact that we are slow to recognize the technological convergence taking place. By definition, technological convergence is the tendency for different systems to add features and move toward performing similar tasks (Wikipedia, 2010f). For instance, phones once facilitated communication. Cameras once captured images. Tape recorders once captured sound. Video players once displayed moving images. These started as separate technologies. Now, it is possible to acquire devices that cross over and perform additional functions. And with the advent of smart mobile devices, the convergence of many separate technologies is almost complete.

Digital computing and miniaturization have enabled this revolution to take place. Smart mobile devices are quickly becoming platforms that enable, facilitate, and inspire the tech-savvy millennials to possess a different set of cognitive skills and characteristics that in turn strengthen the cycle and require even better platforms with more sophisticated digital tools and communications capabilities. Many experts believe the convergence has just begun and will soon permeate all aspects of society, business, and education.

In Livingstone's 2009 article, after commenting on how higher education is missing the mobile revolution, he provides examples of ways smart mobile devices can and are being used. Among these are "multimobile services." Multimobile services allow the user's preference of voice, text messaging, instant messaging, email, and Web interfaces to drive a series of applications for class registration, tuition payment, scheduling, advising, athletic and theater ticket purchases, and accessing a number of other university services.

Livingstone and others also suggest the use of smart mobile devices to replace clickers as classroom interaction devices so polls and questions can be answered in class (Tremblay, 2010). Mobile devices can permit questions to be texted in during class without interrupting the lecture and posted on a public screen. Mobile devices are ideal for contacting class members with cancellation notices or reminders. These devices also could be used to track attendance, interface with virtual learning environments such as Blackboard (Young, 2010), download course material, and record class lectures. The possibilities are nearly limitless.

Acquisition and use of class materials such as electronic textbooks becomes feasible with the availability of e-readers, tablets, and netbooks. Games for learning, simulations, illustrations, practice quizzes, and a multitude of other material can be distributed to students using these technologies. Many universities are adding wireless infrastructure with the belief that, if tablet computers such as the iPad catch on and if textbook publishers make digital versions of their books and chapters available for purchase or rent by students, much greater demand could be placed on university networks during class time (Peck, 2010). Mobile learning and distance learning can also be enhanced in that environment (MLearning Website, 2010).

In my opinion, the combined forces of convergence and evolution of technology into the private layer will push higher education to find a basic platform for teaching and learning. The iPad or similar device seems poised to accomplish this. The ultimate outcome may depend on whether an infrastructure such as iTunes Store emerges to support the buying and selling of educational material. In any case, a large number of apps supporting education are emerging for the iPad and other devices. These are explored in more detail in chapter 5.

Virtual Learning Environments

Virtual learning environments are widespread in higher education. At its most basic level, a VLE is computer software and hardware to facilitate learning online. VLEs are often called learning management systems (LMS), content or course management systems (CMS), learning support systems (LSS), or learning platforms (LP). VLEs were initially developed for use with distance learning but have been widely adopted as supplemental tools for traditional face-to-face classrooms. This practice is known as *blended learning*. Features were developed to house course content for use over the Internet and enable students to have a space where online faculty and peer interaction could take place.

A goal of most VLEs is to provide teaching and learning tools that enhance a student's class experience and promote learning. VLEs have a range of tools to accomplish learning objectives. Often included is a content management subsystem that enables courses to be broken into modules (e.g., curriculum mapping) and served over the Internet in an organized fashion. Frequently, digital audio or video lectures are posted together with material such as PowerPoint slides, reading assignments, videos, and other material to form the core of a module.

Other components also comprise a VLE. Generally, tools to track student use of material and progress are included. Communication facilities such as threaded discussion boards, email, chat rooms, blogs, and message facilities are present. Group management software for student projects, assignment creation, management, and grading features will be available. Other items such as a syllabus system, notice boards, Internet links to the outside world, grade books, assessment management systems, automatic exam grading facilities, questionnaires, rosters, calendars, and other tools will be present. Some VLEs incorporate new Web 2.0 tools such as blogs, wikis, RSS feeds, and 3-D virtual-world interfaces. Users are assigned roles (e.g., teacher, teaching assistant, visiting lecturer, student, guest, and so forth) that permit access to varying privileges on the system. For instance, teachers may be able to create or upload new content but students may have viewing privileges only.

Many VLEs support Shareable Content Object Reference Model (SCORM) to enable course content sharing. Class content objects can be developed either by a teacher or by a commercial provider and then loaded into a course.

Open Source Systems

A number of VLEs are free or open source. Examples include Dokeos, Moodle, and Sakai. Of these, the best known is Moodle (abbreviation for Modular Object-Oriented Dynamic Learning Environment). Moodle is widely used, with a base of 50,293 installed sites, 3,594,463 courses, and 35,801,861 users as of July 9, 2010 (Moodle, 2010b). Moodle was released in 1999 by Martin Dougiamas from Curtin University in Australia. Since that time, a number of developers (including Todd Ballaban and Alex Trivas) have contributed to the software (see Figure 3.3).

Commercial Systems

There are a number of commercial VLE software packages available (see Figure 3.4) including Blackboard, CyberExtension, and Axio Learning (see Figure 3.5).

Figure 3.3   Moodle Features

Assignment Module: Assignments can be specified with a due date and a maximum grade.

Chat module: Allows smooth, synchronous text interaction among teachers and students.

Choice module: Similar to a single question poll; used to vote or to get feedback from students.

Forum Module: Discussion threads and group support features are available with this module.

Glossary Module: Allows participants to create and maintain a list of definitions, like a dictionary.

Lesson Module: Allows a series of pages and objects to be presented to the student.

Quiz Module: Database of questions for course quizzes or for lessons. Includes grading features.

Resource Module: Displays many types of media content files (PowerPoint, Flash, Videos, et cetera).

Survey Module: Provides instruments for analyzing online classes.

Wiki Module: A series of web pages that anyone can add to or edit.

Note. Adapted from *Moodle Features*, by Moodle, 2010, retrieved July 8, 2010, from http://docs.moodle.org/en/Features.

Of these, Blackboard is generally acknowledged as the market leader (Jaschik, 2009a). Blackboard is a Web-based server platform that includes features such as course management tools, an open architecture, and scalable design intended to permit integration with university student information systems. Blackboard's stated goals are (1) to provide online elements for courses delivered face-to-face and, (2) to enable faculty to develop and deliver online courses without face-to-face meetings (Blackboard Inc., 2010a). Blackboard provides the following features that are typical in most VLEs (see Figure 3.6).

Figure 3.4   Sample Commercial Virtual Learning Environments

- **Axio Learning**—www.axiolearning.org—Virtual managed learning environment originally from Kansas State University

- **Blackboard**—www.blackboard.com—A family of virtual learning software

- **CyberExtension**—http://rightreasontech.com/virtual-learning-environment/CyberExtension.aspx-virtual learning environment

- **FirstClass**—www.firstclass.com—Messaging and communications solution

- **WebCT** (Now a part of Blackboard)—www.blackboard.com—Software applications designed to enhance teaching and learning

- **WebTrain**—www.webtrain.com.au—Virtual live classes, enrollment, attendance, and attention monitoring.

Figure 3.5   K-State Online, an Implementation of Axio Learning

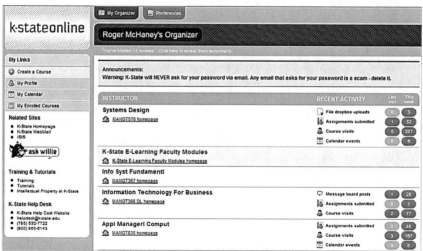

Note. Kansas State website, faculty-only access. For more information, see http://ome.ksu.edu/applications/axio_learning/

Figure 3.6   Features Found in BlackBoard

Communication Announcements: Announcements for students under a tab or as pop-ups.

Chat: Synchronous chat between students (or with instructors) in class sections.

Discussions: Discussion threads and replies within class sections.

Mail: Allows students and teachers to send E-mail to one another.

Course Content: Allows teachers to post videos, lectures, PowerPoints, articles, et cetera.

Calendar: Allows teachers to post due dates for assignments and tests.

Learning Modules: Allows postings of different lessons for students.

Assessments: Allows teachers to post quizzes and exams for students.

Assignments: Allows assignments to be posted and students to submit finished work.

Grade Book: Allows posting of grades.

Media Library: Videos and other files may be stored for use in learning modules and other locations.

Goals: Allows teachers to post class goals and objectives.

Roster: Provides a list of students enrolled in the course.

Syllabus: Allows posting of class syllabus.

Who's Online: Permits students and teachers to view anyone currently online for a particular course.

Helpful Hints: Provides links to information technology webpages.

www.blackboard.com

Moving Outside the VLE

VLEs have done a great deal of good by enabling distance learning and blended learning delivery. Further, by most accounts, VLEs are ubiquitous landmarks on higher education's new digital shoreline. In spite of these pluses, academia is filled with rumblings of dissatisfaction with the constraints placed on teaching and learning by these systems.

First, VLEs create an environment where the ownership of teaching material created by professors and teachers must eventually be determined. For example, if you leave the university, does the material on the VLE belong to the teacher that created it or the university? A colleague who taught at a southern U.S. university once related what he called the "dead professor story" to me as a reason why he was hesitant to teach a distance course. In his story, a distance class was listed on the line schedule with a deceased professor as the primary instructor. As gruesome as that seems, prior to dying he had taught a member of the secretarial staff to administer the course (e.g., post his prerecorded lectures, administer and grade exams, and post the final grades). After he passed away, the department kept the class going. Other than a few complaints regarding the professor's proclivity to ignore email messages, there were no problems with the class, and it provided the school with a fine income stream. I am not sure how long this continued, but after a while the students caught on, and it became fashionable to take the "dead professor's class."

Another complaint about VLEs is how they are becoming increasingly commercialized. Some professors worry that high-quality instructional material bundled with textbook packages will be directly ported into their institution's VLE, effectively cutting them out of the equation. This disintermediation effect could be the first step toward making many university professors obsolete and replacing them with sets of quality learning material administered by low-paid instructors or assistants (Stiles, 2007).

Due to these and other worries, a movement known as "loosely coupled teaching" has arisen to reduce the influence of VLEs and instead to move learning into the spaces where students will be working when the course is complete (Leslie, 2007). Although VLEs provide the ability to monitor student progress, ensure authentication, and provide the convenience of having all course material in one location, these systems also do remove students from learning in the broader world. Loosely coupled teaching retains some advantages of VLEs (particularly the course management aspects such as grade posting and so forth) while leveraging contemporary-education practices of infusing Web 2.0 tools into an edu-cational experience. Loosely coupled teaching seeks to develop and pro-mote a personal learning environment (PLE) based on readily available Web 2.0 tools and mobile apps with which students control and manage their own learning. This marks the beginning of a lifelong learning experi-ence using tools that aren't left locked behind institutional walls following the conclusion of a course. Blogs, wikis, social networking, podcasting, mashups, and other tools can be used to help promote authentic, person-alized learning, as well as demonstrate problem solving and critical think-ing in the "real world." This connectivist learning approach is described more in chapter 7.

Teaching Implications of Virtual Learning Environments

There is little doubt that the VLE has reshaped tech-savvy millennials' learning experience and indeed their view of what constitutes the class-room and the "face" of the university. Because I teach a number of courses online and as blended learning through VLEs, I can make several observations regarding student experiences in these systems.

First, the classes they take are far from uniform. In my interviews with university teachers and students, I discovered a range of class arrangements using VLEs. Some classes are disappointing to students. David Stewart, assistant dean of continuing education at Kansas State University, calls these the "set 'em and forget 'em"–type classes. Some professors see the VLE as a way to promote independent studies, post their PowerPoint slides together with reading assignments, and then just give periodic exams. Of course, these classes are not prevalent and are being phased out wherever possible.

Other classes employ audio messages, video lectures, video supple-ments, reading material, and special learning objects constructed with Flash Animation or tools such as SoftChalk, and have clear learning paths established (ELATEWiki, 2009). These classes provide students with structure and important content and are consistent with the expectations of the tech-savvy millennials.

Second, students are beginning to pick and choose classes from a variety of institutions. They feel comfortable doing this because the VLE interface is very similar no matter where they "virtually attend." The motivations behind this vary, but I have discovered some interesting reasons.

1. If a particular course or instructor is perceived as unreasonably difficult or incompetent, students may take the course elsewhere and transfer the credits back to their home institution.
2. Some universities have policies against on-campus students taking distance classes. Students may seek to get schedule flexibility by taking distance classes from another university and then transferring the credits back to the home institution.
3. Students who are studying abroad may take an online course from their home institution to ensure they don't fall behind or "lose a semester."
4. Students may be putting together a custom program that requires taking specialty classes from a variety of different institutions.
5. Students may be hunting for cost savings.
6. Students may have heard about a particular class or professor at an institution other than their own and want to include that experience as part of their degree program.

Although the VLE has changed higher education and is largely embraced by the tech-savvy millennial, it does have some shortcomings. These are being addressed by advocates of loosely coupled teaching who believe the use of publicly accessible Web 2.0 tools provide a superior learning environment for students. Student reactions to using public tools have been favorable in my experience, provided it happens in one or two courses only. Some students have told me that learning in this manner for all their classes would become a logistical nightmare because they would have to learn a variety of systems and keep each course straight. For loosely coupled teaching purists, this would not be a problem, because they would advocate the students' choosing the tools for their learning, resulting in a common set of tools for all courses. However, the reality is that, often, instructors specify the tools that should be used, so that grading and assessment won't become a nightmare for *them*. To address these issues in part, VLEs are now adding Web 2.0 capabilities to their stable of tools.

Summary

The tech-savvy millennial lives at a time when technological advances bestow magic on the landscape. This is certainly an interesting, transitional time to start along a path of lifelong learning. Currently, higher education's new digital shoreline has been influenced by a number of changes including classroom interaction devices such as clickers, content development tools, video game consoles, mobile devices, and virtual learning environments. Many of these technologies are converging toward an inevitable mobile, digital learning platform, which could take the form of a tablet computer like Apple's iPad. This convergence has already captured the attention of tech-savvy millennials as technology moves from the personal layer to the private layer (Stone, 2009). This movement has encouraged students to integrate technology into their everyday private lives. For education to be lifelong and relevant, it too must enter the private layer of their lives and become part of the social system that shapes their world.

This chapter has examined the platforms that are enabling technology to penetrate tech-savvy millennials' private lives and their educational experiences. As their teachers, we need to do a better job of understanding how teaching and learning are being altered and then enhance our practice without losing good pedagogy.

In addition to the platforms for learning, today's tech-savvy millennials have access to an enormous range of application tools that are driving the Web 2.0 revolution. Chapters 4 and 5 examine the software and social systems that are being developed to leverage the capabilities of our ubiquitous, worldwide, interconnected, mobile, and rapidly changing technology infrastructure.

Notes

1. Defined as the ability to create and understand visual messages.
2. http://school.discoveryeducation.com/schrockguide/gadgets.html
3. Earlier mobile phone systems were in existence at this time using other technologies. For instance, the world's first mobile phone system was launched in Stockholm on April 25, 1956, by MTA. The Motorola system was significant because it marked the beginning of modern cell phone systems.
4. The tech-savvy millennials do text frequently. While I was writing this, a friend of mine sent me a message that her daughter had run up over 18,000 text messages in the past month. That averages out to about one text message every minute and a half for 15 hour days over an entire month. Whew!

CHAPTER FOUR

THE NEW SHORELINE'S TOPOGRAPHY

Web 2.0 and Social Learning

One of the primary forces behind the changes in higher education is Web 2.0. The concept behind Web 2.0 is important to understand for what it really is: a new way of using Internet technologies. The term Web 2.0 *doesn't refer to a technical update of underlying software and hardware but rather to changes in the way the Web is being used by businesses, universities, and society in general. Web 2.0 comprises five major, interrelated components: social computing, social media, content sharing, filtering/recommendations, and Web applications. These components can be integrated into classroom pedagogy to provide richer knowledge delivery to the tech-savvy millennial. This chapter looks at Web 2.0, social computing, and social media applications for higher education.*

Web 2.0 Overview

CHAPTER 3 DISCUSSED the technological platforms that are making today's new digital shoreline a reality in higher education. The Internet provided a worldwide communication network. Mobile computing infrastructure took this a step further moving personal computing to private layer computing. This promoted the integration of technology into the tech-savvy millennials' everyday lives. This chapter moves the discussion to the next phenomenon, which is consistent with a "tipping point" as described by Malcolm Gladwell. Higher education can no longer expect its constituents to learn in isolation nor can it ignore that information is now omnipresent and highly accessible. Higher education's new shoreline is largely shaped by new paradigms for social computing. The term *Web 2.0* is used to describe this new way of using Internet technologies.

I like to view Web 2.0 as comprising five major, interrelated components: social computing, social media, filtering/recommendations, content sharing, and Web applications. Chapters 4 and 5 discuss several examples in each of these categories to help us visualize how tech-savvy millennials view the world, starting with social computing and social media in this chapter. As we consider these, remember that the Web is in its infancy and will change form with future advancements.

Social Computing

Web 2.0 concepts make it possible to move the inherent social nature of humans onto new digital platforms. Social computing is based on the premise that people are profoundly communal and have a need to interact using voice, gesture, and written language. Not only do people seek social outlets, they rely on social clues in decision making, planning, and communication. Social computing supports a variety of interactions in digital environments by making it possible for users to supply, aggregate, filter, and consume information in various forms. New computing paradigms are emerging to support what people want to do. The most prominent of these include social networking and various virtual environments.

Social Networks

KatBird is a 20-year-old college student who studies business at Kansas State University. Throughout the day and even during her classes, she uses her mobile phone to post text messages to her friends' "walls." Most days at around 4:00 P.M. she heads to her dorm room and logs on to Facebook to see what her friends have posted for her. She spends a little time reading their notes and visits their pages to see recently posted photos. She might add a few tags to describe people she recognizes in these photos so others can find themselves more easily. She also leaves comments teasing her friends about what she's seen. Sometimes she hears a new song on her friends' pages or finds out about their evening plans. Facebook is a central point for her social group, and it provides an event calendar, a message center, and a photo album documenting their good times together. Facebook helps her track and organize her busy social life.

Although KatBird's actions don't sound out of the ordinary or amazing, they represent a new mechanism for communication that has dramatically changed human interaction. In fact, the years 2004 to 2010 may be remembered as the era of social networking or, depending on what the future holds, the advent of the social networking age.

Social networks are essentially linked websites that provide virtual space for a community of people to share information about themselves and/or their interests. The sites can be public or restricted to a circle of friends. Generally, social networks exist to enable people to gather in real time and use chat tools (text, voice, or video, sometimes embedded and other times using third-party software such as TinyChat, AIM, Stickam, BlogTV, MSNMessenger, or Yahoo Messenger) to shoot the breeze with their friends or asynchronously leave messages on "walls" that might have pictures, songs, or other rich media attached. Members usually create online profiles that may or may not represent their true identity (Thomas, 2007). These profiles can contain biographical information, pictures, likes, dislikes, current "status," and any other information the user may choose to post.

One of the first true online social networks, Friendster (www.friendster.com), was started in 2002. Another site, MySpace (http://myspace.com), followed about a year later with explosive growth. Facebook came out in 2004, quickly developed into a favorite of the college student demographic, and eventually expanded to a much wider audience.

Since its inception, social networking has opened doors for students to redefine the way studying, homework, reading, and discussions can take place. Nearly every student I interview emphasizes how important social networks are to their daily life and how interwoven their academic experience is within their network of friends. Students no longer go home and study alone. They continually interact and seek out information with a group of peers.

Little is done in isolation anymore, and information is shared across school, university, state, national, and international boundaries. Students study for exams together. They write papers together, and they have access to a wide variety of friends, and friends of friends, who may be rich and diverse sources of knowledge. This social interaction provides an emergent set of behaviors and facilitates knowledge creation. What we see is just the tip of the iceberg. In 1999, in his book describing how new interconnectedness had begun transforming the business world, Thomas Petzinger included a chapter titled "Nobody Is as Smart as Everybody" (Petzinger, 1999). Since that time, a new connectedness fueled by technology has empowered the social user. Our students have realized that collectively they can access more knowledge than the best professors and educators in the world possess individually. Let's look more closely at three social networks, Facebook, LinkedIn, and Ning.

Facebook   Facebook is the world's most popular social networking site, with over 400 million active users (Facebook, 2010). Facebook was developed by a tech-savvy millennial, Mark Zuckerberg, who created the software in his dorm room at Harvard. It started as a tool for Harvard University students to socially connect but went on to attract a wider audience ranging from school children to senior citizens. Businesses, universities, clubs, and other organizations have also embraced Facebook. According to website-traffic-analysis statistics, on July 11, 2010, Facebook was the second most popular destination on the Internet (Alexa, 2010).

Facebook provides each member with a profile to decorate with various color themes and photos as they share aspects of their personal interests and life story. Personal space on Facebook can be used to house photos, video clips, messages, status updates, comments, and countless third-party applications. The arrangement of these items and ability of various categories of users to access these items is defined by the profile owner. Facebook profiles can be searched by names, locations, keywords, memberships in groups, and other criteria. If a Facebook member locates a person they want to connect with, or want to "friend," an invitation can be sent. If the recipient of the invitation accepts, the two members become linked as "friends." This will enable the linked person to access additional areas of the Facebook profile, post messages on their linked friend's "wall" and provide mechanisms to remain in touch. It becomes much easier to keep up with what your friends are posting, doing, saying, where they are going, and so forth. Facebook also allows blocking certain people from seeing a profile or sending messages.

One of Facebook's strengths is the ease with which personal relationships can be maintained and information communicated. Built-in filtering capabilities enable a user to control the flow of information coming in from their friends. In addition to connecting with friends, relatives, and colleagues, an enormous range of application programs can be used via a Facebook profile. These applications (or apps) range from games, surveys, and organizing tools to helpful reminders and horoscopes. Facebook also provides tools to form and join interest groups. Once a group is created, it is provided with a space for photos, videos, text-based information, and other capabilities. Many civic and nonprofit organizations have taken advantage of these features. Additionally, groups can be created for purely social reasons. Events can be created for groups. For instance, universities often create groups for various academic majors, career fairs, athletics events, and other venues. After members join the group, they can be contacted easily with invitations via email.

Facebook also permits businesses and organizations (such as universities) to create pages. If a user becomes a member of a page (i.e., a "fan") then the business or university logo will be displayed on that user's profile page (if they wish). This helps create networks of people affiliated with different organizations.

Although universities and teachers have long brainstormed ways to integrate Facebook into the classroom, students resist. I have spoken at length with students about this topic, and the response is generally the same: they don't want professors, parents, and people from outside their social circle getting into their daily personal lives. Facebook is squarely situated in private layer technology applications, and unlike mobile smart devices, which distribute specific messages at the request of the sender, information flow out of Facebook is much broader.

LinkedIn   This popular social networking website differentiates itself from Facebook and MySpace by specifically targeting professional relationships, career development, and networking among business colleagues. LinkedIn was released in May 2003, and in 2008 had over 70 million members from more than 200 countries. In fact, LinkedIn reports that executives from all Fortune 500 companies belong to their network (LinkedIn, 2008).

LinkedIn allows its members to develop a professional profile and then link themselves to contacts derived from universities (e.g., student cohorts, professors, advisors, etc.), prior or current professional positions, and a number of other places. It also has a mechanism to self-promote skill sets and often is used by recruiters to find matches for job openings. It is also possible to send messages to personal contacts. Recommendation letters, resumes, work histories, accomplishments, and other information can be posted and shared.

Users who can view a profile can also see contacts they have in common. This makes it easier to reach potential references, should they desire. As on Facebook, LinkedIn users can create and join groups. Groups provide discussion forums and often house information pertinent to particular business and career interests. Third-party applications are available to users so they can add RSS feeds from blogs, view local events, remain apprised of job postings, offer polls, and perform other tasks.

LinkedIn continually monitors its membership and suggests a connection to people it believes you might know. My personal experience has been that this works very well, and I have been reconnected to countless colleagues and former students. LinkedIn provides information regarding how many degrees of separation exist between users on the system. Depending on your degree of separation you may have more or less capability for directly contacting particular people via the network. LinkedIn also permits a variety of functions to help in job searches, locating partners and potential business ties, and finding service providers. Company profiles together with demographic statistics can also be found on the system.

I have discovered that, unlike on Facebook, where students prefer to keep their lives private, most are more than willing (and in fact actively pursue) to be linked to professors' or advisors' profiles in LinkedIn. LinkedIn is very different from Facebook because it is specifically aimed at career maintenance and advancement. Tech-savvy millennials recognize the importance of their university ties to potential future employment. For that reason, there is no hesitation to mingle with those outside their intimate circle of friends. In my opinion, LinkedIn provides an excellent example of how social networking (in another, separate social network) could successfully exist for the higher education community. In fact, a LinkedIn-type application for education that begins with a student's elementary education experience and follows them throughout their life would be an amazing tool. The required elements already are present. Groups related to educational institutions could be initiated and students linked together in that way. Class groups, events, and opportunities could all be incorporated into the system. Apps for textbooks and course material could be made available together with mobile device interfaces.

Ning Ning is a social network creation tool developed by Marc Andreessen (co-creator of Mosaic, the first true Web browser) and Gina Bianchini and released in October of 2005. Ning is the Chinese word for "peace" and is meant to convey how this social networking site can promote greater understanding and better connections among people. Ning is not intended be a comprehensive social networking platform like Facebook or MySpace. Instead, it permits users to design a topic-specific social network that can benefit a specific group or interest.

At one time, Ning provided a free service if users were willing to allow Ning-controlled ads on their site. A premium ad-free service was available with a subscription fee. In April of 2010, Ning announced it was suspending its free service (McCarthy, 2010), causing a number of education-related networks to move to Facebook and other social networking venues (Peirano, 2010).[1] Ning initially generated wide interest with educators and was used for class-specific social networks and by groups in the higher education community.

In my classes I have used Ning for project purposes and found it widely accepted and enjoyed by tech-savvy millennials. Of course, they see it as a limited-use social network for connections related to class activity. They accepted it more enthusiastically than they would a group in Facebook. With the phase out of Ning's free services, its usefulness for classroom-specific social networks is questionable.

Instant Messaging (IM)

Not long ago, the preferred Internet-based communication method was email. Ask any student today what they prefer, and you'll get an answer that is consistent with the move from personal layer to private layer computing: IMing (from a computer) or texting (from a mobile device).[2] The advantage of IM is, of course, the instant part. IMing allows people to communicate via text in real time. It is possible to instant message between individuals (if one is offline, the messages queue up and wait until the recipient logs on) or, using chat rooms, between members of either a temporary or more permanent group. Although the idea of IM was invented prior to the Internet, global networking has allowed the technology to gain widespread use and acceptance.

Like most Internet technologies, IM providers have expanded their capabilities, and many of them (such as MSNMessenger and Yahoo Messenger) provide added features including group chats, voice, video, file transfers, and links to mobile phone systems. Most IM systems also permit users to save conversations for later review. This gives educators another tool in their arsenal. Saved instant messages can be posted to a message board for access by others unable to attend an educational exchange synchronously.

Web Videoconferencing

Similar in nature to IM, web videoconferencing adds a visual component to the IM interface. Services such as Yahoo Messenger and MSNMessenger have used video to modernize existing capabilities and to better utilize the Internet's bandwidth expansion. Web videoconferencing and messaging ranges from personal video chats to chat rooms displaying multiple videos.

Skype is a well-known web videoconferencing tool. It not only enables free online conversations (audio and video), it also can connect to mobile phones and landlines. Skype also enables file transfers and text messages. Skype software was developed by Estonians Ahti Heinla, Priit Kasesalu, and Jaan Tallinn (also known for developing Kazaa). In 2003, Skype Limited was established in Luxembourg by Niklas Zennström, from Sweden, and Janus Friis, from Denmark (Thomann, 2006). According to Skype.com, Skype users made "6.4 billion minutes of calls to landlines and mobiles in the first half of 2010" together with "88.4 billion minutes of Skype-to-Skype calls," of which approximately 40 percent were video calls (see Figure 4.1) (Skype, 2010).

In addition to Skype, numerous other Web videoconferencing services exist. This market is relatively young, and heated competition will

Figure 4.1   Skype Web Videoconferencing

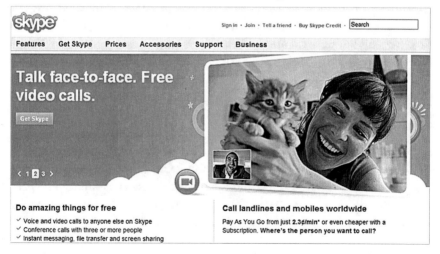

www.skype.com

determine which companies, products, and features eventually will become consumer favorites. Other Web videoconferencing applications include the following:

ooVoo—Allows video conferencing with up to three people for free or six for an upgrade fee. It also permits leaving recorded video messages.

iChat—This instant video messaging application interacts with AIM or MobileMe. It comes standard with Mac OS X.

WebEx—This product is targeted to business videoconference users. WebEx is owned by Cisco, and it provides on-demand collaboration, Web conferencing, online meeting support, and various videoconferencing applications.

Chatroulette and Omegle—These are applications that randomly pair strangers into Web videoconferences.

Metaverses

In his 1992 sci-fi novel *Snow Crash*, Neal Stephenson describes a virtual 3-D world where humans (represented by avatars) interact in various scenarios with each other and with software-based agents. He calls this the Metaverse. Stephenson's book has been moving rapidly from the imaginings of a fiction writer to a reality for millions of users who now inhabit a wide range of virtual worlds created by the intersection of computing power and network capability. Additionally, graphic resolution has improved in these worlds to the point where avatars[3] can look and act realistically, and users can interact in a wide and startling array of ways (see Figure 4.2).

In general, virtual worlds require a user have access to a computer, which presents the world via its screen and through sounds and text. The user can manipulate virtual objects in the world with various keystrokes, voice commands, and controller devices such as joysticks.[4] The worlds are generally developed with a set of rules (e.g., gravity) that limit users' actions. These rules might be based on real-world limitations or may endow its denizens with superhuman qualities such as the ability to fly or change shape and size. In virtual worlds, users generally communicate through avatars using text messaging, expressions, color, gestures, and sounds. Virtual worlds often are viewed as game environments, but more are becoming social networks, educational platforms, and commerce centers. The changes that are taking place in virtual worlds promise to transform all aspects of society, including higher education.

Figure 4.2   Author's Second Life Avatar

Although many different types of virtual worlds exist, most offer the following features (Virtual Worlds Review, 2008):

shared space   Many users can participate at once.

graphical user interface   Space is depicted visually, ranging in style from 2-D "cartoon" imagery to more immersive 3-D environments.

immediacy   Interaction takes place in real time.

interactivity   Users can alter, develop, build, or submit customized content.

persistence   Virtual world exists regardless of whether individual users are logged in.

socialization/community   The world allows and encourages the formation of in-world social groups like teams, guilds, clubs, cliques, housemates, neighborhoods, and so on.

porous boundaries   Boundaries between the real and virtual worlds are porous because users bring their unique set of behaviors and attitudes to influence their virtual world interactions.

A number of virtual worlds exist, the best known being Second Life (Mansfield, 2008). Other worlds growing in popularity are listed in Table 4.1.

All told, over 200 virtual worlds either exist or are in the late stages of development. More and more people are using virtual worlds, and researchers report a growth rate of 15 percent per month that does not appear to be slowing (Bray & Konsynski, 2007; Noor, 2009). Designers are working on enabling avatars to travel between virtual worlds and have a presence in multiple places (Virtual Worlds Review, 2008). To better understand virtual worlds, the next two sections look at two of those relevant to higher education: Second Life and ActiveWorlds.

Second Life   One of the most popular and well-known virtual worlds is Second Life (SL). After a less-than-inspiring virtual tour five years ago, I decided to pay a return visit in 2008. During my initial experience, I wasn't impressed with the slow, clunky way my avatar struggled to place one foot in front of the other and the impossibly slow rendering of the graphics my computer struggled to throw up on the screen. But time had passed, and a colleague of mine at K-State, Larry Jackson, suggested starting a user group to bring Second Life enthusiasts together from across

Table 4.1   Virtual Environments

Environment Name	URL	Target Audience	Platforms
ActiveWorlds	www.activeworlds.com	Teens and Adults	PC and Linux
Barbie Girls	http://barbiegirls.com	Kids and Younger Teens	PC
Club Penguin	www.clubpenguin.com	Kids and Younger Teens	PC and Mac
Forterra Systems	www.saic.com/products/simulation/olive	Training Application	PC
Gaia Online	www.gaiaonline.com	Teens and Adults	PC and Mac
Habbo Hotel	www.habbo.com	Teens and Adults	PC and Mac
Kaneva	www.kaneva.com	Teens and Adults	PC
Neopets	www.neopets.com	Kids and Younger Teens	PC and Mac
Second Life	http://secondlife.com	Adults	PC, Linux, and Mac
The Sims Online	http://thesims.ea.com	Teens and Adults	PC
Whyville	www.whyville.net/smmk/nice	Kids and Younger Teens	PC and Mac
World of Warcraft	www.worldofwarcraft.com/index.xml	Older Teens and Adults	PC and Mac

Note. Derived in part from www.virtualenvironments.info/list-of-virtual-environments, retrieved on December 24, 2008.

campus. Being unable to pass up meeting colleagues of this ilk, I wholeheartedly joined in and revived my avatar under another name.

As you might guess, both the entire landscape of SL and the limberness of my avatar had greatly changed. In fact, Second Life had improved remarkably during my absence and become decidedly more commercial. I was able to fly and move easily, and I was surprised by the amount of commerce and the number of interesting people I encountered. Strange and amazing things popped up on my screen everywhere I visited. In fact, after a few delirious weeks, I had to pull the plug on my wanderings in order to get some academic work done—or at least the type of academic work that has measurable results.

Let's talk about SL for a moment. If you've never heard of it or haven't experienced it, you are in for an eye-opening treat. SL is essentially a user-created virtual world that resides on the Internet. This virtual world is driven by imagination and allows residents to interact in a variety of ways including simple communication and more graphically oriented and content-rich alternatives. Residents in SL create an identity, meet people, socialize, buy/sell land, and develop or buy their surroundings, including homes, art, furniture, accessories, and clothes.

SL's initial release was in 2003. Philip Rosedale (known as Philip Linden "in-world"[5]) of Linden Research, Inc., in San Francisco developed this environment in which residents can create their own worlds. In essence, SL is a MMORPG[6] in which most of the rules are determined by the users.

To start, a potential user must download SL client software to their machine. After logging in, they create an imaginary first name and select a last name from a list provided by Linden Labs. They then run software to create a default avatar to be used in-world. At this point, the user is free to roam public areas and purchase (or acquire for free) clothes, new skins, fashion accessories, and even additional body parts.

Newbies to SL can be identified easily because they appear as default avatars; however, these are highly customizable with regard to height, facial features, arm length, weight, color, and dozens of other attributes. More seasoned users typically develop a unique appearance for themselves. In fact, some users spend real-world money to buy photorealistic skin and features. Companies specializing in taking full-body photographs of users and porting these into SL for use on an avatar have sprouted up recently. This blending of reality and virtual reality offers a great deal of promise in a variety of ways.

An avatar is controlled in SL from a keyboard, with various keystrokes enabling the user to walk, run, perform tricks, fly, and even teleport instantly to new locations. The avatar can explore new locations to meet friends or shop and buy things. All land and objects such as clothes, furniture, houses, cars, boats, tattoos, skin, and body parts are purchased from Linden or from third-party developers that have set up stores in SL. All transactions are conducted in Linden Dollars, which are purchased from Linden Labs using real-world currencies. The value of Linden Dollars floats like any currency exchange, and Lindens can be changed back into U.S. dollars. This has encouraged the growth of a "real" virtual economy that makes real money for its owners. Many large companies and universities have purchased land in SL and constructed virtual buildings, storefronts, and created information centers to give themselves a virtual presence.

In addition to buying objects and services in SL, residents can use programming tools to develop houses or other objects for sale. Offline images and code can be ported into SL, and new movements, actions, and features can be added to users' inventories. The programming in SL is conducted using Linden's scripting language. This enables users to create SL environments ranging from traditional houses to futuristic discos to lifelike biological models.

One of the main reasons SL has become popular is because users can self-organize and find like-minded friends. In the few years of its existence, countless subcultures ranging from vampire wannabes to cat lovers to religious scholars have emerged to create arts, games, sports, clubs, fantasy adventures, educational journeys, museums, concert venues, and other social organizations. Corporations have formed branches in SL, and numerous universities have created online classes, admissions centers, and informational kiosks. Countries have even created virtual embassies in SL. People get married in SL and virtual sex of all sorts is available.

Virtual worlds allow users to experiment with various identities and behaviors that are too risky or violate social norms of their real-world families or peer groups. By becoming an anonymous avatar, features such as age, gender, sex, and race can be modified and different behaviors tried. Similarly, people with disabilities or disease can assume a form where these conditions are left behind. This provides a safe environment offering emotional and physical freedom not available in the real world: Through the use of an avatar, no distinction can be made based on real-world appearance. It becomes possible to socialize, find friends, and form relationships without real-world obstacles normally associated with disabilities.

Education in SL comes in a wide variety of forms including recreations of historic buildings and cathedrals, 3-D versions of museums and art galleries, computer-programming tutorials, lectures and videos, virtual libraries, online classrooms, and meeting spaces for university courses (DeMers, 2009). Additionally, several universities now conduct admissions operations or at least provide admissions information in SL. Others have recreated portions of their campuses for prospective students to wander through. Still others are building games and educational experiences for their students. Researchers from universities use SL as a venue for gathering information to help develop human behavior models and perform other forms of academic research. SL's potential as an online learning environment promises to be a huge part of education's future.

ActiveWorlds   Like Second Life, ActiveWorlds is a 3-D world where the user defines and creates his or her environment. This 3-D world was initially released in 1995 and has gone through a range of name changes and versions (Wikipedia, 2010a). ActiveWorlds is accessed through an ActiveWorlds Browser that runs on Windows operating systems. Several classes of users can be found in ActiveWorlds. The first, Tourist, is a free membership that allows the user to enter the world and create buildings and other structures. However, anyone can delete a Tourist's work. Tourists have limitations regarding their avatar appearance and cannot preserve their name should someone else wish to use it.

To gain more privileges, a user can pay a fee (about 70 dollars per year) to become a Citizen. Citizens have several key protections. For instance, only they themselves can delete their construction. Citizenship grants the citizen access to any public world in the universe. Citizens can use voice chat and can bring bots[7] into the world for use. They have several communication options such as file sharing and telegram capability. They also can engage in collaborative construction projects more easily than Tourists.

Online Game Worlds

Second Life and virtual worlds find more acceptance among baby boomers and Gen Xers, but online game worlds are clearly the domain of tech-savvy millennials. The Pew Research Center reports that daily video game use by millennials is more than double that of any other generation (Pew Research Center, 2010, p. 25). These games focus on a particular theme (often fantasy-related) and involve making an avatar achieve particular tasks in order to progress through an interactive and dynamic storyline influenced by actions, decisions, and peers. Generally, progression through various levels in a world is competitive and involves winning contests or beating foes. In addition to fantasy-themed worlds, there are science fiction and anime genres.

Nearly all sizable virtual game worlds are commercial because of the need to maintain a programming staff to keep the games fresh and innovative. These games are called MMORPGs and are much larger than single-player or small multiplayer games. The virtual worlds in them continue to change and evolve even when a player's character is not being used. This causes some players to remain in-world for excessive amounts of time, afraid to miss something significant. In 2008, it was reported that subscribers to MMORPGs paid more than $1.4 billion in fees to game producers (Harding-Rolls, 2009). Example MMORPGs include World of Warcraft and Guild Wars.

World of Warcraft   World of Warcraft, known as WoW, produced by Blizzard Entertainment, is the most popular MMORPG (see Figure 4.3), with more than 11.5 million paying monthly subscribers (Cavalli, 2008). It was first introduced in 1994 and has regularly published major expansions. World of Warcraft runs on Macintosh and Windows platforms. The premise of WoW is that players must develop skills that will help them succeed in a quest. This will yield rewards such as experience points, WoW money, or other useful items. Quests also provide connections to other players, new skills, and exploration of new territory. Additionally, WoW quests may involve groups of up to five players. This promotes group learning, teamwork, and group decision-making dynamics (World of Warcraft, 2010).

Guild Wars   Like WoW, Guild Wars is a popular MMORPG. According to some sources, it has over 4.5 million paying monthly subscribers (Guild Wars, 2007). Guild Wars, though technically classified as a MMORPG, is defined by its developers as a CORPG (cooperative online role-playing game) because it incorporates cooperative and competitive game aspects. Cooperative game play (e.g., via the "guilds") encourages players to form social units closely linked with the game theme. Players do not have to join guilds but will have additional camaraderie and a broader range of experiences if they do. Guilds enable players to gain experience and learn from more seasoned peers. In-world communication is used to learn the nuances of the system. The competitive-play part (known in the gaming community as *player versus player,* or *PvP*) allows individuals to battle one another in specific areas of the virtual world. Guild Wars was first released in April of 2005 and was created in part by a group of senior developers that broke away from the original World of Warcraft team (Baker, 2006). They formed a company called ArenaNet that developed the software, which was published by NCsoft.

Figure 4.3 WoW Avatar

Teaching Implications of Social Computing

In tandem with the mobile device revolution, social computing has changed the way tech-savvy millennials spend their time and the way they foster social connections. Social computing can connect people, it can provide access to information and material, and it can provide a space where long-term interaction can take place.

There is no doubt social computing impacts higher education in a number of ways, but its potential is far from being fulfilled. Nearly every university student has a Facebook or MySpace account. Many have LinkedIn accounts that aid them in finding and maintaining jobs after graduation. Faculty members and their recommendation letters are welcome in this venue. Universities have attempted to integrate Facebook groups and pages into their operations to interact with students "on their home turf." Although this can be successful in some contexts (e.g., student advisors, campus clubs, athletics, and other organizations), students send a clear message to professors and administrators to stay out of their Facebook world.

Unlike regular friendships online, faculty–student relationships rely on an external, real-world system that is not peer based. Because of this, students may experience the feelings of intimidation or obligation that can accompany "friending" someone in authority. Further, students may feel powerless in the situation and will be conflicted regarding an online invitation and how to set their privacy controls. I don't believe faculty members should attempt to friend most students nor accept their invitations. Facebook experts Ana M. Martínez Alemán and Katherine Lynk Wartman concur with this advice:

> It is important to realize students manage their self-presentation on Facebook in many ways and to greater and lesser degrees. Some students use the site's privacy settings to restrict and regulate information, while others don't restrict much of anything. Students' self-presentation on Facebook takes place across a spectrum of transparency adjusted to meet the user's needs. (Alemán & Wartman, 2008)

A group on Facebook provides a code of ethics for faculty members in an attempt to clarify these issues further (*Faculty Ethics on Facebook*, 2010).

Members of the higher education community envision social networking websites as ideal platforms for reaching out to students with messages and other information. Having online portfolio tools, class discussion groups, alumni relationship groups, and many other features seems to be a natural fit, but perhaps not on the same site where weekend parties and social events are discussed and documented. Higher education can learn from the tech-savvy millennial and benefit from social networking attributes that are less intrusive and more in line with the technology and its current use, such as the following:

1. *Listen to the buzz.* Use Facebook to determine what perceptions (good and bad) are being discussed about an institution or programs. These can be obtained using groups to solicit information and through other means. This should be viewed as data collection

not an excuse to contact Facebook members to ask them to defend their comments or positions.

2. *Share content.* Make useful information available to those who might be interested in a class, institution, or club.

3. *Develop an identity.* Brand an institution or class on Facebook so it appeals to the tech-savvy millennial. This will result in more interaction and a connected community.

4. *Be available.* Answer messages, have up-to-date and easy-to-locate information.

5. *Relax and have fun.* Remember, most tech-savvy millennials are not conducting business on Facebook. They want to have fun and connect with their peers.

Some universities have begun to monitor student comments regarding their experiences on campus (Creeley, 2008). This is particularly true regarding student athletes that may become public figures (Ruppenthal, 2010). These uses have further soured some students on opening up their private lives to their teachers.

Other social networking sites such Ning, which permit the development of custom, specific applications, are more welcome by students because they won't intrude in their private lives. The advantages of connecting are present without threat of exposing one's personal life. This is consistent with the tech-savvy millennial's characteristic of experimenting with multiple online identities.

Social computing is not limited to just social networks. Online virtual worlds are also impacting higher education. Are tech-savvy millennials leading the charge into these worlds? Surprisingly, the answer appears to be no. According to Linden Labs, the developer of Second Life, approximately 15 percent of its user base (in terms of hours online) are in the 18- to 24-year age group, 34.5 percent are between 25 and 34 years of age, and 49.6 percent are 35 and over (Linden Labs, 2008; see Table 4.2). Of course in other virtual worlds aimed at children, a different result will be demonstrated. But, still why are the tech-savvy millennials a minority in the largest online 3-D world?

I teach a segment of Second Life to my master's of business administration students in an introductory technology course. Surprisingly, in a class of 25, usually only 2 or 3 will have used Second Life previously. When I ask them why, the answer is usually related to time constraints. They view metaverses as being time sinks and already use Facebook, MSN

Table 4.2   Second Life User Ages

Age Range	Percentage of Total User Hours
13–17	0.32%
18–24	15.07%
25–34	34.51%
35–44	28.51%
45 plus	21.14%
Unknown	0.45%

Note. Adapted from *Second Life Demographics,* by Linden Labs, retrieved November 2008 from http://secondlife.com/statistics/economy-data.php

Messenger, texting, and other tools to fulfill their social needs. Others tell me their choice is WoW, where socializing takes place around a game theme. WoW's user demographics appear to be a closely held secret, but casual observation indicates a much younger crowd populates that world.

Other types of online games are being used in higher education. A good example occurs in the business field. Helping students learn how to operate the vast computing platforms and complex software systems typical of Fortune 500 corporations is a daunting task. To help with this, ERPsim was developed at the international business school HEC Montréal.

According to the ERPsim.net website,

The ERP Simulation Game is an innovative "learning-by-doing" approach to teaching ERP concepts.[8] Using a continuous-time simulation, students are put in a situation in which they have to run their business with a real-life ERP (mySAP ECC 6.0) system. Teams of five to six students operate a firm in a make-to-stock manufacturing supply chain[9] and must interact with suppliers and customers by sending and receiving orders, delivering their products and completing the whole cash-to-cash cycle. A simulation program (ERPsim) was developed to automate: (1) the sales process, so that every firm receives a large number of orders in each period of the simulation, (2) part of the production process in order to account for production capacity, and (3) part

of the procurement process to account for delay in delivery and payment. Using standard and customized reports in SAP, students must
analyze their transactional data to make business decisions and ensure
the profitability of their operations" (ERPSim, 2010).

This simulation game uses the actual software (SAP/R3 from German
software giant SAP AG (www.sap.com) together with a simulation package to create a realistic game experience. A competition between student
teams allows them to develop the best approach to conducting business.

An interesting article describing why tech-savvy millennials seem less
enamored with Second Life, a blend between a video game and social
networking, supports my own observations (Epstein, 2008). Epstein states
that, "more people from Generation X participate in Second Life than
from any other generation . . . [i]t's harder for Millennials to make contact with other Millennials in this scene, since they constitute a minority
of the population . . . and [they] feel somewhat uncomfortable interacting
socially with folk outside their own generation." Epstein also believes that
tech-savvy millennials (at least many middle-class members of this
group) were raised amid a flurry of regimented tasks, by "helicopter parents" who constantly hovered about, attending too closely to every minute aspect of their child's experiences. "Second Life is an environment in
which you need to be able to set goals and tasks for yourself in order to
get anything out of it, it is a non-directed playground in which to let the
imagination run free" (Epstein, 2008).

What does this mean for higher education? The possibilities are exciting, but there is much work ahead. Virtual worlds provide new ways to
interact with content as collaborative creators and learning peers. A virtual world appeals to the sense of becoming an explorer and having freedom to encounter new material in innovative ways. For instance, I was
talking with an anatomy professor who leads a field trip of students
through a virtual colon. They are all represented as avatars that can talk
as they slog through a colon, observing polyps and other anomalies as
well as healthy colon conditions. Did the students learn more? According
to him, way more! Being able to visually interact with your surroundings
while chatting with peers and teachers seems to be an ideal mix for learning. I tend to agree.

Multiple successful uses of metaverses in education have been documented. For instance, at the 2009 WCET Conference, Stephen Bronack
of Clemson University demonstrated a class structure developed in

ActiveWorlds. Students would enter the virtual world, learn various technology lessons, and then complete related assignments in-world. He has used this approach successfully for more than five years (Tashne, Riedl, & Bronack, 2005). A well-received class called Field Research in Second Life is taught at Bradley University. Students learn applications of field research methods by conducting research in-world (SL Education, 2007). The Ann Myers Medical Center uses a virtual clinic to educate medical students and nurses in Second Life. Students learn from educators through interactive and clearly visualized 3-D case presentations (Ann Meyers Medical Center, 2010). The University of Kansas teaches medical students bedside manner and patient interaction through a Second Life interface. These and thousands of other educational examples demonstrate why it is important for higher education to consider the benefits 3-D virtual worlds can offer our students. According to Chris Collins, ". . . many educators see virtual worlds as a tool that might help instructors connect students to the real world through the technology of the virtual world. . . . it gives students the ability to play, to practice, to pretend, to be creative and imaginative, and to do things that they [can't] in real life" (Collins, 2008).

Jeffrey Young (2008), in the *Chronicle of Higher Education*, provides teaching tips for professors derived from video games: (1) give frequent and detailed feedback; (2) test before going live (e.g., especially in online courses, make sure everything works!); (3) use a narrative (story line) to answer the question "Why are we learning this?"; (4) don't be afraid of fun; and (5) not every subject works as a game.

Social Media

The tech-savvy millennial has access to a tremendous amount of content on the Internet. The content includes text, audio, and video that social media originators have disseminated and published with the purpose of encouraging user interaction. Many tools using Web 2.0 concepts enable individuals to publish and distribute materials in ways only available to large organizations a few short years ago. Social media promotes the democratization of information and knowledge and allows students, teachers, and everyone else to become content producers rather than just consumers. Social media can be categorized in various ways. The following sections provide examples of several popular areas and applications related to tech-savvy millennials and higher education.

Blogging

The blog was one of the first tools associated with the transition from the World Wide Web to Web 2.0. Although initially not a collaborative technology, in many ways the blog has become a focal point for synthesizing and mashing material from a variety of sources. Unlike other instances of magic appearing in cyberspace, the blog isn't new, nor did it materialize suddenly. Rather, its early roots can be traced back to the 1980s when Usenet, bulletin board systems, and moderated newsgroups emerged. In the mid-1990s, online journals began appearing. In 1997, the word *weblog* was used to describe these journals, and a couple of years later it was shortened to *blog* by Jorn Barger (Wortham, 2007).

Why should higher education pay attention to the blog? Several reasons come to mind. First, it gives professors, administrators, students, alumni, and others in education a voice. The voice is immediate and can be heard by anyone, anywhere, around the (free) world without edit or filter. Most blogs promote open dialog with readers by inviting their comments, opinions, and suggestions. The blog's author can choose to acknowledge this feedback, edit it, or delete it. Blogs created in the classroom can have impact in the real world and can help stimulate students' interest in participative learning experiences.

Blogs have been embraced by educators, and numerous useful teaching blogs can be found. A couple of my favorites follow:

http://teachersteachingteachers.org—This blog is written by four teachers: Paul Allison, Lee Baber, Susan Ettenheim, and Thomas Locke. On their website they say, "we are searching for the most effective practices in technology, studying research, and improving our knowledge of new media by using it ourselves. We have two purposes: developing teacher knowledge and leadership in our own schools and districts and putting this knowledge and leadership to work to improve student online reading and writing through the use of blogs, wikis, podcasts and webcasts" (TeachersTeachingTeachers, 2008).

www.facultyfocus.com/topic/articles/teaching-professor-blog— Maryellen Weimer's blog about professors and their teaching mission is excellent. This blog by the author of *Learner-Centered Teaching: Five Key Changes to Practice* provides practical entries about teaching topics. The blog cites teaching literature frequently and reflects her experience as both a scholar and classroom teacher.

A quick search using Technorati.com (a great search engine for blog content) will yield hundreds of other excellent blogs that dispense information about teaching and classroom administration.

Additionally, education-related blogs have been developed for specific classes. A typical classroom blog might be developed by the teacher to distribute information or by students to build a relevant knowledge base. Because it belongs to the entire class, it fosters communication and collaboration. A classroom blog contains thoughts by the whole class but is often guided by the teacher. Because its content and entries can be tracked by contributor, the teacher will have insight regarding the performance of individual students. Some classroom blogs are emptied of content at the end of a semester and started fresh with a new group of students. Others are intended for the long term and require students to build on the work of their predecessors.

In many classroom blogs, teachers will provide prompting entries to stimulate discussion. Students can leave their comments below the entry. The teacher can quickly assess the collective knowledge and understanding of the class. Students can read comments left by their peers to become aware of different perspectives. Often, blogs enable shy students to participate in ways they would avoid in face-to-face interactions. Blogs also permit the teacher (and students) to post links to relevant material including images and videos. This creates learning opportunities for both the student and teacher.

Student blogs can also be created as individual projects or online portfolios equivalent to electronic term papers or projects. In this instance, students can learn from their peers, and teachers can create a collective space that gives a sense of cohesion to the individual projects.

Blogger is a development and storage website that provides users with the ability to create free blogs. Blogger was launched in 1999 by Pyra Labs as one of the first websites to successfully promote blog publishing. It is credited for standardizing and popularizing the format taken by most blogs today. In 2003, Google purchased Blogger and integrated it with Picasa to enable users to post photos. Since that time additional improvements have given Blogger a wide range of widgets that make it easy to post multimedia material and import RSS feeds from other sites. Blogger is a favorite tool of teachers who use classroom or student blogs (see Figure 4.4).

Figure 4.4 Blogger Website

www.blogger.com

RSS

By enabling more people to disseminate information and create content, Web 2.0 tools have added exponentially to information overload. No one person or even an army of people would be able to track everything posted and make sense of it all. Tech-savvy millennials are no exception. RSS offers a mitigating solution.

RSS stands for *Real Simple Syndication* and is something every teacher and student should have in her or his inventory of tools. In fact, every member of the higher education community, from students to university presidents, should be using this as a mechanism for filtering and pulling relevance and meaning from the mountains of new information filling cyberspace.

To understand RSS, it is necessary to think about how the Web works. XML is used in the background of most modern websites, including blogs, wikis, and podcasts. RSS feeds use XML to identify user-specified digital content. Links to that content are aggregated on a specific website (or feed reader) so the material comes to the user instead of the other way around. Potential readers can acquire the information from a variety of sites and centralize it for viewing. The reader no longer needs to visit a specific blog. Instead, the centralized content is updated every time a user visits the Web, and new items are automatically collected.

For example, imagine a teacher who has located 20 blogs or other websites relevant to her area of study or interest. If she visits each of those every day searching for new items, it would require a large investment of her time. With RSS feeds, the new content can be piped directly to her personal, aggregated collection. This aggregator software, sometimes called a feed collector or news reader, can work even while the user is not on the Web, and depending on the specific software (like Blogbridge or Newsgator), new feeds will be pulled at preset intervals. In fact, most major news services now use RSS for content distribution (some use Atom, a similar technology). In particular, RSS provides news headlines and stories to other partner sites and enables new material to be acquired from corporate sources and news databases. Most websites with RSS feeds provide special links that can be loaded into an aggregator (Richardson, 2006). Usually the RSS symbol, shown in Figure 4.5, indicates the availability of RSS feeds. An RSS feed URL may look like this one retrieved from CNN.com: feed://rss.cnn.com/rss/cnn_topstories.rss.

Podcasting

Web 2.0 has grabbed the attention of the tech-savvy millennial because it enables the creation and use of rich media. Many technologies I had growing up—newspapers, magazines, radio, records, albums, telephones, and television—to name most, have been recreated in digital forms on the Web. With blogging, the parallels to the newspaper industry are apparent. While a blog's structure is comparable to an individually published newspaper, the interconnectedness of the Web also recreates its distribution infrastructure at an inexpensive, global level.

Podcasting can be compared to radio infrastructure, except without costly barriers to entry and without FCC oversight. Podcasters have instant connections to millions of potential listeners with virtually no startup cost. In a sense, podcasting has allowed anyone with Internet access and a reasonable computer to become a broadcaster. A quick search of a website like Podcastalley.com reveals thousands of regularly produced digital audio feeds where individuals have transformed themselves into disc jockeys, political pundits, comedians, talk show hosts,

Figure 4.5   RSS Feed Symbol

information providers, recording artists, and commentators. Although the quality of many "broadcasts" is amateurish at best, professional-level material can also be found. Podcasting provides an example of how Web 2.0 may lead to the disintermediation of broadcasting and help move control from corporations into the hands of individual producers.

The concept behind podcasting is relatively straightforward. In the past, as Internet connections became faster and software improved, people wanted to create audio blogs to save time and add interest. To accomplish this, digital audio files (generally in MP3 format) were created and uploaded to a server where Internet users from around the world could access the material and then play it on their audio player, mobile phone, or computer.

Like blogs, as more podcasts appeared, tracking and downloading new ones became problematic. Synching these files with audio players was also tedious. To simplify the process, former 1980s MTV video jockey Adam Curry suggested automating the process of locating, delivering, and syncing audio content. He also advocated updating feed technology to enable MP3 files posted to a blog to be downloaded via RSS feeds.

Although the details are murky, Curry spoke with Dave Winer, an early developer of RSS, who provided a "file enclosure" feature to feed technology, making it possible for a computer to determine where to obtain the audio file. Next came Curry's podcatcher software, called iPodder, which tracked subscriptions and collected desired podcasts. This software looked for new episodes, downloaded files, and then transferred the MP3 to an iPod or other device. As with most new technologies, additional developers improved on these ideas, and podcasting grew in functionality and popularity (Watson, 2008). Adam Curry is still involved with podcasting and hosts a popular feed called *The Daily Source Code* (Newitz, 2005). His iPodder software gave way to a new implementation called Juice (see Figure 4.6).

The latest podcatching software (including the well-known iTunes program from Apple, Inc., automatically downloads new episodes as they appear. Most podcasts now include a "subscribe" feature to ensure these episodes will be waiting on a subscriber's mobile device when the listener is available.

In spite of its popularity, podcasting remains the domain of the small broadcaster. Several corporations and big media organizations produce

Figure 4.6 Juice Receiver for Podcasts (formerly iPodder)

http://juicereceiver.sourceforge.net

podcasts, but typically, listeners comprise small niches, and the podcasts cater to the Web's long tail. This keeps listeners loyal and coming back for more.

Video podcasts have augmented audio podcasting with a visual element. Video producers including artists, educators, hobbyists, and large corporations have been able to capitalize on new, inexpensive digital video technology to create high-quality visual media with cameras, various editing software, and an Internet connection. From the user's perspective, a video podcast works the same as an audio one except that a video file type is used.

From their inception, podcasts have been embraced by higher education. On the teacher side, lectures can be easily recorded and loaded to the Web for use by students wishing to hear the lecture again or by students who missed class. Tutorials and other material can be posted online and assigned as homework instead of using classroom time to disseminate them. Items like exam reviews and readings are also common podcast applications (King, 2007).

Online courses are often constructed of lectures in podcast form so students can download the material to their mobile smart devices. This helps ensure time and geography independence for the user.

Screencasting

Useful in the classroom, a screencast is a close relative of the video podcast. Screencasting digitally captures a computer screen display and stores it in a video file. More sophisticated screencasts may include a voice track narration.

In my field, where information technology is often the topic of a lecture, screencasts provide a useful method for demonstrating software usage. Tutorials are easily created and posted for students to use online, to illustrate tricky or subtle software features that generally result in numerous questions or loss of productivity during class time (Richardson, 2006). A number of popular screencasting software packages exist, including: Camtasia, ScreenFlow, Snapz Pro X, and CamStudio (see Figure 4.7).

Microblogging: Twitter

Another tool that has burst into the higher education arena is microblogging, specifically Twitter (www.twitter.com). Twitter is the combination of social networking (like MySpace and Facebook), instant messaging,

Figure 4.7   Camtasia Studio Records Lectures in Various Ways

www.camstudio.org

and blogging that created a phenomenon called microblogging. Microblogging involves sending out brief, personal messages that interested people can view on either a webpage or mobile device. Twitter is a free microblogging service that enables users to send and read updates known as *tweets*. A tweet is a text message displayed on the sender's profile page and delivered to subscribers via the Twitter website, instant messaging, SMS, RSS, email, or an application such as Facebook (Wikipedia, 2008a).

To understand Twitter, think of a constant status update regarding a selected topic or purpose. My daughter's pet pug, Otis, would probably send the following tweets to update his followers about his exciting life:

About to nap 11:00 am
Almost asleep zzzz . . . 11:05 am
Hungry 1:00 pm
Eating a few kibbles 1:02 pm
Eating a few more kibbles 1:04 pm

About to nap 1:07 pm
Almost asleep zzzz . . . 1:12 pm

Microblogging allows a single sender to create brief updates for immediate Web publication. Twitter calls the recipients of these updates, limited to 140 characters, "followers." So, if a Twitterer has a large number of followers (who, incidentally, call their leader a "friend"), she can quickly climb the ranks of Twitter popularity. A person has to send out her or his own updates, unless she or he employs a personal assistant (as do the many political figures using Twitter). Depending on the frequency of transmission, this can become time-consuming. However, the tech-savvy millennial is no stranger to sending out short, frequent messages, and Twitter can be configured to allow messages to be sent out via text messaging from a mobile device. According to some sources, Twitter's user base is primarily in the over-35 demographic (Mansfield, 2009). A recent report by Pew Research disputes this finding, showing that tech-savvy millennials are nearly 40 percent more likely to use Twitter than the next-closest generation of users (i.e., Gen Xers) (Pew Research Center, 2010, p. 25).

Of course, detractors point out that Twitter's technology is nothing new, and they are right. In programming terms, Twitter is an updated way to tie instant messaging or chat to a Web database and webpage. In a sense, these applications have been available since 1997. However, it hasn't been until recently that the utility of this application has seized the imagination of the Web 2.0-savvy public.

Evan Williams, an entrepreneur originally from my neighboring state of Nebraska, marketed this idea and has convinced a large number of people and businesses that status updates about various activities, movements, and thoughts can be useful (see Figure 4.8). Add the mobile revolution, and you have a mini tipping point, giving this technology the push needed for wide-scale adoption.

To some extent, Twitter has been embraced by the higher education community. Digital mavens manufacture uses for it, and connectors love its power to reach out to others. Several uses appear to be relevant and helpful to the tech-savvy millennial. At the university level, Twitter can be used to develop a sense of community by relaying important information to students. Deadlines, reminders, and safety information can be quickly distributed. Twitter can be used similarly at the classroom level. However, good teachers suggest other uses. Among these are using Twitter to develop a sense of community. Some say allowing students to

Figure 4.8   Kansas State University President's Twitter Site

http://twitter.com/kstate_pres

receive and send tweets related to class will push discussions beyond the walls and time constraints of the classroom. Other teachers advocate students' using Twitter as an information-gathering tool by becoming followers of people important to the material being studied. Business professionals can be virtually shadowed with Twitter, and other forms of learning can be encouraged by subscribing to tweets (Young, 2008).

Wikis

Blogs are essentially a one-to-many technology, in which someone communicates to a group via a website. Many blogs enable reader feedback and comments that can be seen by all other readers. This fosters the creation of a community with multiple communication channels.

Wikis take this further, unleashing the collaborative power of the Web by allowing a community of people to develop a "group blog" or group website filled with informative content. This enables a many-to-many technology. Users can create and edit a webpage using their browsers. Like blogs, wikis support images, hyperlinks, and other web-page features. Wikis can be either completely open or limited to a specific group of users. Allowing a group of users to cocreate and edit a webpage encourages democratization of the Web, but it also necessitates care be taken to prevent inaccurate information from being added to the site.

Ward Cunningham developed the concept for wikis[10] to create a shared repository of software design knowledge. He envisioned this material to be accessible and changeable by those who would share in the long-term benefits of having tacit knowledge maintained. In other words, why reinvent the wheel for each software development project when certain lessons can be captured.

In time, Cunningham's wiki, the Portland Pattern Repository, became recognized in the software development community as a synergistic example of giving control to those who would directly benefit from accurate and useful information. The idea spread, and soon many organizations and groups adopted wikis (Bishop, 2004).

Probably the best known wiki application is Wikipedia, a web-based, free-content, collaborative encyclopedia anyone can edit. Wikipedia was founded in January 2001 by Jimmy Wales and Larry Sanger, who wanted to "create and distribute a multilingual free encyclopedia of the highest quality to every single person on the planet in his or her own language" (Wikipedia, 2008b). Wikipedia provides evidence that a group-created knowledge repository is a viable method of codifying, maintaining, improving, and collecting information.[11]

Of course, Wikipedia has been criticized for its potential to include incorrect information and for furthering commercial or political causes. Like any encyclopedia, it should not be used as a primary source for academic research papers. But, over time it has improved, with fewer errors and more entries. Wikis are primary examples of the cumulative effect of many people making order out of chaos.

As an experiment, I placed a brief entry about my uncle Wilson Sawyer, composer of the Alaskan Symphony, in Wikipedia. Within a few days, the article had been added to, edited, streamlined, and strengthened with citations. It was amazing to watch the process in action, which reminds me of an intelligent machine, except in this case humans provide the computing power.

Wikis have a bright future in higher education (Parker & Chao, 2007). From a teaching perspective, students must be taught to evaluate the accuracy of wiki-based material and understand its limitations. Additionally, students with expertise and knowledge on a particular topic can be directed to make meaningful and useful contributions to wikis such as Wikipedia (Notari, 2006).[12]

Also, I support the development of wikis specific to a class. I encourage group projects developed by the entire class or groups within the class. I post exam notes that can be improved and modified by the entire class as students prepare for a test. An advantage is that students can work from anywhere at any time. They build on each other's knowledge, and as a teacher I can track and assess who made the changes and contributed in meaningful ways, because wikis possess history and contribution tracking tools.

Two of the tools I find useful for these exercises include the sites Wikidot and PBWorks. Both provide excellent tools for building, maintaining, and sharing wiki websites. For more comprehensive applications, the open source tool Mediawiki is very useful.

Wikidot Wikidot was developed in Poland by Michal Frackowiak and was initially released in August of 2006. Soon after, in 2007, Wikidot Inc. was incorporated in the state of Delaware. Since that time it has grown into the "world's third-largest wiki farm, with almost half a million users running 120,000 sites and serving about 40M unique visitors per year" (Wikidot, 2010). Wikidot wikis are noted for their ability to morph into various forms such as traditional wikis, forums, and blogs. Wikidot software is well known for its capability to have a website up and running in minutes. It provides a variety of modules, themes, site templates, and software add-ins to facilitate ease of use and power. Wikidot sites have low-cost pricing structures that include free use for educational applications in the classroom or for research (Wikidot, 2009).

Wikidot also provides an active community of users who answer questions, develop new software add-ins, and offer new ideas for future development. Each community member has "karma," a composite indicator of activity, interaction with other users, experience, and contributions. Those with the highest karma levels are considered Wikidot Gurus. Wikidot also is ideal for classroom use because it requires little student training but enables sophisticated collaboration and development and sharing of class projects. Based on its offerings and history, Wikidot seems committed to preserving this capability (see Figure 4.9), unlike another wiki provider, Wetpaint, which recently refocused itself as a celebrity news hosting service (Cook, 2009).

Figure 4.9 Wikidot Wiki Development

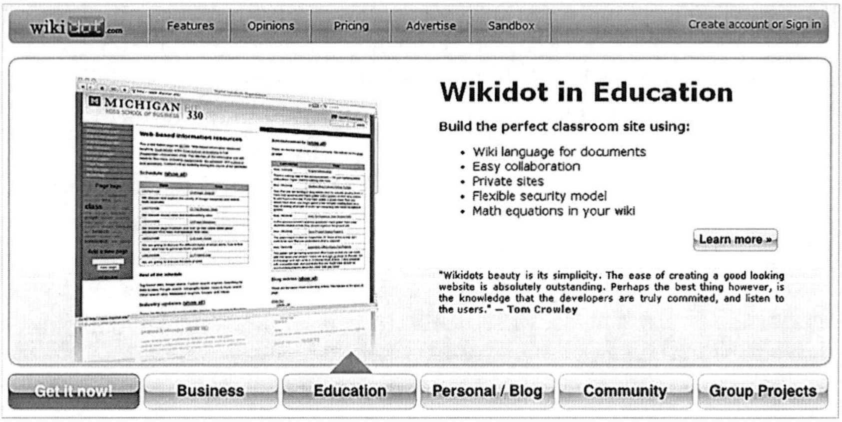

www.wikidot.com/learnmore:education

PBWorks PBWorks, originally called PBWiki, was developed by pro-grammer David Weekly, who thought creating wikis should be as easy as assembling a peanut butter sandwich (hence the *pb* in PBWorks). David Weekly devised a nontechnical way to implement wikis through a central website. A beta version of PBWorks went public in May of 2005, and the site was launched in June of the same year. In 2010, PBWorks housed over 1 million wikis. According to their website, "The company is the world's largest provider of hosted business and educational wikis, ahead of other hosted wiki providers like Wikidot and Google Sites. The com-pany also competes against on-premise software such as Microsoft Share-Point" (PBWorks, 2010).

PBWorks has always paid close attention to the higher education community and actively markets its free edition to professors and stu-dents alike. Recently, PBWorks announced a campus addition. According to Kem Barfield (a blogger with links on the PBWiki website), "Unlike its basic free account, PBworks Campus Edition provides unlimited pre-mium workspaces for $799/year. The premium version offers centralized control, centralized account creation, centralized monitoring of accounts, branding of the PBworks accounts, and easy site administration. A planned add-on will be plagiarism tools. In effect, PBworks is nudging more into the realm of the LMS."[13] This offering provides insight into the direction PBWorks is heading in and its plans to strengthen ties with higher education.

MediaWiki   MediaWiki is the open source wiki technology underlying Wikipedia. This system is in wide use and offers numerous multimedia extensions as well as easy methods to tag and categorize complex content. Further, MediaWiki is regularly updated and offers strong security features. MediaWiki is not a simple system to use (compared to PBWorks and Wikidot). It requires knowledge of scripting, selecting skins (themes for the wiki's appearance), and programming expertise. However, it is powerful and robust. Many professional-grade wiki sites run MediaWiki (Barrett, 2009). It is designed to run on a large server farm and the software is capable of managing millions of visitors per day. MediaWiki is scalable software that uses PHP code to process and display data stored in its MySQL database (MediaWiki, 2010).

ELATEwiki   In early spring of 2009, Kansas State University publicly released ELATEwiki, the Electronic Learning and Teaching Exchange. ELATEwiki facilitates the creation and documentation of innovative teaching approaches used by individuals and organizations interested in advancing the use of technology in teaching. This synergistic exchange hosts a wealth of freely available information categorized and organized into e-learning and e-teaching topics. It is useful to teachers, scholars, students, and administrators seeking to understand the dynamic and changing higher education landscape. During the first few months following its release, the number of entries on ELATEwiki went from 0 to more than 150, and over 200 individuals have registered as users. ELATEwiki can be found at http://ELATEwiki.org (McHaney, 2009a). See Figure 4.10.

Teaching Implications of Social Media

Technological convergence is impacting social media in the same way it has impacted mobile phones and smart devices. The tech-savvy millennial is often left wondering what, if any, differences exist between blogs, wikis, and other social websites. I made this observation first in a class when I taught a unit on blogs followed by a unit on wikis. After completing the first unit, students used Blogger to create a blog. After the wiki session, they were assigned a wiki-development project using Wikidot. Although the wiki assignment stressed the technology's collaborative nature, the two websites with their collection of features, wizards, and interaction tools resulted in nearly the same development process. This convergence had students wondering why there should be differences.

The answer I give them is this: Perhaps there shouldn't be differences. We are moving toward a common social media platform that will include

Figure 4.10   ELATEwiki

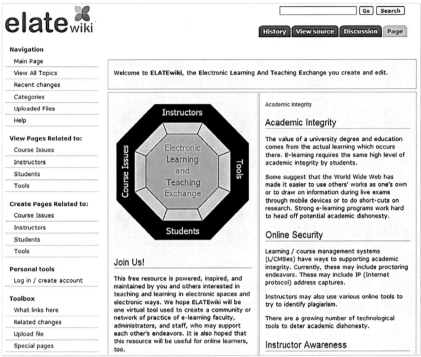

http://ELATEwiki.org

a variety of features. Word processing is a good example from my generation. At one time text was entered using one system. Spelling could be checked with a separate program. Mail labels and mail merges were done with yet another piece of software. Graphics were created in still another program. Over time, these features were absorbed or combined until all could be found in a word processor. Technology convergence is a process of social learning and acquiring/adapting best practices.

Summary

The emerging shoreline is the reality for the tech-savvy millennial. Our role is to teach this generation of students what we know and cooperatively learn with them what we don't know. We can help them make sense of what they experience and ensure mistakes made in the past are not repeated, so that innovations can be taken to the next level. This chapter has looked at technologies related to the Web 2.0 revolution, specifically *social computing* and *social media*. In mobile computing and various hardware platforms, technology convergence is occurring, and technologies within and between various Web 2.0 categorizations are blending and merging toward common implementations. In fact, technology convergence is occurring on all levels: hardware, software, and conceptual.

An excellent example of convergence is illustrated by Mentira, a game that uses mobile smart devices and a concept known as *augmented reality*. Mentira was created by Christopher Holden and Julie M. Sykes at the University of New Mexico and was built on a platform called Augmented Reality and Interactive Storytelling (ARIS) developed by David Gagnon from the University of Wisconsin in Madison. Mentira uses a fictional murder mystery together with iPod Touches to teach Spanish. The premise is that students travel to Los Griegos, an Albuquerque neighborhood near campus, and through a combination of interviewing Spanish-speaking residents in the real world and entering their physical locations on the iPods, they are able to acquire clues and solve a mystery while learning the language (Li, 2010).

Pedagogically, this incorporates gaming elements, group dynamics, social learning, technology, and a number of other concepts to create a complex learning environment that captures the imagination of the students. This is only possible because of the convergence of various gaming, mobile, and Web technologies. This trend of reality being blended with virtual worlds can form a powerful teaching and learning tool.

The next chapter continues the discussion of Web 2.0 technologies, looking specifically at *content sharing, filtering/recommendations*, and *Web applications*.

Notes

1. The popular College 2.0 Ning network moved to Facebook after the pricing restructure took place. Several alternatives were considered before Facebook was selected as the best option.

2. Over 90 percent of the high school students I've surveyed prefer IM and texting over email.

3. In cyberspace, avatars are a graphic representation of a user. The term comes from a Sanskrit word used to mean the incarnation of a god on earth (Free Dictionary, 2010).

4. Full-body sensors are being developed and tested, too.

5. The term *in-world* is commonly used by virtual world enthusiasts to refer to their activities while inside the environment.

6. massively multiplayer online role-playing game

7. Bots are automated programs that can appear as avatars or other entities. They can be used for collecting information or for performing tasks in-world.

8. An ERP is an "enterprise resource planning" system that integrates an organization's databases and improves the performance of resource planning, sales, purchasing, accounting, management control, and operational control.

9. A make-to-stock (MTS) manufacturing process focuses on commodity-based products. In this situation, production is started prior to sales orders based on forecasts. This means controlling inventory is critical and that warehouse and distribution operations play a key role in controlling costs.

10. The word *wiki* is derived from the Hawaiian word for *fast.*

11. Another excellent wiki (with which I am affiliated) is ELATEwiki.org. This wiki provides an electronic learning and teaching exchange.

12. A favorite assignment I give my students requires they become Wikipedians and contribute in a meaningful way to Wikipedia.

13. An LMS is a learning management system, another name for a virtual learning environment.

CHAPTER FIVE

THE NEW SHORELINE'S TOPOGRAPHY

Web 2.0 Content, Filtering, Apps, and Emergent Behaviors

Vast amounts of free information have made the Internet a powerful resource for learning. Information nodes form the basis for personal learning networks and change the way people work and interact. Information comes in many forms including text, photos, videos, e-books, classroom material, and other items. In order to effectively use this emerging information, tools have been created to find, filter, and sort what is needed. Among these, social bookmarking and tagging have become indispensible. With abundant information comes a variety of applications for personal computers and mobile devices. This puts the tech-savvy millennial in the middle of an emerging world filled with new possibilities and behaviors. This chapter explores these topics in a higher education setting by looking at content sharing, filtering/recommendations, Web applications, and resulting emergent behaviors.

Content Sharing

IN CHAPTER 4 WE STARTED A discussion of Web 2.0 and described this new way of using Internet technologies. Content sharing has become an important aspect of this use and takes many forms. Among these, text, photos, videos, multimedia, e-books, course material, and all sorts of artifacts are created and, often, made freely available. This abundance of information has an important impact on higher education and the way people learn.

Video and Photo Sharing

Video- and photo-sharing services have gained societal acceptance faster than many other Web 2.0 applications. Essentially, these sites allow users to upload video clips and digital photos to a website. Tech-savvy millennials rely on these sites in their daily lives and have very little hesitation when it comes to posting and sharing their media. These sites generally provide settings that enable a picture or video to be viewed according to rules regulating privacy and ownership. In most cases, the media is either made public or remains private so only invited guests possessing a password may view the material. Some sharing sites stipulate all images are public domain and may be used in any way. Others are strict about usage. It is important for the user to determine her or his level of comfort with sharing and the potential for an organization to harvest the picture for their commercial use before agreeing to the terms of service.

In general, pictures and videos stored on these sites are either viewed by a user visiting the site or used as embedded media on other websites. This flexibility permits bloggers, website developers, or anyone with limited bandwidth to serve the pictures from a faster, central site.

In the past few years, photo- and video-hosting services have increased enormously in popularity. This is due in part to sites such as Facebook, Flickr, and YouTube (see Table 5.1).

Another reason for the increased use has been the widespread availability of digital cameras, camera phones, webcams, and digital video cameras and the ease with which images and videos can be created. Computer users fear their home computer might crash and their video and photo collection might disappear, so sharing sites are viewed as reliable, free backup. On the other hand, worries about consigning their collection to a company that may not be around in a few years or that might use their photos and videos for other purposes are also concerns.

In recent years, other low-cost storage venues have emerged. Tech-savvy millennials often use "the cloud" via sites such as Box.net and Mozy.com for storing their files. So what impact do photo and video sharing have on higher education? These sites are frequently used by tech-savvy millennials, so it seems natural for them to use these tools in their educational experiences. As teachers we can educate our students on the

Table 5.1   Example Photo- and Video-Sharing Sites

Photo	Video
Flickr www.flickr.com	*Big Think* www.bigthink.com
Photobucket www.photobucket.com	*Blinkx* www.blinkx.com
PictureTrail www.picturetrail.com	*Crackle* www.crackle.com
Shutterfly www.shutterfly.com	*Daily Motion* www.dailymotion.com
SmugMug www.smugmug.com	*Hulu* www.hulu.com
Snapfish www.snapfish.com	*MetaCafe* www.metacafe.com
Webshots www.webshots.com	*YouTube* www.youtube.com
My Photo Album www.myphotoalbum.com	

Note. Of course, MySpace and Facebook can be used for video and photo sharing as well.

types of sites available and integrate photos and videos into assignments, projects, lectures, and more.

Textbooks and Tech-Savvy Millennials

Educational content has been housed in textbooks in their traditional paper form for hundreds of years (Wakefield, 1998). Many of their primary characteristics that were once strengths may ultimately be what lead to changes in their form and use. Textbooks have traditionally been static entities that can't be easily changed, manipulated, altered, or co-opted. They are generally juried by professionals and held to a particular standard. They are widely available and portable. They are not impaired if the power is cut or if a copy falls into a bathtub or is accidently stepped on or dropped. Some people find it comforting to open a book, bookmark a page, highlight and annotate sentences, and interact with paper in the way we're accustomed to. In fact, people from my generation will probably never completely dispense with textbooks, but ask a tech-savvy millennial his or her opinion. You'll find millennials are much less sentimental about paper-format books.

For example, a student pulls a mobile smart device from a coat pocket and lays it flat on her desk. A new article from a magazine is waiting on the screen, together with her textbook. In the five minutes before class starts, a shoe commercial plays. A minute later, a school-generated reminder that Friday is an early-release day appears. Rather than dwell on the reminder, she pulls up the magazine article and begins to read. Next to her, a student with thick glasses listens to the same article through earphones.

It hardly requires a technological leap to imagine how students will use textbooks and other educational material in the future. If the current textbook market disintegrated, what would come next? I can envision several possible scenarios. Given the pace of technological change, what emerges may be driven more by the development of new devices and interfaces, economics, and user preference than by the intentions of faculty and publishers. Several possibilities for providing textbook-type content exist. These are explored in the next few sections.

E-Books   Electronic books, or e-books, emerged in 1971 when Michael Hart developed a method to store written material on a computer (Lebert, 2004). The first e-book was a copy of the Declaration of Independence and became the foundation of Project Gutenberg, a repository holding thousands of free e-books. Since that time, e-books stored in numerous formats, including Adobe PDF, EPUB, Mobipocket MOBI, Microsoft Word DOC, hypertext, and others, have been distributed on the Internet (Barker, 1993).

Early e-books were developed by a variety of companies, each using proprietary formats. Lack of standardization led to fragmentation of the market, with no real consensus regarding how books should be published and displayed. This kept e-books from going mainstream. Around 2001, major publishers began looking into electronic book distribution and established partnerships with online book stores such as Ebooks.com. Sales slowly increased, and by 2009, the Association of American Publishers reported yearly e-book sales had become a $169.5 million market. Although this represented fewer than 3 percent of all books sold, the 2009 figures represented a 176.7 percent increase in sales. This suggests a tipping point could be at hand (Timpane, 2010). As the tech-savvy millennial asserts her- or himself more in the e-book marketplace, these numbers will increase, particularly regarding textbooks and electronic educational journals. Nicolas and Lewis (2008) reported that 45 percent of millennials use e-journals for completing their school-related research and would be more likely to make the jump to e-books if they put fewer restrictions on printing and copying text.

Google Books   Google has a program to make all books on the planet (within the constraints of copyright law), available for free on the Internet. As a result, thousands of out-of-print, obscure books are now downloadable in PDF format on the Web. During my experimentation with Google's book service, I located a number of old books about Mount Athos, some published almost a century ago. Being able even to ascertain the existence of these books was tricky a few years ago, and now I can read them for free on my Kindle. It is also possible to create a personal online library using Google Books, so once you find an interesting book it is kept in a list for easy access in the future.

This is an incredible resource for educators. It becomes possible to make reading lists of original material available through a simple hyper-link. Students can access material without cost and without attempting to borrow the limited library copies that might already be in the posses-sion of classmates.

Google Book Search accompanies the Google Books service. Not only can books be found by title or subject, but a full-text search of any word in the book can be conducted. This is an incredibly powerful tool. Activi-ties that would have taken the most dedicated scholar years to accomplish now can be quickly performed in minutes. I have already used this search engine to find obscure material in unexpected books. In the past, only chance and good luck would have allowed someone to stumble across hidden material of this sort.

Google Books not only provides the full text of many out-of-copyright books but also offers sample pages from copyrighted, newer material. The user can specify in a search whether he or she wants to search all material or just full-text books. If all material is searched, results also may be pulled from sample pages of copyrighted books. I was surprised to see how much material was available from a book I wrote in 1991 (McHaney, 1991).[1] In addition to material from the search, Google Book Search brings up places where the book can be purchased. Google tracks the number of page views and limits printing and copying in order to adhere somewhat to copyright laws (Duffy, 2005).

Of course Google Books has to generate revenue somehow. Content-related advertisements are used to promote items associated with key-words used in searches or that are tied to the books chosen. As another revenue source, Google offers Google Editions, an e-bookstore for selling directly to the public. Users are able to purchase digital copies of books they discover through Google Book Search. Additionally, book retailers, including independent stores, are able to offer Google Editions from their sites. Google gives its selling partners the bulk of the revenue. The premise behind Google Editions is consistent with the tech-savvy millennial's mindset and their habit of searching online for content. Evan Schnittman, vice president of global business development for Oxford University Press, was quoted in the Wall Street Journal as saying, "[Google Editions represents] whether the ability to search, find and instantly buy content will generate significant gains in revenue" (Vascellaro & Trachtenberg, 2010). Google is looking ahead to how online content will be discovered in the future and then attaching a revenue model to that process.

Google Books has to be careful of copyright laws and ensure it errs on the side of the copyright holder. Meanwhile, it continues to build a database of books, and as these books become part of the public domain, Google will release them. The books are scanned from hard copy at high speed—over 1,000 pages per hour according to some estimates (Kelly, 2006). By October of 2010, it was believed that Google had already scanned over 15 million books (Crawford, 2010).

What does this mean to higher education? It means full-text searches of vast numbers of both in-print and out-of-print books can be conducted to find specific extracts. If the full text of a book of interest is available for free, it can be read online or downloaded to an e-reader. If the book isn't in the public domain, details about where to acquire the full text are usually available. Teachers will be able to enhance their research bibliographies, find more source material for lecture development, and introduce their students to a low-cost, nearly limitless library. Student research will be enabled and fortified. What took me months to research for my Ph.D. dissertation written back in 1994 and 1995 would take significantly less time with superior results! Rare books and collections will be more readily available. The ability to filter, sort, and discover is consistent with skill sets possessed by teach-savvy millennials.

Wikibooks I was extremely excited when the prospect of Wikibooks hit the Web. Wikibooks is a community for collectively creating free textbooks so students can access content without charge. Although in its infancy now, the potential exists for capturing and collecting textbook-type information and making it available at no charge. Not only could a system like this completely realign the textbook publishing industry, it could potentially provide superior books drawing on the combined expertise of a multitude of practitioners, enthusiasts, professors, instructors, and students. Of course, some problems do exist. For instance, the contents may be in various stages of completion, and inaccuracies may creep into the material. However, studies have shown the contents of Wikipedia, the online encyclopedia wiki, in the area of science to be as accurate as *Encyclopedia Britannica*'s (Giles, 2005). I would suspect, over time, the same phenomenon would occur with textbooks: More content would be added, fine-tuned, and made increasingly accurate with each group of students and teachers that uses them.

Although the idea of students being able to access free educational material and knowledge is appealing, I do have mixed feelings on the subject. I have made money selling textbooks and know the days of supplementing my income this way are nearing an end. (However, since Wikibooks began on July 10, 2003, good-quality wiki textbooks in my fields of study still have not become available.) Also, although Wikibooks includes over 30,000 pages in a multitude of subjects, most of its books are not yet competitive with those being sold by academic textbook companies. I think a few more things have to happen before this textbook revolution really takes hold. But I do believe community developed and maintained textbooks will eventually compete with the best commercial publications.

Website- and Community-Based Classroom Material I remember when Course Technology, a book publisher specializing in information-technology-related textbooks, began posting supplemental faculty and student information on a website. I thought the world of publishing, and textbooks in general, had changed forever. That was back in the late 1990s, and now, even though most publishers offer material on the Web, paper textbooks remain their leading products. Still, various groups are dedicated to promoting Web-based course material distribution. In the nonprofit arena, organizations are posting material online to reduce the financial burden on students and learners. Among profit-seeking companies, most material placed on the Web is used to indirectly support sales efforts and add value to published material. Several interesting trends in these areas give a glimpse of what may emerge. OCW, Connexions, and CourseSmart provide examples of these.

OCW. A recent development comes from an organization called the OpenCourseWare Consortium (OCW). OCW promotes the free and open digital publication of high-quality educational materials, organized into courses. The consortium comprises more than 200 international higher education institutions and organizations hoping to advance education and empower students through free accessibility to digital course material. OCW has several goals including:

- Extend the reach and impact of OpenCourseWare by encouraging the adoption and adaptation of open educational materials around the world.
- Foster the development of additional OpenCourseWare projects.
- Ensure the long-term sustainability of OpenCourseWare projects by identifying ways to improve effectiveness and reduce costs. (OCW Consortium, 2008)

Although the courseware is free to anyone wishing to use it, in order for a university to become a contributor, it must commit to publishing material from at least 10 courses in a compatible format. To satisfy my own curiosity, I browsed through available resources and found a number of items readily available for use in a variety of areas. I paid particular attention to teaching material on the subject of international business, being unable to locate anything related to my own specialties. Although I didn't find anything specifically resembling a textbook, I did find a number of helpful readings, handouts, and classroom presentation material.

In my opinion, OCW has begun the dialog that must eventually become part of all higher education institutions. Rather than reinvent the wheel each semester at each university, social networks of teachers and learners will benefit from sharing resources and building better versions of material on a regular basis. OCW will need to make locating resources easier and more uniform, but I think they have an admirable goal and a great start.

CONNEXIONS.   This is another up-and-coming environment for sharing collaboratively developed, timely teaching content on the Web (Connexions, 2010). Connexions was started by Richard G. Baraniuk, an engineering professor at Rice University, after he received a $6 million grant from the William and Flora Hewlett Foundation. He sees the future of textbooks as being similar to what is occurring in the music industry, with its *rip, burn, and mash* mindset. He envisions textbook publishing as being a changing and growing ecosystem rather than a profit-producing pipeline (Cohen, 2008).

Connexions has created a "Content Commons" to house educational material for anyone from preschool teachers to professors at Carnegie Research I universities. This material is arranged in modules connected to larger collections, courses, or books depending on the authors' paradigms and needs. Material is free under the Creative Commons "attribution" license (Connexions, 2008). Connexions has the following features and philosophies regarding educational material (adapted from the Connexions website; see Figure 5.1).

- *Modular and Non-Linear Content.* Most textbooks are a mass of information in linear format. However, human brains are not linear. People learn by linking new concepts with familiar ones. Connexions mimics this by breaking down content into smaller chunks, called modules, that can be linked together and arranged in different ways.
- *Sharing.* Why reinvent the wheel? When people share their knowledge, they can select from the best ideas to create the most effective learning materials.

Figure 5.1 Connexions Homepage

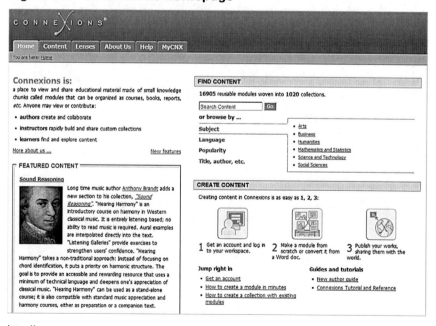

http://cnx.org

♦ *Technological.* Content is stored in XML to ensure it works on multiple computer platforms.

♦ *Legal.* Creative Commons open-content licenses make it easy for authors to share their work—allowing others to use and reuse it legally—while still getting recognition and attribution for their efforts.

♦ *Educational.* Authors are encouraged to write each module to stand on its own. This is so others can adapt material for use in different courses and contexts.

♦ *Collaboration.* Just as knowledge is interconnected, people don't live in a vacuum. Connexions promotes communication between content creators and provides various means of collaboration. Collaboration helps knowledge grow more quickly, advancing the possibilities for new ideas from which all can benefit.

CourseSmart.   CourseSmart LLC is a new for-profit venture founded and supported by five higher education textbook publishers including Pearson, Wiley, and McGraw-Hill. Their mission is to improve teaching and learning by providing instructors and students with better exposure and access to digital course materials. This model for textbook sales attempts to maintain the current top-down publishing system whereby editors work with authors to develop and maintain a textbook pipeline to ensure current, accurate, and cutting-edge material distribution to students. CourseSmart maintains the royalty model and pays authors for new content. According to the CourseSmart (2008) website, this approach to digital material provides the following benefits:

Instructors: CourseSmart provides instant access to review and compare textbooks and course materials in their discipline without the time, cost, and environmental impact of mailing examination copies.

Students: CourseSmart helps students find assigned e-textbooks at savings averaging 51% versus the print version. Another value of CourseSmart is web functionality. Search, instant access, note taking, and a lighter backpack are some benefits of an e-textbook.

Institutions: CourseSmart provides benefits related to a large selection of e-textbooks in a common format from a single provider and helps lower the total cost of education through a more "wired" campus.

Web 2.0 Textbooks: BookBooN, Textbook Revolution, Scribd, Flat Earth

The concepts of collaborative development, information sharing, and social computing are reshaping many aspects of higher education. Innovations that combine e-book technology and delivery have emerged in the form of Web 2.0 educational publishing applications. A variety of new ideas are being tried as people rethink how books can be written, published, and distributed in education marketplaces (Young, 2009). In one example, BookBooN (see Figure 5.2), run by the Danish company Ventus Publishing ApS, provides a venue for professors to publish books that remove students from the revenue stream. Textbooks are financed using advertisements sold to carefully screened organizations. BookBooN works with authors to deliver material according to guidelines that more closely resemble how modern students want to use books on computers and handheld devices that read PDF files. BookBooN ads are placed on select pages of the online books, and then usage, downloads, and clickstreams are monitored to determine how much revenue is generated, which is shared with book authors. BookBooN further adds the advantage of allowing authors to quickly and efficiently update their books (McHaney, 2009b).

Figure 5.2   BookBooN Homepage

Textbook Revolution is an online organization cooperating with BookBooN and other Web 2.0 textbook publishers. Textbook Revolution was developed and is operated by university students. The original intent of the site was to locate free educational materials for students and professors and then create a central location to promote moving these materials into the classroom. The site tracks the popularity of various textbooks and brings attention to the best free classroom material (Textbook Revolution, 2010).

While BookBooN and Textbook Revolution focus on the academic world, other social publishing websites provide access to a wider range of online books and textbooks, some of which are free. The largest and most active of these is Scribd. Scribd, often called the YouTube of the written word, reports that more than 60 million people visit its website each month to share original books, documents, and articles. Scribd has a vision of "turn[ing] everyone into a publisher and creat[ing] the best possible reading experience on the web and mobile platforms" (Scribd, 2010). In addition to providing free online books, Scribd sells commercial works of fiction and nonfiction for Web and mobile platforms. Scribd's books might be published by a company or an individual. Reader comments and ratings help propel the best items into more prominent locations where users can more easily find them (see Figure 5.3).

Another upstart textbook company is Flat World Knowledge Inc. Flat World provides free textbooks on the Web or for iPhone but charges if print copies are ordered. In fall of 2009, Flat World textbooks were used by more than 40,000 students at more than 400 institutions of higher education, with 65 percent of the students buying a book and only 35 percent choosing the free option (Weir, 2009). Authors receive a 20 percent royalty on sales. Another innovation by Flat World was their use of paid college student interns to convince college professors to adopt the free online textbooks in their classes (Park, 2010).

Teaching Implications of Content Sharing

To teach tech-savvy millennials there must be an understanding of their characteristics and worldview and its core. To most of them, the concept of social media makes sense. They appreciate core features that encourage

- Discovering existing content.
- Contributing new content.
- Combining and organizing all content.

Figure 5.3   Scribd Is the "YouTube" of Printed Material

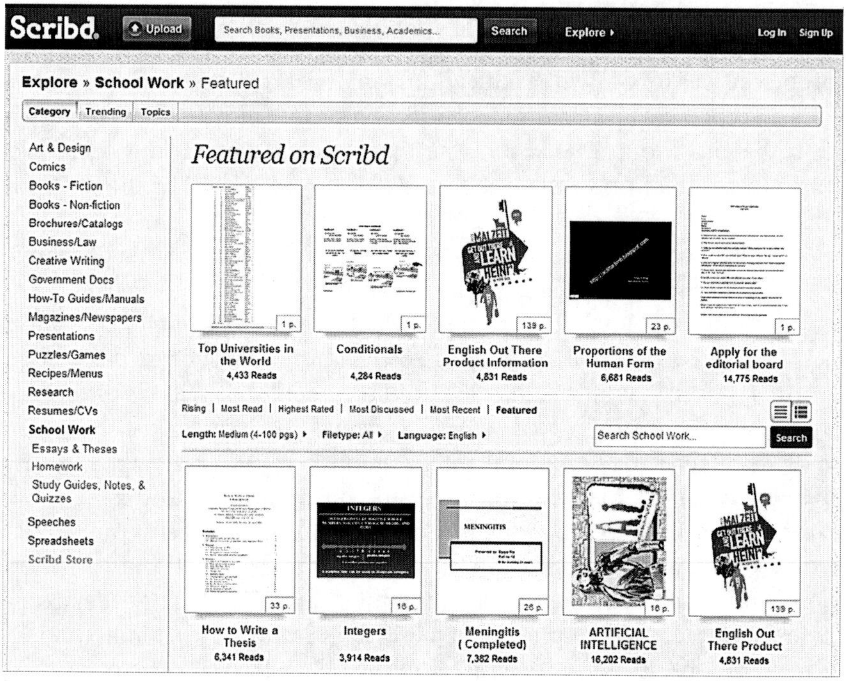

http://scribd.com

- ◆ Directing others with reviews and ratings.
- ◆ Creating groups and collaborating.
- ◆ Sharing opinions, thoughts, and questions.

This can constitute elements of a sound pedagogical approach that integrates social media concepts into teaching. First, social media lends itself to personalization of learning and the development of a personal learning environment. Social media, with blogs, wikis, and RSS feeds, permits the uncoupling of knowledge and removes barriers to integration. Knowledge can become location and device independent so it is accessible through any number of platforms and channels. Further, social media permits the blending and construction of new synthesized concepts (chapter 7 discusses this idea of constructivism in more detail). As teachers in higher education, we can encourage this uncoupling and synthesis within a community of learners. In essence, what results is scaled content adapted to specific learning needs at the time/place needed on whatever device that is available. Around this infrastructure is a community of learners.

What does this mean for shared social media and online content relevant to higher education and the tech-savvy millennial? Several things are occurring simultaneously:

Revitalization of existing content. Many out-of-print books will be resurrected as tools such as Google Book Search and e-book formats make consumption feasible and keep costs low.

Uncoupling content from physical formats. Class material is being freed from physical format constraints and is available for consumption on multiple platforms. The tech-savvy millennial has enjoyed this advantage with music and other multimedia for some time. Class material will certainly follow.

Assembled material sets. More professors are assembling their own source material based on available journal articles, material posted on professional websites, news articles, blogs, and open content courseware. This material might be compiled so it can be printed at local locations, or it might fall to the student to print anything desired. Assembled material sets might pose a problem regarding copyright depending on the diligence and beliefs of the professor.

Specialization of knowledge. The Web has given us the long tail (Anderson, 2006), and the ability to specialize has made personal learning networks easier to construct.

Community-developed/improved books and material. The Connexions and Wikibooks models are sure to become more important and more widely used as the idea of community-based development and upgrading becomes the norm. Already these are gaining acceptance by mainstream academics.

Student-developed material. The idea that course material can be developed from the collective projects of prior classes is becoming more popular. This approach is taking shape on venues such as ELATEwiki, where student-developed entries are created by a class one semester, then read and edited by classes in subsequent semesters. In the future, this material will be bundled into a booklike structure that can be assembled and printed.

Filtering and Recommendations

As discussed earlier, Web 2.0 concepts have made it possible for individuals to collaboratively develop recommendations and filter information in ways once limited to several powerful individuals. For instance, in the past, news organizations could decide which stories to run and which to bury. Now, social news websites such as Google News, Digg Top News, and others permit users to determine which stories rise to the top (see Figure 5.4).

In the emerging digital landscape, grassroots or viral movements are placed on equal footing. By collecting the wisdom of multiple people, different ways of using and looking at the information becomes possible. Social bookmarking and tagging illustrate how these concepts have been implemented.

The tech-savvy millennial has this expectation for her or his education as well. With websites such as RateMyProfessors.com and others, millennials have empowered themselves in new ways. For instance, students

Figure 5.4   Digg Is a Social News Website

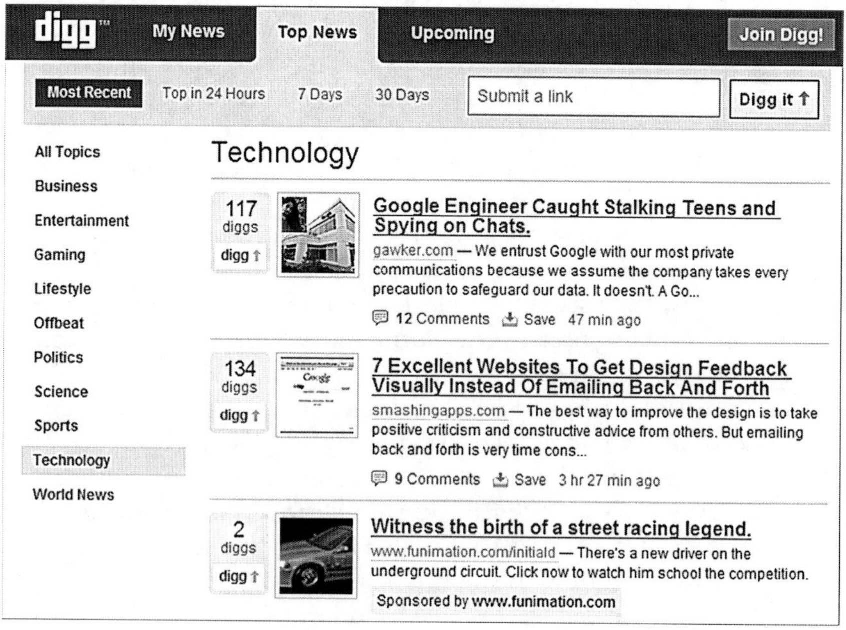

http://digg.com

want to be sure their professors are competent and are teaching relevant material. Rating professors and classes is not the only way these technologies come into play. Tech-savvy millennials are able to use rating tools to find the most informative articles, to purchase the best mobile devices, and to construct cooperative information-sharing sites. What results is an informed cohort of students.

From a pedagogical standpoint, teachers need to ensure these tools are integrated into teaching and learning so students understand how to use them appropriately. We can also use these tools ourselves to help maintain currency and relevancy in our fields. Filtering tools create a knowledge base acquired from our peers that would be impossible for one person to assemble on his or her own. Several primary tools exist in the category of filtering and recommendations.

Social Bookmarking

Social bookmarking uses the power of a self-organizing Web 2.0 community. The idea is simple. When someone locates a particularly helpful website, they bookmark it so returning will be easier. Social bookmarking takes this helpful individual tool and expands it collectively. This makes it possible to share and categorize large numbers of bookmarks and create an index of helpful websites. These sites can be ranked by the number of bookmarks indicated for a URL or by most recent bookmarking or other criteria. Each user of the system has an individual goal of sharing information about helpful websites she or he has encountered. No one knows what overall pattern will emerge from everyone's collective knowledge. System users essentially work together as distributed social agents to organize a complex and otherwise amorphous set of information into a more coherent body of material using many different criteria. The resultant collection resembles complex, intelligent design but is a result of these individual, distributed processes.

Social bookmarking yields value to individual users because it provides an online venue for storing valuable collections of bookmarks. These bookmarks are available on any computer with an Internet connection. Some see social bookmarking as a way to democratize the Web and move the power held by search engine companies such as Yahoo and Google back into the hands of the individual. Because classification and tagging are done by people who understand the content of the pages being viewed (unlike in commercial search engines, where general algorithms are used to determine the content of a website), the tags are more meaningful.

Some people believe the commercialization of the Web has compromised search integrity and that social bookmarking will, in the long run, create more stable and useful systems.

Many social bookmarking sites permit bookmarks to be saved privately or to be shared with specified people or groups (see Figure 5.5). RSS feeds are often tied to specific tags and allow interested people to keep up with new websites they might find interesting. The following are several popular social bookmarking sites:

> http://delicious.com
> www.diigo.com
> http://digg.com
> http://faves.com/home
> http://spurl.net

Of course, drawbacks to social bookmarking exist. Among these are misspelled tags, misclassification, the lack of standard tags to describe similar content, the lack of standard word forms for tags (e.g., plural vs. singular), and so forth.

Tags

Tags and social bookmarking go hand in hand. Tags are the nonhierarchical keywords assigned to help describe an item. Tags are meant to make

Figure 5.5   Diigo Is a Social Tagging Website

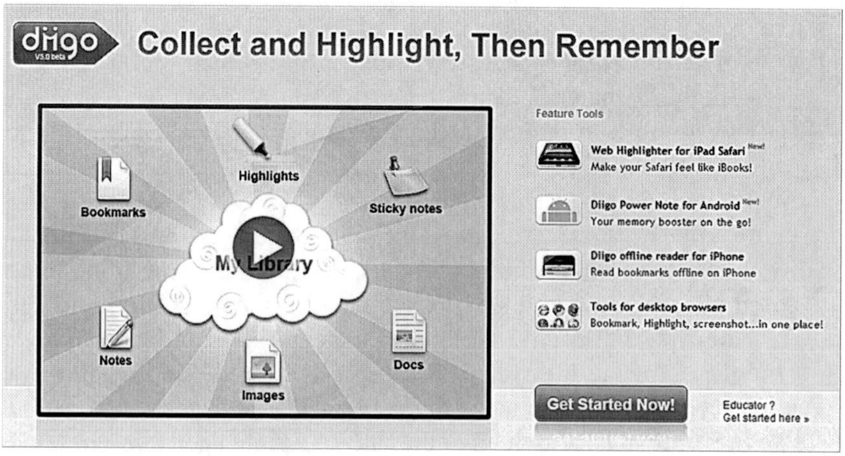

www.diigo.com

it easier to find something again or illuminate a topic for future searches. Tags are selected informally by an item's creator or by someone viewing or using the tagged object. Websites, photos, videos, animations, paragraphs, documents, and numerous other information objects can be tagged. As a collection of tags grows, it becomes known as a *folksonomy.* Tagging has become vastly popular with Web 2.0 and collaborative applications and is the primary feature of many collaborative websites. Figure 5.6 shows an example tag cloud generated by Wordle (www.wordle.net) for ELATEwiki.

Recently, tagging has been extended to the real world, with mobile devices being used to take pictures and to read bar codes that are then linked to geospatial databases with GPS coordinates. A virtual database of tags attached to real-world objects has resulted. Museums, parks, businesses, and other entities are exploring and using these ideas to virtualize the real world. Some believe this could eventually form the basis for recreating the physical world in cyberspace and metaverses.

Teaching Implications of Filtering and Recommendations

In higher education, social bookmarking is a way for classes, disciplines, and groups of classes to create a knowledge base of websites and useful information marked with descriptive keywords and predetermined tags. For instance, if a class is studying Beaver Island and students discover a

Figure 5.6   Wordle Tag Cloud for ELATEwiki

helpful site, the teacher might want to save it as a bookmark and at the same time attach key words such as "Beaver Island," "education," "King Strang," "Mormon" and other relevant tags. This means a class of students is to generate their own bookmarks for a semester project or list of readings. The tags become meaningful metadata that help describe topics covered on various websites and encourage students to think about classification schemes. This makes organization a meaningful exercise and benefits the larger community of Web users.

Web Applications (Apps)

When a tech-savvy millennial wants to solve a problem, play a game, take notes, create a to-do list or accomplish any number of other tasks, he or she pays a visit to the Apple or Android App store.

The Web has enabled a software revolution, facilitating cross-platform development and implementation of applications that run in browsers rather than on specific computer or mobile platforms. In general, Web applications make software conveniently available over networks and drive down distribution and maintenance costs. Common applications in higher education include virtual office tools, webmail, graphics manipulation software, video and audio editors, and countless others. The flavor of this aspect of Web 2.0 is described in the next two sections: Virtual Office Tools and Mobile Apps.

Virtual Office Tools

One of the next huge explosions on the Web will be the mass acceptance and use of Web 2.0 versions of office applications such as word processors, spreadsheets, and presentation-support tools. These tools typically are expensive to install, both in terms of space and costs, and tricky to maintain. This is changing, as users now expect their productivity software to resemble other tools they use every day. In other words, the features of Web 2.0 that are most valuable to them—collaborative tools, communication capabilities, wiki-like features, and interactive tracking ability—are not currently in versions of MS Word, Lotus 1-2-3, Power-Point, or other tools. But that is changing.

A number of Web-based versions of office-productivity tools are now emerging, and many of these are low cost or even free. Although these young tools lack many high-end features of Microsoft's tools, they are evolving rapidly and offer the strengths of Web 2.0, which means a focus on connecting users and fostering collaboration.

In a sense, the race is on in this marketplace. Open Office (although not really Web 2.0 focused) was an early competitor. Its development began over 20 years ago as a single piece of software. Its goal was to run dependably across all major computing platforms: Microsoft Windows, GNU/Linux, Sun Solaris, and Apple's Mac OS. This cross-platform robustness reflects the goals of the newer Web 2.0-focused packages.

Although rumors about Microsoft's eventual transition to Web-based platforms for its MS Office suite of products continue to whirl, and it appears to be imminent (Harvey, 2010), Google has gotten an early foothold in this area.

Google Docs is an example of productivity software that may soon become a major contender. In general, Google Docs offers free, Web-based word processing, spreadsheet, presentation, and form-application software. The idea is to enable the creation of familiar documents on Google servers rather than local drives. Further capabilities permit multiple users to interactively, simultaneously collaborate on these documents (see Figure 5.7). This opens the door to massive, worldwide collaborative development (Solomon & Schrum, 2007).

Figure 5.7 Google Spreadsheet

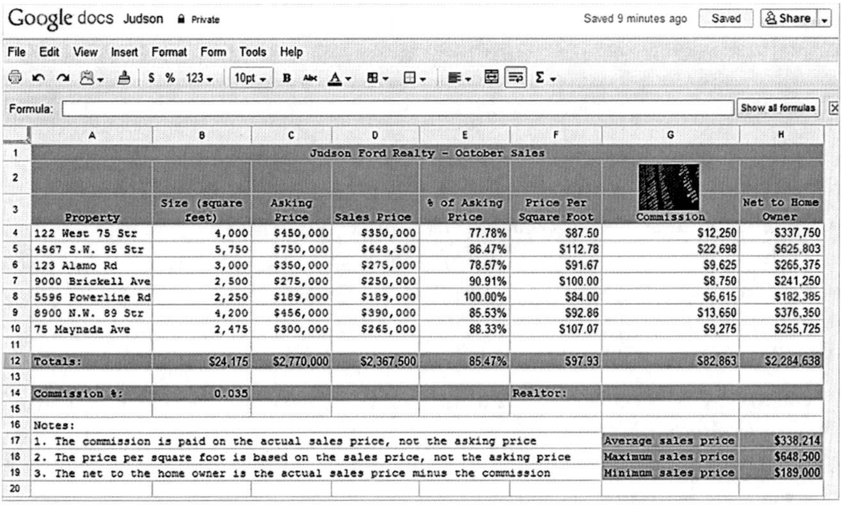

	A	B	C	D	E	F	G	H
1	Judson Ford Realty - October Sales							
2								
3	Property	Size (square feet)	Asking Price	Sales Price	% of Asking Price	Price Per Square Foot	Commission	Net to Home Owner
4	122 West 75 Str	4,000	$450,000	$350,000	77.78%	$87.50	$12,250	$337,750
5	4567 S.W. 95 Str	5,750	$750,000	$648,500	86.47%	$112.78	$22,698	$625,803
6	123 Alamo Rd	3,000	$350,000	$275,000	78.57%	$91.67	$9,625	$265,375
7	9000 Brickell Ave	2,500	$275,000	$250,000	90.91%	$100.00	$8,750	$241,250
8	5596 Powerline Rd	2,250	$189,000	$189,000	100.00%	$84.00	$6,615	$182,385
9	8900 N.W. 89 Str	4,200	$456,000	$390,000	85.53%	$92.86	$13,650	$376,350
10	75 Maynada Ave	2,475	$300,000	$265,000	88.33%	$107.07	$9,275	$255,725
11								
12	Totals:	$24,175	$2,770,000	$2,367,500	85.47%	$97.93	$82,863	$2,284,638
13								
14	Commission %:	0.035				Realtor:		
15								
16	Notes:							
17	1. The commission is paid on the actual sales price, not the asking price						Average sales price	$338,214
18	2. The price per square foot is based on the sales price, not the asking price						Maximum sales price	$648,500
19	3. The net to the home owner is the actual sales price minus the commission						Minimum sales price	$189,000
20								

http://docs.google.com

Mobile Apps

A wide array of applications has been developed for mobile devices. Mobile applications run on handheld and laptop devices such as personal digital assistants (PDAs), mobile phones, smart mobile devices, and tablets. These applications are intended to either run independently or use server software from a connected location. They may be preinstalled on a device or downloaded by users from websites or app stores.

Many universities have responded to the desires of the tech-savvy millennial and rolled out mobile Web interfaces with apps to support student life experiences. Several of these provide good models for the higher education community regarding transmission of campus information. Some of my favorite mobile sites include:

Ohio State University—http://m.osu.edu
West Virginia University—http://m.wvu.edu
Texas A&M—http://m.tamu.edu
Texas Tech—www.ttu.edu/mobile

Just as all universities have websites, within a short time frame, all will have mobile websites. The demand for mobile services is growing exponentially, and university technology staff members are scrambling to respond (Fienen, 2010). Students' expectation for apps relevant to their educational experience has skyrocketed. Some apps will come from developers and third-party commercial sellers. Others will be developed at universities or customized with their branding and local culture (see Figures 5.8 and 5.9).

Leading in this area is Blackboard Mobile Central (Blackboard, 2010b). This software is customized and used to serve campus information to students. For instance, Texas Tech's mobile Web runs Blackboard Mobile Central software (Blackboard Video, 2010).

These mobile webs are helpful but should be viewed as a first-generation implementation (recall that most first-generation websites were also informational). They are not m-learning applications nor do they directly mediate educational exchanges or pedagogical approaches to learning. Most mobile Webs at universities provide the following information (Feldstein, 2010):

♦ Campus maps
♦ Course catalog information

Figure 5.8   Mobile Web Interface for Texas A & M University

www.blackboard.com/Mobile/Mobile-Central.aspx

Figure 5.9   Mobile Web Interface for West Virginia University

http://m.wvu.edu/about/

- Campus calendar
- Campus photos
- Campus news
- Campus sports info (e.g., scores, game schedule, etc.)
- Campus directory

Higher education will learn from its initial foray into mobile Webs. Initial success as measured by student use and general adoption will drive the development of teaching and learning-related mobile apps.

Blackboard has adapted many of its learning management system (LMS) features to mobile platforms. Blackboard Mobile Learn (clearly branded to reflect pedagogical use) was initially released for Sprint Network Android and BlackBerry phones and iPhone OS–powered devices over a WiFi connection. Among Mobile Learn's capabilities are the following (Blackboard Mobile Learn, 2010):

- Announcements—Instructors post instant, on-the-go access to anywhere, anytime news for students.
- Discussions—Discussion Board engages students and promotes learning. Students ask and answer questions, and instructors can respond to one student for the entire class's benefit. Instructors and students can review and post to threaded discussions on the go.
- Grades—Students can view grades.
- Blogs—Blogs can be read and comments posted.
- Tasks—Students can track and manage the progress of various tasks, from turning in homework assignments to remembering to pick up a midterm or purchase a textbook. Also allows students to track projects.
- Roster—Class roster displays class member lists.
- Media—Directly on their mobile device, students can access music, videos, and images uploaded by their instructors.
- Journals—Students can read and reflect on Journal posts. Students and instructors can comment on Journals from a mobile device.

Some of these items are building blocks that a teacher can use to construct a sound pedagogical approach for their class.

Teaching Implications of Web Applications

The implications of apps (both mobile and Web-based) for higher education are staggering. Further student interaction with faculty and peer teams is enabled through the use of Web and mobile applications. Web apps such as Google Docs make team projects easier to coordinate and complete. Changes to the documents are maintained so older versions can be recovered and individual contributions to the finished product can be tallied. Pedagogically, this will enable learning communities, and constructivism (discussed in chapter 7) will be fostered as students build meaning and understanding in group settings.

So why hasn't large-scale adoption of Web apps already occurred in higher education? Mostly because these tools (e.g., Google Docs) don't yet have the full set of features and power that MS Office applications offer. But this appears to be forthcoming.

Although the users are not paying for the software out of pocket, tool use does provide revenue to Google. Google generates revenue with small advertisements that appear alongside a document as a user types. Some users may not find this acceptable because it also means software is tracking the words used in a document.

I have required my students to use Google Docs on several assignments and found the outcome to be very satisfactory. I plan to use more and more of these tools in my future classrooms. For many tech-savvy millennials, the idea of using free online office tools that store documents "in the cloud" makes perfect sense. As educators, these tools can foster online collaboration and remove constraints related to platform, time, and location.

Like Web apps, mobile apps are poised to have a huge impact on higher education. Tech-savvy millennials and their teachers are using apps to enhance their capabilities and perform many tasks associated with teaching and learning. Supported areas range from virtual books and course materials (via CourseSmart, Stanza, Amazon's Kindle app, and iBooks from Apple) to homework, studying, and note-taking applications (Evernote, MyHomework, and iStudiez and gFlashPro for creating flashcards) to reference materials (Dictionary.com, Wikipanion, and Chemical Touch Lite) to virtual calculators and other tools.

Although no shortage of mobile apps exist, there does seem to be a shortage of understanding how to integrate these new technologies into classroom pedagogy. Many students are not allowed to use mobile devices in classroom settings because of their disruptive nature and the recreational options available on most. One thing is certain: Higher education needs to find a way to integrate and make use of these tools, because they offer so much power and flexibility and have the potential to support pedagogy and learning in exciting and effective ways!

Emergent Behaviors on the Web

One of the most incredible things about today's Internet is how well suited it is to self-organizing behaviors and interaction between distributed, independent agents. Scientists and researchers have compared the buzz of activity surrounding this hive of information to bee or ant colonies, where individual insects don't know much about the "big picture" but by completing their own small tasks, an amazing outcome emerges.

Kevin Kelly, in his prescient book *Out of Control* (Kelly, 1994), describes emergent behaviors and how these behaviors can't be predicted or understood until a certain threshold is reached. For instance, studying an individual ant won't provide any insight into its colony-creation behavior. Likewise, studying a bee will yield very little information about how it participates in hive creation, caring for a queen, or swarming. Although Kelly's book predates the current Web 2.0 phenomenon, his ideas translate smoothly to what we are seeing today. The connection of people in worldwide networks has resulted in behaviors and systems that were never conceived but instead emerged.

With the Internet, the collective impact of millions of distributed, separate efforts by individuals over time have impacted the way information is created, stored, and organized. We have already explored one example—wikis—and talked about how groups of people, often separated by geography, time, culture, and other factors, come together and create a useful body of knowledge without needing a supervisor or even common vision. This emergent behavior was not truly predictable when small numbers of users existed. It wasn't until a certain threshold was reached that the true nature of the system began to be revealed. We are seeing how large collections of small actions can shape the Web and produce online communities in ways no one could have forecast. Imagine what could be accomplished by our students if we were to use their small, individual efforts in a way that creates a larger, more meaningful whole. What emergent behaviors will a "flock" of students display? Perhaps the result will be a future of education in which doing replaces memorizing and creation replaces review . . . one can only hope.

Summary

If this chapter has given you reason to pause and think about the future, then I have accomplished my goal. The next chapter of this book steps back and provides a view of how these platforms, transformations, convergences, and software tools might come together in a holistic way to support strong teaching and learning practices. Like all futurists, I am taking some risk by presenting my viewpoint, and without a doubt, some of my observations will prove to be no more than hopeful speculations. But as William Arthur Ward once said, "If you can imagine it, you can achieve it." Let's imagine something amazing and watch new learning theories and pedagogical practices emerge in this time of incredible potential and possibility.

Note

1. View *Computer Simulation* (McHaney, 1991) here: http://books.google.com/books?id = tZl9CeMJXAkC.

CHAPTER SIX

WHAT STUDENTS ARE FINDING ON THE NEW SHORE

Students are experiencing a mixture of old and new when it comes to class delivery on the new shoreline. Rather than being offered well-thought-out pedagogies rooted in learning theory, students often find themselves at the receiving end of experimentations with technologies that vary widely from course to course. The new shoreline offers opportunities that allow higher education to become more relevant and effective in its interaction with students, but typically students don't perceive this as happening.

Student Expectations of Higher Education

STUDENTS EXPRESS FRUSTRATION with their perceptions about higher education's response to technology. Fairly or unfairly, often they view their teachers as behind the times and out of touch with new media and the mobile revolution.

Tech-savvy millennials have spent their formative years in an environment where informal learning is widespread, easy, and almost second nature. They expect to work in a variety of different, potentially unrelated fields during the course of their lifetime. They know their jobs may involve technologies and ideas that have not been developed yet. For this reason, they realize that informal learning and self-learning will be a significant component of their success. They believe formal education is a portion of their lifelong learning experience but may not be the most important piece. Their learning occurs in a variety of ways, through networks of friends, online searches, communities of practice, and through social networking. They know learning and work are not separate but rather two aspects of a lifelong process (Bisoux, 2009).

I recently attended a lecture given by a brilliant colleague of mine at Kansas State University, Dr. Michael Wesch, a cultural anthropologist, media ecologist, and creator of the highly acclaimed YouTube video, *Web 2.0 . . . The Machine Is Us/ing Us* (Wesch, 2007). Dr. Wesch provided insight into how higher education needs to change in order to remain relevant to the next generation of students. Based on student classroom surveys and discussions, he concluded that most of them believe the following:

- ♦ To learn is to acquire information.
- ♦ Information is scarce and hard to find.
- ♦ Trust educational authority: in other words, *obey and follow your teacher.*
- ♦ Authorized information comes from the front (based on how desks face forward, toward the teacher).

Most of these unfortunate misconceptions are contrary to the reality of the emerging world, and this leaves tech-savvy millennials seeking relevance in their educational experiences. Wesch (2007) says their lives outside of higher education has placed these students in the center of a world where instead the following is true

- ♦ Acquiring information doesn't equal mastering it.
- ♦ Information is ubiquitous, easy to find, and abundant.
- ♦ Some educational authorities are behind the times.
- ♦ Relevant and highly useful information emerges from a community of peers, not an authority figure.

In order to understand higher education's situation, let's investigate what forms teaching has been taking recently. We'll start with a short story to illustrate different ways of coping when change is thrust upon you.

Driving Lessons

"Yikes!"

My wife, Annette, used her left hand to wrestle our used Nissan hatchback into third gear as she bumped up over a curb and bounced back into the left lane of a busy North Shore city street in Auckland, New Zealand.

I moaned a little and looked up at her through glazed, puffy eyes and wheezed out some encouragement.

She swatted at me for a second before gripping the wheel with whitening knuckles. "I didn't expect to learn left-lane driving quite like this," she said through clenched teeth, with a warning-like growl emanating from deep in her chest, before she sped through an intersection.

"You're doing great," I said weakly.

"Better than you," she said, glancing at my shaking silhouette hunched in the passenger seat. "You're lucky I know where the hospital is . . ."

In 2003, my wife, Annette, our three children—Mark, Matt, and Megan—and I accepted a one-year appointment for me to teach and do some research at Auckland University of Technology while on sabbatical from Kansas State. This constituted an exciting time for our entire family. We settled into a great condo overlooking the harbor on the north shore of Auckland in a village called Devonport. We watched the America's Cup sailboats flash by from our living room windows and enjoyed the amenities of a beautiful country while being visited by a steady stream of family and friends from home.

At first, life went well, with the kids adjusting to Kiwi schools and us making great friends with our neighbors—Tim and Anne on one side and Kelly, Mickey, and John on the other—and other faculty members, like John and his spouse, Kris.

Then, things went a little strange—at least for me. I started to lose weight and feel sick all the time. I became exhausted and was constantly breaking out in skin rashes. I couldn't eat much and had a number of other problems you don't really want to hear.

My personal tipping point came at about 9 P.M. on a Sunday night when I suddenly blew up like a balloon and began having breathing difficulties. That was when Annette had her first driving lesson with our used, left-sided, stick-shift Nissan while she rushed me to the hospital.

On our arrival, the nurses rushed me past a couple of other unfortunates in the emergency room. They hooked me up to an IV, and after a quick appraisal, gave me adrenaline, steroids, and antihistamine shots.

"You're in anaphylactic shock," someone said. I shook and shuddered uncontrollably.

"You're one big hive," my wife said matter-of-factly, poking at my arm with her finger.

"What's anaphylactic shock?" I asked after a while.

"Anaphylactic shock is severe anaphylaxis," remarked a young doctor who just entered the room. "It's usually in response to allergic reaction. Your body has experienced a quick release of immunological mediators, most likely histamines, and that has resulted in dramatic systemic vasodilatation, hence the big drop in blood pressure and the hives covering your body, and the edema of bronchial mucosa which results in bronchoconstriction and your trouble breathing. You're fortunate your wife brought you in. Anaphylactic shock can become deadly in a big hurry."

Huh? I wasn't sure what his jargon all meant but was grateful I hadn't experienced the deadly part yet.

"Now we need to find out what triggered it," the doctor said. "Unless you've been stung by an insect, it's probably something you ate."

And so started the process of doctor visits, dietary restrictions, blood tests, skin prick tests, and a number of other diagnostics. I'll save you the details of the long and drawn-out process, and instead get to my point that is relevant to teaching and learning.

My allergic reactions (I went through several more before arriving at the root cause) were related to food. Through a blood workup called a RAST (Sears, 2008) that measures the antibodies forming in response to certain food allergens and skin prick tests, my doctor was able to determine I had developed allergies to several food items, including beef, lamb, pork, and dairy products. He shortened the list for me to, basically, "everything mammal." So my life, at least in terms of my diet, had to change dramatically. It had nothing to do with New Zealand but probably was related to genetics and some triggering factor, like me reaching my fortieth birthday and my body becoming less tolerant and unable to manage the consumption of certain foods any longer.

Where's the tie in to education? We're getting there.

Educational Alternative Diets

In my personal life, I was forced from a diet of steak, chili, milk, cheese, desserts, and lattes to something different. Did I have a choice? Of course! I didn't have to follow the doctor's advice and could have continued to eat the same foods I had enjoyed my entire life. I wouldn't really be hurting anyone but myself. I could have limped along taking large quantities of antihistamines before each meal and stocking up on EpiPens to help manage symptoms. My liver and intestines would probably deteriorate over time, and I'd slowly waste away at an age much younger than if I had taken care of myself and adapted to my new reality.

Ah, so there it is. Our educational institutions have suffered an anaphylactic reaction to old technologies and must change their ways or suffer in slow agony until they deteriorate. Or, that is one analogy you could take from my story, but mine isn't quite so dramatic. I don't think most institutions of higher education are in the emergency room or on life support at the moment. But, there are some things worth considering.

After learning I could no longer eat my favorite foods, I began looking for alternatives. As you might imagine, cutting all things mammal from your diet is a dramatic change. Particularly when pizzas, nachos with cheese, roast beef, and dozens of other items suddenly become taboo. Added to the list were the thousands of foods at stores and restaurants that have hidden ingredients like whey or milk fat or gelatin in them.

At first, I sought out replacements. Instead of hamburgers, I went for soy shaped like hamburger patties. There were vegan hotdogs, fake breakfast sausage, soy "milk," and a cornucopia of products meant to resemble items from my old diet. Even though I could still eat poultry, during my searches for new foods I even discovered tofu shaped like a turkey for a vegan Thanksgiving dinner. I encountered genuinely helpful people who told me it wasn't the dairy and meat I was allergic to but rather the chemicals and toxins introduced into the food chain and that I needed a deep colonic cleansing (even though the protein-related antibodies are in my blood!). I even had to sheepishly admit, when addressing the Kansas Beef Cattle Association, that I couldn't eat any of the delicious-smelling beef they were serving during the meeting. After my talk, which included comparisons of beef, soy, tofu, and the aptly named meat substitute *seitan* (which I pronounce *Satan*—"sáyt'n"!), they didn't give me the gift they had ready (I think it was a package of steaks!). Needless to say, I lost weight and became a little depressed.

That is until I changed my worldview. I had to progress through four stages to adjust to my new environment:

Stage 1. Realization of situation
Stage 2. Coping
Stage 3. Substitution
Stage 4. Reengineering and continuous improvement

I've already taken you through stages 1 and 2, during which the problem came to my attention and I had to take immediate action to cope with my new situation. This left little time to deal with a longer-term solution. When I entered stage 3, I sought substitutions. I tried to keep my world the same and find replacements that could do the same things for me. When my family ate roast beef, I would substitute roast chicken. When they had hamburgers on the grill, I would grill a veggie burger. I used fake cheese in my omelets and substituted dairy and beef ingredients in my casseroles. You get the picture: I continued doing pretty much what I always had but with substitutes. It worked, but my world had changed, and it was hard to imagine spending the rest of my days eating the way I currently was eating.

That's when I entered stage 4—I had to in order to remain sane. During this stage I tried to rid myself of my old notions of food and eating and tried to reconstruct the possibilities from scratch. I started watching Food Network programs and investigated new foods previously off my radar screen. I experimented with a variety of seafood as well as Asian and Indian foods. I visited vegan and vegetarian websites. My sister-in-law, Jeni, bought me some cookbooks including one perfectly named *What to Eat When You Can't Eat Anything* (Sweetman & Sweetman, 2005). I joined several social networks like GroupRecipes.com and Open-SourceFood.com. My perceptions of what constituted food changed. Soon, I moved beyond eating according to the established traditions in which a meal consists primarily of a main meat dish with a starch (like potatoes or rice) and a side vegetable. Instead, I went back to the basics and recreated a healthy meal within the constraints of my new environment. I used the knowledge of those who ate according to different traditions and eventually became a "pescetarian.[1]" So, in other words, I adapted. Let's apply this situation to higher education, where we need to travel through several stages and determine how to cope with our new environment.

Tech-savvy millennials often find themselves facing teachers who have entered stage 2 (coping) or perhaps stage 3 (substitution). This frustrates them and results in learning experiences that fall short of their potential.

The Reality of New Media

I could have dealt with my food allergy in various ways, and so too can higher education deal with the reality of the new media emerging from

Web 2.0 technologies, the mobile revolution, and the integration of people into the Internet's fabric. Here are different ways tech-savvy millennials view their professors in regard to their teaching practices.

Example 1: Professor Luddite. (Food Allergy Equivalent: *I'll ignore my problem and deal with the emergency room visits when they come; I'll take antihistamines to prevent any deadly situations and live as I always have, although my lifespan may be shortened or even end abruptly.*) Professor Luddite's arrival to class is predictable because a small swarm of graduate assistants enter the room about two to three minutes prior to take attendance. Generally, his primary tool for course material delivery, besides his resonant voice, is the whiteboard, which he grudgingly accepted some years ago when the last chalkboard was removed from the building. On rare occasions, he has engaged a graduate assistant to project an overhead slide of a diagram onto a screen, but generally he provides handouts instead. Professor Luddite wishes the Internet was a fad and would fade into the mists of time. He recently concluded that won't happen but still has a hard time admitting it. When he misses important information posted to a website or sent by email (which he rarely uses, having assigned a grad student to print out anything of value and place it in his departmental mailbox), he generally finds a way to recover. He has no intention of changing. He has always worked the way he does and won't consider doing anything different. Professor Luddite simply is coping with the new reality and biding his time until retirement.

Example 2: Professor Emulate. (Food Allergy Equivalent: *Replace favorite foods with something that looks the same—soy hamburgers, fake steak, etc.*) Professor Emulate is in transition. She imagines her students are stunned to learn she is not more Internet savvy but has little time to retool herself and fully integrate these new technologies into her classroom. She attends conferences and workshops where the new technologies are lauded and terms like Diigo, Qoop, and Netvibes are thrown around. She has seen a number of demos and would like to try some of these things in her class but generally runs short of the time necessary to have them ready before the next semester rolls around. Professor E, as her students call her, is well liked and wants to move into the future but is doing so carefully and slowly because her classes have always gotten good ratings and she has won several teaching awards. She knows students are different than they used to be and are generally more receptive to the idea of using technology in a vast number of different, innovative, creative ways. She learns a little more each semester and is careful not to look dumb, but sometimes, over a glass of her favorite pinot noir, she wonders how far behind she is when it comes to "Internet stuff."

To prevent being relegated to Professor Luddite's peer group, Professor E has started doing a couple of new things, such as using the university's course management system to post class documents and PowerPoint slides. She has started a discussion board and has a class blog. But all of these things are being used as 1:1 substitutes for what she has always used. Her foray into classroom technology began after she had lifted her ban on laptops from her class. More students brought their computers to class and she believed, at first, these machines prevented them from focusing on her lecture and detracted from analysis activities. She thought students were transcribing rather than thinking and interacting. And she still believes she was partially right. However, a classroom discussion one day revealed some students were transcribing into their email; others were notating her PowerPoint slides, and yet others were typing notes into MS Word (and, of course, some were Facebooking!). After the discussion and following a meeting with campus educational technology specialists, she decided to adapt and accept the new reality rather than fight it. This led to the enrichment of her lectures, because students were Googling her facts and contributing to the discussion in increasing ways. Professor Emulate would like to use the new media in her classroom world but still substitutes the new tools for existing learning methods. She runs the risk of using the Web as a shortcut to provide limited and very specific information without getting into the "meat" (or, in the case of the food example, "soy meat substitute") of the topic.

Example 3: Professor Digital. (Food Allergy Equivalent: *Assessing the situation and developing a paradigm for assembling meals in healthy, tasty ways without worrying too much about the past.*) Professor Digital is a digital maven. He loves tinkering with applications and developing new, exciting ways to introduce technologies to his students. He is a firm believer that change is constant and part of being a professor is to be on the forefront of new possibilities. He sometimes gets carried away with methods and temporarily loses sight of the material he wants to teach. His students ascribe these faults to his enthusiasm and are forgiving of this professorial trait, finding him inspiring and his excitement contagious.

Professor Digital recently used new media literacy possibilities and Web 2.0 as a baseline for reevaluating teaching and learning. He deconstructed his class then rebuilt it from the ground up. He wanted to take the strong collaborative possibilities found in these new technologies and leverage them in his student's educational experience to provide both better knowledge of the subject material and a stronger grasp of ways the world will communicate, collaborate, and work in the future.

Professor Digital still lectures during class time, because he believes in face-to-face interaction, but has developed a learning community to help his students collaboratively and collectively discover and understand new material, do their homework, do projects, and study. He has helped them develop a classroom wiki where class notes and other important information regarding their exams and assignments can be collectively constructed. He encourages students to tag useful articles and readings with Digg, Diigo, and other social tagging software. He has shown them how to integrate RSS feeds into their classroom wiki and provided incentives (with grades and classroom peer encouragement) for participation. Many student projects involve creating resource material used widely outside the class. He has enjoyed great success publishing projects to YouTube and other websites. He has experimented with games, simulations, mobile apps, and new 3-D worlds for learning. Professor Digital has adopted a new paradigm based on emerging collaborative technologies and believes that, collectively, his class can produce far more intellectual content than can individual students. He wants his students to become active, connected learners that leave their passivity behind.

Example 4: Professor Overenthusiastic. (Food Allergy Equivalent: *Elimination of eating meals altogether in favor of completely different mechanisms for obtaining nutrition.*) In discussing my professor examples with fellow educators, one brought up someone I left off my list. Professor Overenthusiastic is the equivalent of continually trying new non-allergenic food but quickly tiring of it and moving to the next thing. This rapid and random movement doesn't consider an overall dietary plan. In the academic world, Professor Overenthusiastic adopts every new technological innovation without considering its relevance to the pedagogical goals of the course. She confuses the students and often abandons specific tools in favor of something different. Students dislike the uncertainty and start to doubt the promise of Web 2.0 in higher education.

Examples of each archetype probably exist in most institutions of higher learning. Professors are both excited and scared by the prospect of incorporating Web 2.0 ideas into their pedagogy. Although technology can be good, using new media as a primary teaching tool is not without potential problems. Author Susan Jacoby, in her book *The Age of American Unreason* (2008), sees the very foundations of American culture and historic awareness being pushed in a downward death spiral of sorts by a new cultural landscape that celebrates mindless video absorption and devalues critical thinking. She further suggests that Americans' attraction to video-driven "infotainment" has become a "crisis of memory and knowledge" (p. 308). The long-term effects have been the decay of America's intellectual activities, which traditionally have been reading and conversation. 24/7 access to entertainment and digital media gives us quick information but fails to push viewers further, creating passive rather than active learners. She suggests Web approaches to learning can cause students to confuse tools with real knowledge and encourage the learner to move in lock step with the tool itself instead of into deeper and more rigorous learning (Garber, 2008; Jacoby, 2008). Although these concerns might be valid to some extent, we saw in chapters 4 and 5 how this same environment has sparked creativity.

Class Delivery on the New Shoreline

The scope of change taking place in class delivery is not trivial. It is common to hear about blended learning, hybrid approaches, and distance techniques. I use a number of enhancements and new ideas in my own classes, but it is only recently that these changes are really starting to take hold.

I entered the library the week before final exams and noticed larger-than-usual numbers of students peopling the study tables and couches. Not unusual for the end of semester, I thought, but something about it was strange. Then it struck me: Most of them were not holding books, they were cradling laptops. Some of the students gave me *Get away, you creepy freak* looks when I tried to peer discretely at their screens. I had expected to see them viewing Facebook or YouTube but instead was surprised to see them viewing a colleague of mine from K-State, Dr. Sue Williams, lecturing. Some students calmly watched her video and others furiously highlighted material while they listened through earbuds. Still others shared a screen, whispering to each other. I pondered how different exam reviews and the transmission of course material had become. I also realized that, although technology is part of the solution, as the saying goes, *Good teaching is good teaching.* And Dr. Williams is a great teacher.

It is important to make a distinction between inventing new methods to teach in this global and technologically empowered world and just changing a few ingredients in a recipe that used to work. The temptation is, as Nancy Flanagan (2008) says, to "[stick] technology, like shiny stars, [on very conventional] thinking about schools, teaching and learning." Instead, Flanagan continues, "[we need to] abandon the persistent concept of 'teacher as priest,' standing in front of the room (next to the Smart Board, presumably) dispensing knowledge, running the show, [and] controlling the use of technology tools." Susan Jacoby hits the same chord: "When you start confusing tools with real knowledge and stop thinking about how you're using it and how much you're using these tools, that's where the danger is in technology" (Garber, 2008).

Instead, we teachers need to embrace the concept of students' becoming active learners in ways that move beyond rote learning and exploit the new possibilities. Students must be endowed with a sense of being in charge of their own learning. Most university students have good things to say about their social experiences, enjoy their sports teams, and want to be physically present at their friends' parties. These aspects of campus life keep them coming back, but at the same time, they are increasingly conflicted about their learning experiences. Whether we like it or not, in their minds, "education is becoming a private good providing benefits to the individual consumer who then can provide value to an organization; if our institutions don't help this process and don't add value, we become middle men or agents that are candidates for replacement with more cost effective mechanisms" (Rizi, 2007, p. 82).

As we established earlier, students expect two things from their classroom experience. If they don't get these, higher education will become irrelevant, and the economics of spending four or five years in a social incubator will be impossible to justify. The two expected outcomes are

1. relevance to the future job market (which goes against many academics' concept of education); and
2. delivery methods that make sense in the context of a global, interconnected, technologically enabled world.

Many students report getting neither outcome. Why not? And what can be done? And what else needs to be provided? For instance, immediate relevance to short-term job-hiring demands may not best suit students or their employers in the long run. Often, a well-rounded liberal arts education is supported by the business community because it helps develop critical thinkers who can write and communicate, possess cultural competencies, and have a potential for civic engagement.

The Paper Chase

When I was a teenager, I became infatuated with a short-lived television program called *The Paper Chase*. It shaped my expectations for teachers and influenced my eventual decision to become an academic. Some of you may remember it. CBS aired the series for one season (1978–1979), and later Showtime picked it up for three more seasons. In it, John Houseman plays the role of a curmudgeonly, highly intelligent law professor with extreme expectations (and little sympathy) for his students. In various episodes of the series, his students use academic skills to research material and provide answers to real questions during the course of their studies. The problems and deadlines they face sometimes make them choose between finishing contrived assignments and really learning things that impact people's lives.

The television series was based on a movie, which was based on an original novel (Osborn, 1971). The movie version revolves around Hart, a promising Harvard Law School student from the Midwest who becomes obsessed with knowledge and identifies his teacher, Professor Charles W. Kingsfield, Jr., as the embodiment of success in higher learning. After going above and beyond class requirements and engaging in numerous instances of active learning, Hart takes his final exam, which had been the focus of his life. Then it dawns on him that he really has learned something and that the exam is actually meaningless. When the final grade is delivered, Hart makes the report card into a paper airplane and throws it out to sea without viewing his score. Of course, other human elements such as romance, successes and failures, and friendships all enter the drama, but the overarching theme of active learning and the value of knowledge over the value of exam scores really stood out to me and helped inspire me to attend graduate school.

The same premise for learning still applies. Many of the research methods relevant in the 1970s have been updated now, and watching law students perform Google searches may not make good television or movie drama, but the concept of active learning applies more than ever today.

The point is that our students want their academic work to be meaningful. The recent surge in service learning indicates there is a desire for relevance in education (Compact, 2001). Janet Eyler and Dwight Giles (1999) say, "service-learning is a form of experiential education" (p. 7) where "learning occurs through a cycle of action and reflection, not simply through being able to recount what has been learned through reading and lecture" (pp. 7–8). With service learning, students apply what they learn in an attempt to solve community problems. They reflect on their experiences to develop a deeper understanding and new skills. According to the National Service-Learning Clearinghouse (Organization, 2008), service learning experiences

- ♦ Are positive, meaningful and real to the participants.
- ♦ Involve cooperative rather than competitive experiences and thus promote skills associated with teamwork and community involvement and citizenship.
- ♦ Address complex problems in complex settings rather than simplified problems in isolation.
- ♦ Offer opportunities to engage in problem-solving by requiring participants to gain knowledge of the specific context of their service-learning activity and community challenges, rather than only to draw upon generalized or abstract knowledge such as might come from a textbook. As a result, service-learning offers powerful opportunities to acquire the habits of critical thinking; i.e., the ability to identify the most important questions or issues within a real-world situation.
- ♦ Promote deeper learning because the results are immediate and uncontrived. There are no "right answers" in the back of the book.
- ♦ Are more likely to be personally meaningful to participants and to generate emotional consequences, to challenge values as well as ideas, and hence to support social, emotional and cognitive learning and development.

In the same way students in *The Paper Chase* learned far more from engaging in meaningful activities than they could have absorbed from textbooks, service learning and other models can have the effect of pushing our students from rote to active learning.

Michael Wesch, Carnegie/CASE 2008 national professor of the year, said in a recent lecture (Wesch, 2008) that collaborative work by our students can be empowered by new technologies in ways that enhance their learning experiences. He says that to make working collaboratively successful a professor must

- empower students;
- engage them in meaningful projects;
- make room for creativity and play;
- listen; and
- provide inspiration.

That is exactly what Professor Kingsfield did on *The Paper Chase*, only with different methods and tools than are being used today. He inspired his students to go beyond book-based learning and use material to address real-world situations. He empowered them—though often through an informal, "looking the other way" approach—to make a difference in the world. He was an inspirational figure who listened but often didn't seem to recognize them outside the classroom in order to maintain his role as mentor and advisor. He could not be their peer until they completed their studies.

Summary

The best way to think about education today may come from our students. However, it is important to realize there is a difference between what they want and what they need (Tierney & Hentschke, 2007). Given the reality of free access to information of all sorts, we can no longer be gatekeepers to the forbidden kingdom. Instead, we have to be door-openers for our students. We know society will continue to change and today's truths may eventually be forgotten. However, the academic constant is *knowing what questions to ask and encouraging our students to have the courage to discover new answers*.

In my opinion, education is undergoing a fundamental transformation. Teachers must spend less time communicating explicit knowledge and more time demonstrating how to learn. Much of our focus has been on facts, approaches, procedures, and definitions. With the codification of humankind's knowledge and the development of tools that enable access and use, the roles of teacher as door-opener, guide, and adjudicator should trump that of explicit-knowledge verbalizer. In other words, teachers must begin to focus on tacit knowledge, which is much more difficult to communicate.

In the words of well-known scientist Michael Polanyi, "we know more than we can tell," and this is what our students need to know. In general, tacit knowledge comprises the habits, behaviors, expertise, and culture we have trouble putting into words. Web 2.0 has enabled the processing of tremendous amounts of tacit knowledge into explicit form. This process, sometimes called codification or articulation, has become greatly beneficial, particularly when this knowledge is made publicly accessible. More than ever, this transformation is taking place. Our students are already part of it and expect higher education to take them to the next level. Chapter 7 provides approaches for making this transition a reality by looking at learning theories and related pedagogies that will thrive on higher education's new digital shoreline.

Note

1. According to About.com a *pescetarian* is "[Someone] who abstains from eating all meat and animal flesh with the exception of fish. Although the word is not commonly used and a pescetarian is not technically a vegetarian, more and more people are adopting this kind of diet, usually for health reasons or as a stepping stone to a fully vegetarian diet. Pescetarians often believe that moderate consumption of fish or fish oils, which are high in Omega-3 fatty acids, is necessary for optimum health, although vegetarian alternatives, such as flax seed oil, are available." I eat poultry, too.

CHAPTER SEVEN

CONVERGENCE ON THE
NEW SHORELINE

True Knowledge is not attained by thinking. It
is what you are; it is what you become.

—*Sri Auribindo*

The forces of change encroaching on today's universities are a summons to action. Like many transformations enabled by the Internet and mobile devices, changes in education are fueled partially by a bottom-up dynamic. For higher education, this means our students want to see new media reflected in the delivery of learning material on platforms of their choosing. Is this reason enough to enact fundamental changes to teaching and learning? Does it have to be a choice between new technology and sound pedagogy? The answer to both questions, of course, is no. However, we do need to anticipate change and reinvent ourselves while preserving good pedagogical practices, or build a "New Randolph," as illustrated in this chapter. Achieving this will take more than adding technology to our teaching practices. It means stepping back to understand opportunities for improving learning theory and then develop smart approaches that rebuild our practice in ways better suited to the emerging world. In the same way that the small Kansas town we visit in this chapter found itself faced with the prospect of building on a new shoreline or disappearing, higher education must face its new reality and be progressive. This chapter provides guidance for embracing change

from a teaching/learning perspective and offers a fresh look at various learn-
ing theories, using the tech-savvy millennial as a lens. Good teaching is still
good teaching. However, new technologies and what can be called "connec-
tionist ideas" can make it better and relevant.

Metaphorical Visit to Randolph, Kansas

THE TOWN CENTER is an enclosed shopping mall located in down-town Manhattan, Kansas. I couldn't have written this sentence from where I am sitting right now had this been 1951. Apart from the technology issue, I would have been in a different building or perhaps out on the sidewalk, because the Town Center was built in 1987 "to reflect the architectural flavor of Manhattan and the surrounding communities and to maintain and foster the expansion of the Manhattan retail community" (Manhattan Town Center, 2008). On July 15 in 1951, this spot was under almost eight feet of water. A flood inundated the heart of Manhattan's downtown, which now includes nearly 100 retail stores, a food court, restaurants, and other businesses. None of these would exist if changes hadn't been made. During the same time, big floods hit downstream cities including Topeka, Lawrence, and Kansas City, with damages totaling more than $930 million. That translates to more than $5 billion today (Larson, 1984).

Randolph, a small Kansas town, didn't flood that year. It was built in a "safe" area. However, societal forces outside its control would change that reality. Someone living in that town may have said, "Long ago our city founders built upstream to ensure rainfall could never cover our town square or knock our homes down. We built our businesses far enough away from the main shipping routes and flood plains to ensure our safe existence. We were smart people. We watched our neighbor cities flood but were immune to their problems. Then the rules changed. Outsiders didn't view the world the way we did. They built big cities in areas vulnerable to floods. Eventually, they were able to fix their problem with new ideas, but their solutions became problems for us. So now we face the ultimate flood—one that will never go away. In order to preserve Manhattan, Topeka, Lawrence, and Kansas City, our town is going to be flooded."

A construction project was proposed, and 11 years later the Tuttle Creek Reservoir and the Tuttle Creek Dam project was complete. Old

Randolph and 9 other communities were completely submerged. Residents from the 10 cities[1] had staged vigorous opposition, but progress wasn't stopped. They did everything right, but the world still changed.

Academic Floods

Most of us in Academia face a similar situation. The rules are changing rapidly, and we have to make some hard choices. When Tuttle Lake began filling in 1962, 10 towns would be impacted. Many of these were eventually submerged and disappeared. However, one town decided to rebuild. Randolph, Kansas, reinvented itself and moved inland. It recognized the new shoreline, moved the best things there, and rebuilt the rest. The new city's streets were given names to commemorate sister communities lost beneath the waters of the new reservoir. On a calm day, "Old Randolph" still can be seen in the murky waters.

Can academics follow the example of Randolph's residents and rebuild on the new shoreline? Will our teaching practices and institutions end up like Shroyer, Barrett, Irving, and other communities that disappeared after unforeseen changes beyond their control?

New Randolph

After extensive flood control systems were built in the Midwest of the United States in the 1950s and 1960s, this region experienced a renaissance of sorts. New land was opened for development, populations grew, and previously unimagined opportunities became realities. A more recent example is the Town Center Mall in Manhattan, Kansas, where I wrote this passage. Although not a consideration at the time the dam was built, the mall would not have been possible without a system to prevent seasonal flooding. A more significant example is the recent announcement that Kansas State University is to be the home of the premier $450 million National Bio and Agro-Defense Facility (NBAF) to replace the laboratories at Plum Island, New York. This new biosecurity research institute will provide a secure location for the study of pathogens that threaten animal- and plant-based agricultural systems (Richardson, 2008). It certainly wouldn't have been placed in its proposed location if the flood systems were not constructed decades ago.

And so it is for today's universities. We must make fundamental changes without fully being able to foresee the eventual benefits. Our environment has reshaped itself, reflecting the technological convergence arising from the digitalization of various media, personal and mobile computing environments, and synergies with networking technologies. According to some, technology integration needs in education systems and learning are substantial and, unless addressed, will result in traditional schools' being unsuitable to fulfill the needs of our information society (Russell & Holkner, 2000).

Unfortunately, we can't totally anticipate the future. However, many of the trends noted in this book suggest the first steps toward building a "New Randolph" in higher education.

Pedagogy

"I'm here to buy my grade," said the scruffy student in a conspiratorial whisper. He leaned forward, triumphantly pushing a crumpled wad of bills in my direction. "You'll find more than enough for an A."

I examined his smiling, red eyes peering through the beer-scented haze hovering around his head. "Late night," he added hastily, leaning back a little.

Feeling a bit like a pit boss in an illegal gambling operation, I reached for the money and began counting. I finished and looked up. "Definitely an 'A,'" I said.

"Next time, you might want to change some of the rules," he replied with a weary smile. "I guess I'm more of an entrepreneur than a software developer. But that's okay. It's good to know. I learned something about myself this semester, and that's more than I can normally say about a class."

"McHaney Bucks" were a pedagogical technique I used to create an environment for student learning. I would "pay" students for developing IT class projects. A good way for business students to learn business, I thought, is to simulate an economy. Instead of working for grades, students are paid for their projects, required to keep books on income and expenses, and at semester's end, purchase their grades with McHaney

Bucks, not real money. The students can form contracts to license and resell their code to classmates. They can hire consultants from the class to help on their projects (I had established minimum wages). I would "buy" their complete projects and penalize for system failures. The game blended reality and play to inspire meta-learning. The most amusing twist that came to light was a "McHaney Bucks" keg party held by an entrepreneurial but low-achieving student in the class. Subsequent implementations of McHaney Bucks made such uses of classroom currency illegal, of course!

The McHaney Bucks story is an example of a constructivist pedagogical approach. It incorporated active learning, a real-world simulation, teamwork, community building, and a number of other techniques. According to various learning theories, these instructional strategies should result in an environment conducive to acquiring knowledge.

So far in this book, classroom techniques derived from Web 2.0 tools and mobile platforms have revolved around pedagogies and not learning theories. When tech-savvy millennials are asked about classroom effectiveness and what has worked to enhance their learning, most will respond with examples of pedagogy. Although descriptions of teaching styles and methods are useful and can result in excellent outcomes, the changes currently impacting higher education require more. To gain additional insight, the next sections discuss several relevant learning theories on which successful pedagogies for tech-savvy millennials can be based.

Pedagogy Vs. Learning Theory

As suggested earlier, pedagogy refers to strategies of instruction and teaching methods. Often this means developing an approach to support student learning. Other times, the term *pedagogy* is used to describe a style of instruction. In either case, pedagogy approaches the process of learning from the teaching side. Learning theories, on the other hand, are not descriptions of teaching nor do they provide sets of instruction for classroom use. Instead they might be viewed as philosophical approaches that will enable and facilitate learning.

Many educators believe that, in order create an effective learning environment, pedagogies should be consistent with learning theories. Experts in psychology and education have studied learning and developed these theories to explain how knowledge is acquired. Good pedagogies are constructed to support these concepts believed to undergird learning. Three widely discussed theories are behaviorism, cognitivism, and constructivism. A fourth theory, connectivism, is receiving a great deal of attention because it considers learning within the context of the digital age. This makes connectivism a very relevant base for higher education's approach to teaching the tech-savvy millennial and ensuring our teaching provides what they need. A short synopsis of each learning theory follows.

Behaviorism

Behaviorism is rooted in work by Ivan Pavlov, B. F. Skinner, and others. It suggests learning is accompanied by a change in behavior. This behavior is shaped by (1) the environment, (2) how close in time two events occur, and (3) reinforcement (either positive or negative). Behaviorism posits that learning itself is largely unknowable, so the best way to measure it is through a surrogate: *behavioral change.*

Behaviorism has greatly influenced higher education, and various pedagogies are rooted in its sphere of influence. For instance, giving low grades for poor work or high grades for outstanding work can be viewed as reinforcement. Behaviorists are concerned with measurable changes in behavior. Exam scores become measurable surrogates for learning.

Other learning theories (sometimes called *educational approaches* to reflect their applied nature) are closely related to behaviorism. Of these, direct instruction, or instructivism, is commonly discussed and used to represent current behavioral thinking in higher education (Kim & Axelrod, 2005). In instructivist learning theory, knowledge exists outside the learner (typically in another person), and is taught to the student by a teacher. It is teacher centered and focuses on models that facilitate the information transfer from expert to novice. Often this is done using a lecture format. The student passively accepts information as presented by the teacher.

Cognitivism

Cognitivism was developed as a challenge to behaviorism. Bode felt behaviorists oversimplified learning and depended too much on overt behavior. He suggested learning is more complex and involves aspects internal to the individual that result in cognitive changes (Bode, 1929). New understandings of the brain gave rise to the ideas that (1) the brain comprises a memory system that is an active, organized processor of information and (2) prior knowledge influences learning. Cognitivism views learning as more than just behavioral change. It also seeks to understand the physical aspects of memory as a way to explain learning. For instance, cognitivists seek to uncover the physiological origin of encoding information into short-term brain memory and to understand the transfer from there to long-term brain memory.

Cognitivism also embraces the idea that an individual learner, with his or her internal nuances, is central to the learning process. The learning environment is secondary. Cognitivism was very popular during the advent of the computer age, when brain functions were equated to computer systems, with inputs coming from the external environment, being processed in the brain, and resulting in short-term memory followed by permanent storage in long-term memory. This model looked similar to that of a computer and its central processor, RAM, and disk storage.

Constructivism

Constructivism moved cognitive theory to the next level with more focus on the individual. Constructivism sees learning as a building process in which the learner actively constructs new ideas and conceptual understandings based on prior knowledge and current experiences. Learning largely takes place while learners reflect on their experiences. Constructivism views learning as a personal experience that enables an individual to apply the knowledge she or he acquires to the real world. Learning is the journey, not the outcome (Fosnot, 2005).

Social constructivists believe knowledge is constructed also through social interaction between individuals. By talking, communicating, and engaging in shared activities, knowledge can be internally constructed with the result of learning. Social constructivist learning is the process of skilled members of society facilitating knowledge transfer to others (Driver, Asoko, Leach, Mortimer, & Scott, 1994).

Many manifestations of constructivism exist. Among these are active learning, service-learning, self-directed learning, experiential learning, reflective practices, discovery learning, and knowledge building. A common thread among all these variants is that constructivist learning, particularly in higher education, promotes exploration within an appropriate framework. The constructivist teacher is a facilitator who encourages students to build knowledge through discovery and firsthand experience. However, actual learning is the responsibility of the student. Once the principles are established in the learner, knowledge can be used to solve realistic problems.

Connectivism

Connectivism is a relatively new learning theory proposed by George Siemens in 2004.[2] Whereas the other learning theories described so far suggest learning occurs internal to an individual, connectivism posits learning also can occur outside of an individual and that technology can be used to store knowledge and manipulate learning. It moves social constructivism to the next level. Rather than being the responsibility of the individual, connectivist learning takes place at the community level, where the individual is a key element.

Siemen's theory, at its root, has several important characteristics derived from his observations of the digital age. First, when information is abundant, rapid evaluation, together with the ability to recognize and synthesize connections or patterns, is important. Second, when information is scarce, learning in more traditional ways may be required. In the environment of abundant knowledge, technology and connections enable learning. Because so much information now exists, an individual can't personally experience it all. Learning becomes a shared, community experience. This collective learning is mediated via technology. Siemens proposes several principles of connectivism:

- Learning and knowledge rests in diversity of opinions.
- Learning is a process of connecting specialized nodes or information sources.
- Learning may reside in nonhuman appliances.
- Capacity to know more is more critical than what is currently known.
- Nurturing and maintaining connections is needed to facilitate continual learning.
- Ability to see connections between fields, ideas, and concepts is a core skill.
- Currency (accurate, up-to-date knowledge) is the intent of all connectivist learning activities.
- Decision-making is a learning process. Choosing what to learn and the meaning of incoming information is seen through the lens of a shifting reality.

♦ While there is a right answer now, it may be wrong tomorrow due to alterations in the information climate affecting the decision (Siemens, 2004).

Fallacies of Learning Theories

A common fallacy associated with learning theories is that they are in a linear progression—for instance, that behaviorism was superseded by cognitivism, which was superseded by constructivism, and so forth. Depending on the environment and the type of learning required, concepts from certain theories may be more appropriate. In his description of connectivism, Siemens (2004) makes it clear that his learning theory operates in an environment of abundant information. In a paucity of information, he suggests other theories are more appropriate. The good teacher must be familiar with various options and construct a learning environment appropriate to information type and conditions. Tech-savvy millennials have cut their teeth in an environment of abundant information. Siemens emphasizes this:[3]

♦ Technology is altering (rewiring) our brains. The tools we use define and shape our thinking.
♦ The organization and the individual are both learning organisms.
♦ Many of the processes previously handled by learning theories (especially in cognitive information processing) can now be off-loaded to, or supported by, technology.
♦ Know-how and know-what is being supplemented with know-where (the understanding of where to find needed knowledge). (Siemens, 2004)

In the world of tech-savvy millennials, where vast networks of free information are available, connectivist learning may now be the most talked-about practice. The concepts are already being used in their daily lives outside the classroom. The next section looks at how learning theories relate to the tech-savvy millennial's world and create a basis for pedagogical approaches that integrate the best of their world with robust teaching practices.

Learning and the Tech-Savvy Millennial

Our teaching must reflect how the tech-savvy millennial learns. We must also consider the rapidly changing, connected, adapting, and evolving world our students inhabit.

For me as a baby boomer, understanding the thought process of the tech-savvy millennial is often foreign and non-intuitive. Recently, I had a quick lesson in the millenial's take on this interconnected world filled with abundant information. Before I provide the example, it is important to make a couple of points clear.

First, the tech-savvy millennial views his or her world as a series of interconnected nodes. Each node contains knowledge. A node might be a book, an e-book, an expert, someone that has experienced a particular situation previously, a website, a teacher, a scholarly article, a blog, a wiki, or any other number of entities or people that possess knowledge. To be useful, nodes need to be identifiable, accessible, decipherable, accurate, and relevant. Sometimes the same knowledge is held in multiple nodes with varying degrees of completeness and accuracy. Other times, information has to be abstracted from multiple nodes to create a complete picture or be merged into a new node. The primary skill operating here is what Seimens would call "know-how."

Nodes can be found in a variety of ways. Search engines like Google can be used. Tags and filters can provide trails to useful information. RSS feeds can identify nodes, and personal connections can provide links to nodes. Social networks like LinkedIn can provide ties to human experts. Of course, having access to a World Wide Web of interconnected websites provides unlimited ways of connecting, searching, and classifying nodes. Finding one node can lead to another. A piece of relevant information or a person holding that information often can be a starting point for refining and locating more and better information. The more frequently nodes in a particular topic area are sought, the better an individual becomes at locating those nodes. At some point, the seeker becomes a node him- or herself. This primary skill can be called "know-where" (Siemens, 2004).

Confusing? Here is an example. Today, my oldest son, Mark, called me and said his medical school acceptance would be put on hold unless he produced his vaccination records by the next day. That doesn't sound like a difficult problem, until time and geography constraints are thrown in. His records were located in a lock box in our home in Kansas. My wife and I were both in Michigan, one thousand miles away. Each of us had a key—the only two keys to the box. I threw out a number of possible solutions: contacting the family doctor (who informed us their paper records had been moved offsite for digitizing and were not accessible at the moment), breaking open the box with a crowbar, or begging the medical school to give him enough time for the key to be mailed overnight.

My son, being a tech-savvy millennial, had other ideas. He went to the Internet, searched the Web for information about picking locks and quickly found a diagram that described the bends to put into a paper clip in order to create a replacement key for our specific lockbox. A YouTube video provided details about the mechanics behind picking the lock. Within a few short minutes, he had his medical records. I might also add that this was a high-end lock box, so I was surprised he opened it that quickly.

My son had never been trained in lock picking, but as a tech-savvy millennial he had the "know-where" and understood the Web's interconnections enough to quickly acquire the knowledge he needed to complete the task at hand and accomplish his goal. Mark sent messages to his friends about his experience picking the lock and became a node on their information networks. He now is their *go-to* guy for future lock-picking needs! He used know-where to build know-how. This was the connectivist process in action. The learning resided in a community outside the individual but was available to him when he required it.

Tipping Points and Learning Theory

Chapter 1 of this book discusses how higher education is rapidly approaching a tipping point (Gladwell, 2000). We mentioned that three critical archetypes play key roles in differentiating a tipping point from a fad. These archetypes include mavens, connectors, and advocates. Viewed from a perspective of learning theories, each group learns or facilitates learning in different ways. For instance, the digital maven, you may recall, is an intense gatherer of information, ideas, and impressions. It is her nature to detect promising trends. Because of her sensitivity to subtle environmental changes, she is often the first to know about new technologies and ideas. The maven offers suggestions and hints and shares ideas about best practices. She also describes her own experiences and explains her observations. In other words, mavens form new nodes on networks that house knowledge. They specialize in deep learning and make it available to others. A node may take the form of a blog, a wiki entry, or a website or may be a link to the maven's email account or Facebook page. The maven herself becomes a node where community learning is housed.

The digital maven's deep learning may occur using behaviorism approaches (e.g., instructivism and taking tutorials) or constructivism (learning through her experiences and experimentation with new technologies). She may also rely on connectivism to acquire information from a variety of expert sources in her personal networks.

The digital connector, described in chapter 1, is a charismatic person with extensive networks of acquaintances who admire and trust his ability to navigate social waters. The connector, of course, is going to naturally create learning in connectivist ways (or in social constructivist ways). He will seek to create his digital networks and will effectively build know-where skills (Siemens, 2004). The connector will find the best nodes and knit them together into a network of community knowledge. He will reinvent himself to span new worlds. The connector will be largely responsible for building the networks that many people use to acquire knowledge and, ultimately, to learn. As Siemens (2004) has said, ". . . now technology performs many of the cognitive operations previously performed by learners (information storage and retrieval)." From a connectivist perspective, learning can reside in nonhuman appliances, and, "learning is a process of connecting specialized nodes or information sources" (Siemens, 2004).

The digital advocate also will play an important role from a learning theory perspective. Recall that this archetype helps create mass appeal. Whereby the connector creates learning through linking nodes, the advocate will transform the best nodes into widespread phenomena. The advocate throws the spotlight on the know-what the mavens have discovered and the know-where the connectors have linked together.

Together, these three archetypes enable connectivist learning to exist through the integration of the principles of chaos theory, network building, complexity, and self-organization in the emerging digital world. In this environment, know-how and know-where both exist. Siemens summarizes in his blog (Siemens, 2008), paraphrased here:

1. Connectivism is the application of network principles to define both knowledge and the process of learning. Knowledge is a particular pattern of relationships, and learning is the creation of new

connections and the ability to maneuver around existing networks/patterns.

2. Connectivism focuses on the inclusion of technology as part of our distribution of cognition and knowledge. Our knowledge resides in the connections we form, both with people and with information sources such as databases.

3. Connectivism recognizes the fluid nature of knowledge and connections based on context. As such, it becomes increasingly vital that we focus not on premade or predefined knowledge but on our interactions with each other, and the contexts in which those interactions arise.

4. Understanding, coherence, sense making, and meaning are prominent elements in constructivism because of its climate of abundance and rapid flow of information.

Characteristics of the Tech-Savvy Millennial and Learning Theory

Basic characteristics of the tech-savvy millennial provide key insight into this generation's learning capabilities. By understanding these characteristics, we can determine what to provide to enhance their ability to acquire information and to benefit from their higher education experiences.

From surveys and interviews and other material, we learned that the tech-savvy millennial typically is an early adopter of technology. He or she experiments with various online identities and often has multiple personas simultaneously. The tech-savvy millennial is a time shifter and has contacts in various time zones and may communicate or work at any time of the day or night. She or he seeks out information that is stored online in a variety of formats and expects it to be available on a variety of platforms. The tech-savvy millennial is continually monitoring a variety of communication channels and information sources with continuous partial attention (Stone, 2008) resulting in timeslicing behaviors. Many tech-savvy millennials have become nonlinear thinkers and use mobile devices to enable their lifestyles and social connections. This younger generation is highly creative and often links together existing information in new and imaginative ways. So what is the best way to help them learn?

The simple answer would be to say connectivist learning theory would effectively undergird education aimed at tech-savvy millennials.

That statement would probably be accurate but is overly simplistic. Different types of learning need to occur for different phases in acquiring information. For instance, developing a node and connecting to a node are two very different functions, yet both are important to the process of learning. In some instances, a tech-savvy millennial will need to create new knowledge or develop deep, narrow expertise on a particular topic. The process of building this knowledge may require instructivism-based knowledge transfer followed by constructivism-based experience building followed by the development of a lifelong network of connections to other related nodes. Learning approaches are not mutually exclusive.

In other instances, the tech-savvy millennial may need little more than know-where to be able to acquire relevant, accurate, and meaningful facts. Depending on the goal for learning, different approaches may be more useful and better at achieving the goal.

As teachers in higher education, we must be prepared to develop techniques that transition our tech-savvy millennial students in the best possible way. Different learning objectives could require different approaches. Figure 7.1 provides an example.[4]

Instructivism and the Tech-Savvy Millennial   When a subject area is new to a student, certain pieces of information must be transmitted. These are the things they need to know. For instance, understanding fundamental symbols and operators is required for grasping basic math concepts. In the computer field, having general knowledge of input, processing, and output is required. In accounting, debits and credits must be understood. There is very little exploration required to acquire these basic, conceptual foundations. In these types of areas, instructivism still has an important role. Foundational material can be provided in a traditional way. To put it into connectivist lingo, we provide the tech-savvy millennials with initial nodes in their learning networks to give them a foundation for fully understanding basic concepts.

Having a basic understanding of fundamental concepts will provide a starting point for the next level of learning. It will also ensure that initial knowledge is acquired from a reputable source and is accurate. Instructivist approaches can be implemented in a classroom via lecture, through a virtual learning environment in an online course, through tutoring by an expert, and in many other ways. A subject matter expert will ensure the learner has a programmed sequence of material that will take her or him through the basic concepts and provide a sound scaffold

Figure 7.1 Learning Theories With Various Objectives

Learning Math

Instructivism

+ is sign for addition
- is sign for subtraction
= is sign for equality

Constructivism

1 + 2 = 3	3 + 6 = 9
2 + 4 = 6	5 - 1 = 4
5 - 3 = 2	3 + 1 = 4

Connectivism

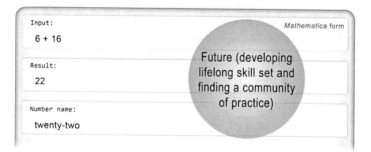

WolframAlpha.com is a great site for accessing and using complex knowledge on the Web.

for future learning. Any novice in a new domain is unlikely to grasp what it is he or she needs to know. Instructivist approaches can transmit important facts quickly and efficiently.

Constructivism and the Tech-Savvy Millennial   Having a foundation of basic concepts permits the leaner to analyze new information, compare it to existing knowledge, and construct new knowledge. In constructivist learning, the focus moves from teacher-centered to student-centered. Constructivism is consistent with various characteristics common to tech-savvy millennials, including their creativity and use of new technologies to construct artifacts. They also build identities for themselves and use a variety of tools such as digital cameras and video recorders to help with their construction efforts. Constructivism permits students to form nodes under the guidance of teachers, who act more as facilitators than instructors. The students take custody of their learning through their own experiences. Constructivism is a useful learning paradigm for those wishing to develop a deep understanding of a particular topic and for those wishing to create new knowledge. The tech-savvy millennial finds learning in this way well suited to his or her lifestyle.

Connectivism and the Tech-Savvy Millennial   In the world of the tech-savvy millennial, constructivist learning has evolved toward connectivism. Connectivism can exist only in a world of abundant information where there is far more knowledge available than can be effectively utilized. The tech-savvy millennial has spent his or her formative years in this long-tail world (Anderson, 2006) and has developed filtering and continuous partial attention skills (Stone, 2008) to cope with information abundance. Connectivism makes intrinsic sense to tech-savvy millennials, who view themselves as intelligent nodes in an interconnected network of people, data, information and knowledge sources. They are continually reinventing themselves as their network expands, morphs, and changes. They don't seek to know everything but instead to create a network of knowledge sources that provide access and information on a variety of platforms, mobile and otherwise, when needed. Millenials view learning as shared and housed in a community. The social aspect of learning is second nature to most of them. They also recognize that a community of learners will arrive at far different results than will a solitary individual. The millenial realizes that gray areas will emerge and change with her or his individual input (Kroski, 2005). Millenials have become connectivists by default and will use these ideas as a basis for lifelong learning. We know the tech-savvy millennial desires education that involves

◆ positive, meaningful, and real projects;
◆ teamwork, community involvement, and citizenship;
◆ complex problems in complex settings;
◆ problem-solving by requiring participants to gain knowledge of specific contexts rather than abstract knowledge from a textbook;
◆ deeper learning in which the results are immediate and uncontrived;
◆ emotional consequences, to challenge values as well as ideas and hence to support social, emotional, and cognitive learning and development;
◆ empowerment of student participants;
◆ creativity and play; and
◆ lasting value to a community.

Table 7.1 summarizes how various learning theories may be relevant to the tech-savvy millennial and may make it possible to develop learning experiences that address their desires.

Technologies and Learning Theory

Various technologies are better suited to supporting certain learning approaches. For instance, a wiki is an excellent tool for a teacher seeking to develop a social constructivist approach to learning in her class. With a wiki, students take charge of their learning and build an online community artifact. The act of construction enhances learning and provides a real experience. Others will interact through the wiki to create a shared experience.

In chapters 3 through 5 of this book we examined a variety of platforms, tools, and technologies that form the topology of higher education's new shoreline. Although many of these tools can support multiple learning approaches, some make more sense in particular contexts. The next sections describe tools from the tech-savvy millennial's realm that can contribute to learning from instructivist, constructivist, and connectivist perspectives.

Table 7.1 Learning Theories and Tech-Savvy Millennials

Learning Theory	Characteristic of Tech-Savvy Millennial	Comments	Nodes and Networks
Instructivism: From expert teacher to student learner	◆ Short attention span ◆ May lack deep understanding ◆ May not understand background/history as well	Instructivist learning is relevant to the tech-savvy millennial in situations where fundamentals and basic concepts need to be communicated. Instructivism-based teaching practices are effective at providing a base for learning and point to accurate, relevant information nodes to form a foundation for personal-learning networks.	Tech-savvy millennials learn about important information nodes.
Constructivism: Learning through individual experience and reflection	◆ Early-adopter ◆ Creative and artistic ◆ Wants to build artifacts ◆ Good at combining and reconfiguring information ◆ Desires to have impact in the real world ◆ Wants experiences and trial and error ◆ Wants authentic tasks to complete and problems to solve ◆ Wants relevance to the real world ◆ All of society is involved in learning; not a secluded, closed classroom with artificial settings	Constructivism-based learning is relevant to the tech-savvy millennial because it appeals to their sense of creativity and desire to build lasting artifacts that are in the real world. Constructivism theorizes that learning occurs through experience and through the process of building knowledge. It encourages deep learning and the development of expertise. Tech-savvy millennials add to information nodes and become nodes for others. Their personal experiences result in learning.	Tech-savvy millennials learn to construct and build information nodes.

Table 7.1   (Continued)

Learning Theory	Characteristic of Tech-Savvy Millennial	Comments	Nodes and Networks
Connectivism: Learning in community	◆ Early-adopter ◆ Time shifter ◆ Experiments with various personas and identities ◆ Mobile and prolific communicator ◆ Uses a variety of platforms for information storage and retrieval ◆ Continually monitors various communication and information channels; timeslices ◆ Good at filtering and searching ◆ Prefers customizable information ◆ Participates in social networks ◆ Wants lasting value from learning ◆ Social learner that belongs to multiple networks	The tech-savvy millennial will ultimately find connectivism-related learning to be a good fit. Given mobile, fast-paced, changing networks of information, learning through identifying information nodes and constructing a personal learning network will provide lasting value. Nodes on their network will be people, information sources, and other resources. Students learn as community expertise is acquired. Nobody can ever know everything, even within a particular domain. Connectivism empowers a learner and extends their knowledge by proxy. They become experts at "know-where" (Siemens, 2004).	Tech-savvy millennials learn to connect nodes that they and others have created. They view learning as a community effort and knowledge as being housed at both the individual and community levels.

Technologies for Instructivism

Instructivism has passive knowledge transfer at its heart. An expert teacher moves his or her knowledge to the learner in a controlled environment. Learning occurs by virtue of this transfer. Students become aware of nodes of knowledge. Teachers also may employ methods intended to engage students, such as Socratic question-and-answer sessions, but the teacher still is leading students toward preplanned learning objectives (Diaz & Bontenbal, 2000). Common pedagogies for this approach include lectures, online course presentations, pop quizzes, video presentations, and a number of other techniques.

A variety of modern technologies are suited to support instructivism. Of these, the most common instructivist tool (and most likely to make tech-savvy millennials groan) is presentation software such as Microsoft PowerPoint, Apple's KeyNote, and others. This software is particularly suited to the "sage on the stage" image associated with lecturing.

Rather than belabor the point, let's step back a moment and assume instructivism is being used appropriately and effectively. This may mean the teacher is using instructivist approaches in small doses to transfer fundamental concepts to students. The students are in the inception stages of developing a node of expertise that will be accessed by others and strengthened through a network of connections. Consider the following modes for instructivist pedagogical delivery: classroom, online, and mobile.

Classroom   Classroom delivery is the traditional approach for instructivism-based pedagogy. The teacher lectures and students absorb. On the teacher side of this equation, presentation software (e.g., PowerPoint, KeyNote) can be a delivery tool in this venue. Other teacher-oriented tools include video and audio recorders that enable lectures to be captured and posted online for later viewing.

A relatively new tool for classroom presentation is Prezi (http://prezi .com). Prezi removes the linear and uniform style typically found in most presentation software and replaces it with a Web-based storytelling tool that uses a single, unlimited canvas instead of a string of slides. The canvas can hold images, audio clips, videos, and other objects. These objects can be grouped, sized for emphasis, and linked with paths. Canvas users can progress either in exploratory fashion or according to a predetermined path. Information can be zoomed in on and out of depending on the depth of exploration desired. A teacher can present the material in the classroom on a screen (without an Internet connection) or post the presentation for access via a browser (Wauters, 2009).

Another modern instructivist approach is called Pecha Kucha (peh-cha koo-cha), the onomatopoeic Japanese word for the sound of conversation (like "chit-chat"). This presentation style involves 20 slides shown in sequence, each having 20 seconds of exposure as the presenter narrates.

This means a presentation will last 6 minutes and 40 seconds. Most presentation software can be set to a mode where the slides switch automatically to keep the speaker on time. This short, concise presentation style has become a craze in many fields and is often used to introduce new topics in an exciting, fast-paced way (Pink, 2007).

Online   Instructivism also has moved online. Most VLEs have facilities to enable instructivist approaches to teaching. For instance, prerecorded online lectures can be posted for the use of class participants. A number of tools exist to facilitate the creation of asynchronous online lectures. Among them, Tegrity is a leading software tool for lecture capture and rebroadcast (www.tegrity.com). Tegrity provides the capability to capture audio, video, and computer screen activity. It is bundled into a Tegrity session, which can be automatically uploaded into a VLE. Many campuses have Tegrity-enabled classrooms, but the same technology can be used from office, laptop or home computers to develop online lectures, demonstrations, student project critiques, and podcasts.

Another leading tool for capturing online lectures is Screenflow for Apple computers (www.telestream.net/screen-flow/overview.htm). This product enables the capture of a computer screen's contents while video camera, microphone, and audio are all running. Added editing tools permit the content to be fine-tuned for rebroadcast. Camtasia Studio is a similar product that runs on PCs and also allows the user to define a screen area to be captured and recorded. Lectures can be recorded using a microphone or speakers while the webcam's video footage is being played on the screen (Techsmith, 2010).

Another tool for creating online lectures is Microsoft's Producer for PowerPoint. This software specifically allows a lecturer to synchronize audio, video, PowerPoint slides, images, and other multimedia for online presentations. Producer also provides powerful content-authoring features (Microsoft, 2010). I have used Producer extensively with good success.

ProfCast is another, easy-to-use, fast tool for creating online lectures and podcasts. The lecturer simply adds a voice track to PowerPoint or Keynote slides. ProfCast transforms the combination into a multimedia file that can be uploaded as a podcast. ProfCast is very inexpensive and is easy to learn compared to the other software packages (ProfCast, 2010).

Other instructivist technologies can be used to deliver online lectures synchronously. Stickam and BlogTV are websites that allow accounts to be created and broadcasts to be streamed over the Internet. Within VLEs, lectures can be streamed synchronously using tools such as Wimba, a live, virtual classroom environment that enables audio, video, application sharing, content display, and MP4 capabilities. While Wimba can promote learning approaches that move far beyond instructivism, it is well suited for online lectures with question-and-answer sessions (Wimba, 2010).

In addition to online lectures, instructivist approaches such as online quizzes, exams, and other assessments can all be developed and delivered using features available in most VLEs and commercial tools such as SoftChalk.

Mobile   Instructivist approaches are well suited for mobile application. Podcasts, vodcasts (i.e., video podcasts), and audio lectures often are developed so students can easily download them to their iPods, phones, or smart mobile devices for listening or viewing at convenient times. Apple's iTunes U provides a distribution system for online lectures, lessons, educational films, labs, audiobooks, and other material. It is positioned as an innovative way to get educational content onto the mobile devices of students and into their hands. Although various learning theories can be supported with these platforms, instructivist lectures are the most easy to move between instructor and student in mobile environments.

Other materials with the goal of moving knowledge between teacher and student are well suited to mobile environments. For instance, e-books, blogs, and online articles can all be accessed via online and mobile platforms from a variety of locations, ranging from Amazon's digital test platform (A. L. Hamilton, 2008) to Qoop[5] to Project Gutenberg's website (www.gutenberg.org/wiki/Main_Page).

Moving Toward Constructivism and Connectivism   Instructivism advocates moving knowledge from teacher to student. As stated earlier, this approach is useful in limited doses to help establish fundamental understanding in areas new to a student, but it has been criticized as ineffective. Teachers using instructivist techniques may seek to improve its effectiveness by adding more interactiveness to their delivery. Many technologies that do this can be classified as *augmented* instructivism-based tools. Although with these the teaching approach is generally instructivist, communication back to the teacher is enabled to a greater extent, and more interaction is facilitated. Tools such as classroom clickers, comment capabilities on blogs, online quizzes, student and teacher discussion-board threads, and other tools promote this additional interaction. VLEs enhanced with tools such as Wimba Classroom permit students to post questions during lectures, asking the instructor for clarification or further information. This level of interaction creates an augmented form of instructivism.

Two favorite tools I use to enhance my instructivist lectures online are VoiceThread and Grapevine Talk. VoiceThread allows an instructor to post a multimedia slide show with images, documents, voice, and video. Students can navigate the slide show and leave comments in five different ways: by voice with a microphone, by voice with a mobile phone or smart device, in text, in an audio file recorded on a computer, or in video with a webcam. The comments are collected as group conversations and shared from a location on the Web. Using this tool, an instructivist lecture becomes a group conversation online. The comments have constructivist elements, and the overall concept can become connectivist (VoiceThread, 2010). Grapevine Talk permits the posting of lectures and has the facilities to enable a conversation to emerge around the lecture. Grapevine is perfect for asynchronous discussions in online venues (Grapevine Talk, 2010). Figures 7.2 and 7.3 show VoiceThread and Grapevine Talk.

Technologies for Constructivism

Constructivist learning environments have been enabled in a number of ways by the digital age. First, students have access to low-cost or free tools

Figure 7.2 VoiceThread Website

http://voicethread.com/

Figure 7.3   Grapevine Talk Website

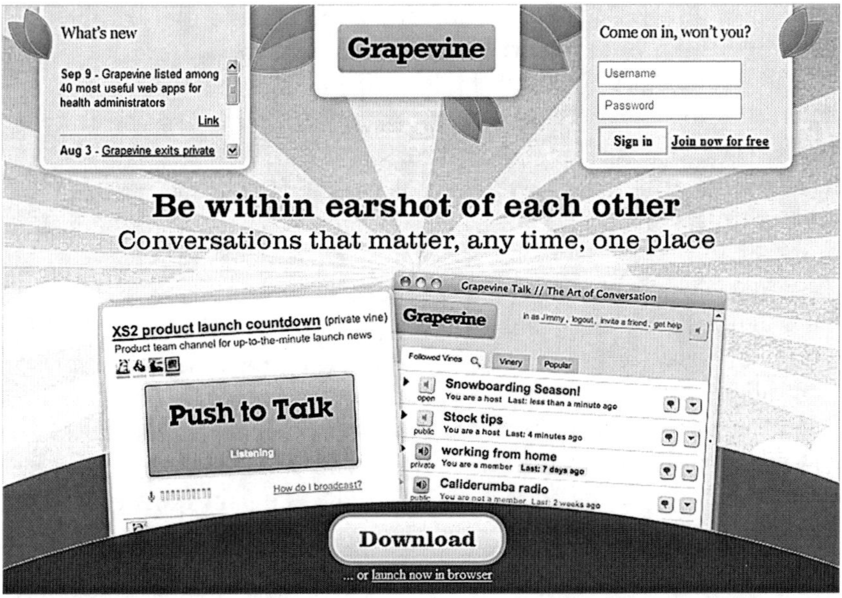

http://grapevinetalk.com/

that can be used to construct meaningful digital content. Second, the collective social construction of knowledge is enhanced by the Internet's connectivity and personal networks. Group projects, service-learning, experiential learning, and a variety of team projects are possible. Constructivism can use technologies to transform students into participants who seek and build new knowledge through their unique, individual experiences. Teachers provide guidance and facilitate students' exploration, discovery, and creation artifacts while building on their base of prior knowledge. Pedagogies for this approach need to ensure activities are interactive and student centered. Students are expected to be responsible and autonomous as they inquire about and build new knowledge through their experiences. Common activities for use in constructivist environments include (1) experimentation; (2) research projects; (3) real-world and virtual field trips; (4) digital content creation (e.g., video, podcasts, e-portfolios, animations, tutorials, etc.); and (5) group discussions and reflections.

A variety of modern technologies are suited to accomplishing these tasks. The distinctions between classroom, online, and mobile tools I used when discussing instructivism blurs when considering constructivism. Teachers empower students. This means the favorite tools of the tech-savvy millennial become part of their classroom experience. In fact, many of the technologies employed by forward-thinking instructivist teachers to create knowledge nodes for students can be deployed by constructivist students to create nodes of their own.

For instance, student research projects can be developed and communicated to classmates via presentation software (e.g., PowerPoint, Keynote, or Prezi). Students can develop Pecha Kuchas or VoiceThreads. Learning will take place through the process of construction of these artifacts and will be strengthened when classmates use, discuss, and reflect on the material. Technologies such as discussion forums, podcasts, wikis, and blogs enable learners to actively construct knowledge and have long been touted as excellent constructivist tools (Seitzinger, 2006). Student broadcasts using the technologies of Stickam and BlogTV are also technologies that can bring constructivism to life. Students can create digital tutorials for online sharing using MS Producer, Screenflow, Camtasia, and Wimba. Content development and compilation is enabled by webcams, digital cameras, and existing Creative Commons licensed material.[6]

Students can work to develop reference material that can be accessed on e-book readers and mobile devices. In some classrooms, course material is developed from the collective projects of current and prior classes. This approach uses venues such as ELATEwiki.org where student-developed entries are created by a class one semester, then read and edited by subsequent classes in following semesters. In the future, this material can be bundled into booklike structures assembled and printed as "free textbooks" for incoming students. Wikibooks is an example of another community-developed platform where course material can be constructed by students under the guidance of an instructor.

Other technologies for constructivist learning approaches include games, virtual worlds, and VLEs. These are examined in the subsequent sections.

Games   A key element of constructivism is learning through experience. "Games confront players with limits of space, time, and resources, forcing them to stretch in order to respond to problems just on the outer limits of their current mastery" (Holland, Jenkins, & Squire, 2003, p. 28). Most MMORPGs increase in difficulty as players master various levels and become more adept at achieving their goals within the environment.

ERPsim from HEC Montreal uses this concept by increasing environmental variability as students learn to use features of SAP/R3, an enterprise-level business computing platform, to compete in realistic business environments and attempt to buy and sell goods and services that will provide greater profitability than those of their rival firms (ERPSim, 2010). As students become better at the game, more difficult scenarios can be enacted to expand their skill set (Squire, 2006). Peggy Sheehy and Lucas Gillespie provide examples of how student learning can be facilitated within MMORPG environments: "[Their methods] force players to tackle a variety of cognitive challenges that scale proportionately as their skill level and proficiency increases. These persistent game worlds are also intensely social spaces, forcing players to work cooperatively in a variety of roles to advance in the game, fostering communication and even leadership skills" (Hargadon, 2010).

Virtual Worlds   Similar to games, virtual worlds can be used as a mechanism to enhance student learning through experience (Girvan & Savage, 2010). Gül, Gu, and Williams (2008) suggest that "providing opportunities for exploration and manipulation in the virtual environments, providing opportunities for discourse between students and other users of the environment as well as providing opportunities to actively build skills and knowledge in relation to their interest" are strengths of constructivist learning in virtual worlds (p. 584). By allowing students to collaborate within virtual environments such as Second Life (www.secondlife.com) and ActiveWorlds (www.activeworlds.com), a variety of experiences can be orchestrated. These experiences allow students to learn content and enhance team-building skills and communication capabilities (Gül, Gu, & Williams, 2008).

Virtual Learning Environments (VLEs)   Most modern VLEs include facilities to enable constructivist learning. Kunz (2004) says, in order for a VLE to facilitate the basic elements of constructivist teaching and learning environment, the following functionalities are required:

- ◆ Workspaces for individuals or groups to support the active construction of knowledge, social collaboration, and negotiation
- ◆ Knowledge construction tools
- ◆ Communication tools such as discussion forums and chat

- Collaboration tools such as electronic whiteboards, brainstorming tools, peer assessment tools, wikis, and polls
- Management tools such as a notification system, a shared calendar, and version control elements
- Cognitive tools to reflect on student experiences such as electronic workbooks, weblogs, or e-portfolios
- Searchable objects repository to foster contextually situated learning using ill-defined complex cases and problems (object repositories provide a way to integrate authentic documents into an online learning environment)
- Templates for games and simulations

Technologies for Connectivism

The application of connectivist learning theory was not possible (at least in a practical sense) prior to the advent of the Internet and the subsequent development of Web 2.0 technologies. Connectivism recognizes that more information exists than one person can possibly access and digest. Therefore many technologies related to implementation of this learning theory involve managing interactions with the vast Aleph[7] that is the Internet. The key becomes using the correct technologies to recognize important and relevant information, and being able to develop a multifaceted network to access stored community learning. Further, these technologies must promote connections, relevant growth, and selective pruning.[8]

Teachers can provide value to tech-savvy millennials in connectivist environments in a variety of ways. Rather than lecture on specific material, the teacher should alternate between roles of network administrator, information curator, and master artist (Blackall, 2007). The teacher can provide tools and technologies that aid in the construction of lifelong personal learning networks that connect relevant nodes. Using this perspective, the following areas become important for the application of technologies: network principles, knowledge sources, fluidity and change principles, and tools for understanding.

Network Principles   A key set of technologies enabling connectivism relate to network principles. For a tech-savvy millennial to fully enjoy the advantages of connectivist learning, she must be able to find nodes, connect to nodes, publicize nodes, and filter nodes. Nodes can be located in a variety of ways. Search engines are commonly used and have become second nature to tech-savvy millennials. However, it has been my experience that most students are not highly sophisticated users. With the acquisition of a few techniques they can become much more effective. Google provides an excellent overall choice for general searches, and it can be very powerful when used in sophisticated ways.[9] Other searches can be performed using specialty search engines. For instance, Technorati is excellent for blog searches. Scirus and Google Scholar work well for academic and scholarly document searches. Some search engines such as Answers.com and Ask.com can provide answers to factual questions. Picsearch helps locate images, as does Google Images. Most university libraries provide electronic database links that enable the most sophisticated scholars to conduct rigorous searches. Teachers should encourage the use of search engines to supplement and enhance discussion during class time and guide students in critically evaluating the suitability of discovered material based on its source.

Other methods for connecting also exist, ranging from making contacts in traditional contexts, such as at conferences and in educational settings, to using technology such as blogs, podcasts, wikis, and Twitter to form relationships with experts worldwide. Mobile devices and the worldwide network of broadband transmission make it possible to use technologies such as Skype and Google Chat to connect to people anywhere in the world at any time. RSS feeds combined with aggregator software such as BlogBridge, Feedreader, Google Reader, and iTunes make it possible to create a filtered network of information sources online that are continually updated as developments occur. New informational nodes created by students can be publicized using technologies that establish RSS feeds (such as FeedBurner,[10] shown in Figure 7.4). Tech-savvy millennials are comfortable creating and viewing podcasts and videocasts. Tools such as Elluminate allow synchronous class discussion and enable a variety of interaction methods. Remote class members and expert guests can use these technologies to connect with students currently online and record sessions for future use.

Like constructivist learning, connectivist methods can make good use of networking and connection capability in virtual worlds, and simulation and game environments. Persistent worlds like Second Life enable a variety of long-term connections to information nodes, people, and community learning centers. For instance, the Second Life Frank Lloyd Wright (FLW) museum (http://secondlife.com/destination/1848) provides a

Figure 7.4   FeedBurner Publicizes RSS Feeds

series of galleries in Second Life to celebrate the work of America's best-known architect. Numerous other examples of information resources in Second Life also exist.[11]

In the past few years, connectivist theory has promoted the concept of personal learning networks (PLNs). PLNs are created by individual learners to provide a persistent and relevant network of community learning. The connections reach interested people and information resources around the globe. PLNs extend knowledge and learning outside the classroom and are being offered by some teachers as alternatives to traditional environments found in virtual learning environments. Students can become PLN consumers by linking and using existing knowledge. As the network becomes stronger and their expertise grows, they can transition into becoming PLN producers who create and share new knowledge. The Innovative Educator (2008) suggests the following for getting started with PLNs:

1. Join a professional social network (examples might include Classroom 2.0 for educators or LinkedIn for business professionals).

2. Pick five relevant and interesting blogs to read.
3. Set up a NetVibes account and subscribe to the blogs you selected.
4. Become a part of the conversation and start commenting on the blogs you read.
5. Join the microblogging phenomena by reading relevant tweets at Twitter.

Wikis and RSS aggregators also can be used to create a PLN on a particular topic (Heather, 2004). Tools such as Questler are emerging to support the idea of creating a learning network. Questler draws on individual experiences and conversations to generate a quest (essentially a mini-blog) that links text, websites, multimedia files, and other resources to create an informal learning experience. Questlers create a learning network based on the website's tool set and their personal contacts (see Figure 7.5).

Knowledge Storage Connectivism posits that learning resides in the connections we form, regarding both people and information sources such as databases. One source of stored knowledge that is growing in importance to higher education has resulted from the open education movement. This "sharing" phenomenon, related to Web 2.0 technologies, was triggered by several high-profile institutes of higher learning and their desire to make educational materials freely available to teachers and learners. This trend represents a change in the control and distribution dynamics related to educational material. In addition to helping to close the educational divide,[12] this mindset represents the idea that most shared knowledge taught at universities is built on the intellect of generations of scholars and doesn't belong to any one person. The concept is that open educational resources, or OERs, are free materials that learners can integrate into their personal learning networks as well as remix, add to, and redistribute. Massachusetts Institute of Technology (MIT) OpenCourseWare and the OpenCourseWare Consortium are key players in the OER movement. MIT provides access to knowledge via 2,000 free online noncredit courses (MIT, 2010). The OpenCourseWare Consortium "is a worldwide community of hundreds of universities and associated organizations committed to advancing OpenCourseWare and its impact on global education" (OCW Consortium, 2010). Members "envision a world in which the desire to learn is fully met by the opportunity to do so anywhere in the world—where everyone, everywhere is able to access

Figure 7.5   Questler Tools for Personal Learning Network Creation

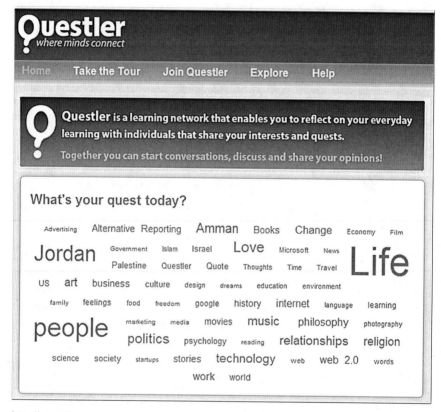

http://questler.com

affordable, educationally and culturally appropriate opportunities to gain whatever knowledge or training they desire" (OCW Consortium, 2010).

Of course, connectivism is not limited to resources developed and released by institutions of higher learning. Knowledge resides in countless databases, scientific websites and journals, libraries, books, e-books, websites, and so forth. The connectivist learner's universe is virtually unlimited.

Another phenomenon for community learning and knowledge storage involves massive open online courses (MOOCs). MOOCs provide an environment where lifelong learners can use various tools to build and manage learning networks simultaneously with a group of peers. A class called Connectivism and Connective Knowledge (CCK08), facilitated by George Siemens and Stephen Downes in the fall of 2008, tested this idea by offering both formal enrollment, for credit, through the University of Manitoba and informal, free enrollment to anybody in the world. The goal was to enable students to develop personal learning networks with others interested in this topic. The "teachers" facilitated connections to preliminary knowledge (nodes) in the subject area and then allowed the students to build connections to peers. Antonio Fini (2009) documents the result in detail.[13]

Fluidity and Change Principles   From a connectivist viewpoint, knowledge and connections are based on context. As such, it is vital that the connectivist learner focus, not on predefined knowledge, but on interactions and the context for those interactions. Modern technologies have resulted in rapid information changes and in dramatic relocation of knowledge resources. Connectivist pedagogies seek to ensure students remain current within their fields by realizing this fact and by promoting skills that can ensure the development of new connections and the pruning of those that become obsolete. Although some individuals worry that too much sharing might diminish their prestige, and undermine the power intrinsic in holding scarce knowledge, others suggest that sharing knowledge yields great returns (Downes, 2008). The more a learner shares, the more others are willing to share in return. This exchange becomes the crux of a PLN, which by its very nature must be fluid and continually changing.

Many Web 2.0 technologies are innately fluid and support change. For instance, social bookmarking systems such as Digg and Delicious are ideal tools for an active connectivist environment. Blogs, wikis, and microblogs are fluid by nature, and when coupled with RSS feed technologies, continually update the knowledge recipient. Social networks and their features are ideal for information updates and remaining current.

Tools for Understanding   A connectivist learning approach may require the development and maintenance of a personal learning network or similar artifact. Several good tools exist that can help in this process. Some, like Questler, facilitate the initial development of a PLN. In other instances, learners might prefer the context of a social network for maintaining a PLN. Still others may find a dashboard environment like Net-Vibes useful for a "connections" repository configured to meet their specific objectives. In my opinion, tools for creating and maintaining PLNs are just beginning to move toward their potential. To understand these ideas better, two example tools are presented in more detail: NetVibes and VUE.

> *NetVibes*—NetVibes, a French company founded by Tariq Krim and Florent Frémont in 2005, is a free website that personalizes Web experiences. The concept is to take everything important found while online—newspapers, blogs, weather updates, email, searches, videos, photos, social networks, podcasts, widgets, games, and so forth—and have them available on a single page, like a personalized dashboard. This dashboard can be set to automatically update every time it opens. In a sense, this dashboard becomes a network hub that provides easy online access to a learner's connections and information nodes (NetVibes, 2010). NetVibes is organized into tabs, each containing a user-defined module such as an RSS feed reader, a calendar, social bookmarks, notes, to-do lists, search engines, email, Web storage (like Box.net), instant messaging, Flickr photos, podcast support, or other options (Calore, 2007; see Figure 7.6).
>
> *VUE*—This tool facilitates the creation and use of mind maps.[14] VUE stands for *visual understanding environment* and was developed at Tufts University and released as open source software. VUE was specifically designed to allow students and teachers to map relationships between concepts and ideas and digital content. It uses the idea of pathways, and presenters can annotate trails through their maps. Expert, guided walkthroughs of information are the result (Frey, 2008). "At its core, the Visual Understanding Environment (VUE) is a concept and content mapping application, developed to support teaching, learning and research for anyone who needs to organize, contextualize, and access digital information. Using a simple set of tools and a basic visual grammar consisting of nodes and links, faculty and students can map relationships between concepts, ideas and digital content" (Tufts University, 2008). A large number of visual mind-mapping software systems are available both as freeware and commercial applications and can help provide documentation for connectivist-style networks (see Figure 7.7).

Figure 7.6   NetVibes Can Be Used to Create a Dynamic Knowledge Network on the Web

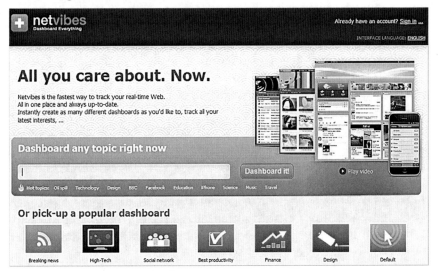

www.netvibes.com

Figure 7.7   Example Mind-Mapping Software from Mind42.com

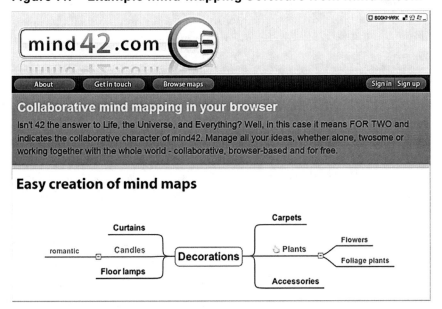

The Connectivist Classroom

Envisioning a connectivism-based classroom can be a challenge. At first glance, it seems difficult to understand the teacher's role and, beyond that, the facilities that might be required. Downes (2008) suggests connectivist influences on the classroom could have profound results. He proposes that schools will become meeting facilities, laboratories, multimedia studios, discussion venues, and workrooms. Rather than rely solely on presentation equipment, tools such as recording facilities, video editing software, and Internet interfaces will be available for community use at the classroom level. Downes (2008) further sees specialty facilities emerging (perhaps in university libraries) where classes will play interactive games and use simulations. The basic structure of classrooms should move away from the "teacher as center" model to a learning ecology resembling the Internet with an emphasis on openness and diversity. Classes will be blended, with some components being offered online and others being done face-to-face.

To be effective, teachers must update their knowledge and be able to communicate within the world their tech-savvy students inhabit. This means teachers must be able to "go faster, use less of a step–by–step approach and be more comfortable and prepared for random access learning opportunities. Instructors should know how to utilize textbooks and then go beyond them. Textbooks should be used to facilitate questioning and discussion, and not for rote memorization" (Darrow, 2009, p. 42).

In *Knowing Knowledge* (2006), George Siemens suggests the connectivist classroom teacher will interact with students in a variety of ways to support learning. One role, *teacher as master artist*, suggests students can create learning in view of their peers and teacher. This makes the classroom into a venue reminiscent of an art studio, where the "master artist" can point out intricacies and specific ideas to the novice. Peers can make suggestions and otherwise influence other individuals' work. This approach can be accomplished both online—using various technologies—and in person.

Another teacher role, adopted by Siemens (2006) from Clarence Fisher, is *teacher as network administrator*. In this learning situation, the teacher guides students in their construction of learning networks. The teacher helps ensure students have the technical and social skills needed for this activity. She or he will also evaluate the students' networks and provide suggestions for improvement. Additionally, students should be encouraged to enter their teachers' professional networks as an example of how learning can be constructed. Students can contribute to the teaching community, and aid in reshaping and updating it. This will impact curriculum and provide a basis for the development of a personal learning network in the topical area being investigated. A jumpstart into an existing learning community is provided by introducing students to an existing professional community.

Siemens also talks about *teachers as curators* (Siemens, 2006). In a traditional sense, a curator maintains collections and prepares items for public display. The curator-teacher has strong domain knowledge and the ability to encourage and guide student exploration in specific areas. The curator-teacher has to carefully balance student autonomy with guidance and interpretation. This can be done face-to-face or with tools such as mind maps. In some ways, the curator-teacher becomes a node in the student's personal learning network that is eventually supplanted with other resources.

Another aspect of many classrooms relates to the use of virtual learning environments. Constructivist and connectivist learning theories have necessitated dramatic changes in how content is displayed and generated. Many VLEs have been updated to encourage student interaction and contributions to learning. More and more VLEs are including tools such as blogs, wikis, and discussion boards. And to accommodate connectivist thinking, restrictions that cut students away from the real world are being eliminated. Social networking tools are being developed and incorporated into VLEs with the idea that personal learning networks created during the course must remain with the students after the class is over (Kunz, 2004).

Summary

I recently ate lunch at a Vietnamese noodle house in Fayetteville, Arkansas. Witnessing my clumsy attempt at seasoning my soup, the waitress determined I needed a general philosophical overview of their approach to eating. She said, "No two people have the same sense when it comes to flavors. Because of this, our cook uses very little seasoning in the initial preparation." She handed me an overflowing plate of herbs, sauces, and spices and suggested I could optimize the flavor for my palate. She educated me regarding each item and made sure I was comfortable with the process. "Most chefs in America and Europe seem to think they know what food tastes like to everyone and that just isn't true," she said as she walked away. The soup was excellent and I am a convert to her way of thinking.

In higher education, we need to step back from the table and listen to those eating our soup. They may have different tastes than we do, and sometimes it is better to allow them to season what they are about to eat.

To me, this means several things regarding learning theory. First, use instructivism sparingly but in key situations where a basic understanding of concepts is needed. Instructivism can be made better by improving student interaction with technology and face-to-face communication techniques. In this venue, we can expose important information nodes, help students connect to these nodes, and form a dialogue. Our use of instructivism should be a starting point in a move toward constructivism and connectivism (Johnson, 2008).

Good teachers can use constructivism to encourage student creation of new nodes in their pursuit of deeper knowledge. Team projects, dissertations, theses, service learning, reflection, and the creation/experience of numerous other artifacts make this possible.

If at all possible, teachers should seek to make connectivism, with lifelong learning practices, a goal. Connectivist teaching means more than grooming students to create and maintain personal learning networks. In order to thrive in their world, our integration of connectivist learning into higher education needs to (1) help tech-savvy millennials avoid distraction and stay focused in spite of information overload; (2) connect with peers and experts through social networking; (3) create and prune information sources; (4) extract and mash important elements of information; (5) stay current; (6) understand the value of relevant and valid information; (7) recognize patterns; and (8) deal with gray, uncertain areas. Tech-savvy millennials should leave our institutions with skills to find and understand information nodes, connect information nodes, and create/become information nodes. We have to be ready to play different roles for our students, and these roles require different uses of technology (see Figure 7.8).

Knowing when to employ each pedagogical approach and in what amount is crucial for the tech-savvy millennial. Good teaching is still good teaching—especially when student learning is the ultimate goal.

Figure 7.8   Roles for Teachers

Instructivism—Teachers are experts and lecturers.

Constructivism—Teachers are guides and facilitators.

Connectivism—Teachers are master artists, network administrators, and curators.

Notes

1. Blue Rapids, Barrett, Bigelow, Cleburne, Garrison, Irving, Randolph, Shroyer, Stockdale, and Winkler

2. Critics say connectivism doesn't qualify as a learning theory. Kerr (2006) suggests connectivism "[uses] language and slogans that are sometimes 'correct' but are too generalized to guide new practice at the level of how learning actually happens" and that "connectivism misrepresents the current state of established alternative learning theories such as constructivism, behaviorism and cognitivism, so this basis for a new theory is also dubious."

3. George Siemens maintains a blog at www.connectivism.ca

4. Wolfram Alpha can be accessed at http://www.wolframalpha.com/

5. Qoop is an up-and-coming publisher that has "cast away the shackles of traditional publishing" (Qoop, 2008) and rebuilt its ideas with the mindset of a digital native in the socially networked world of Web 2.0. According to its website, Qoop "hope[s] to inspire creativity through social commerce." It further says that "QOOP (pronounced que-oop) is an ecosystem filling with content, tools, and products [its] users provide and which offers novel interactions to create unique mash-ups. Art, literature, photographs, poetry, novels, articles, illustrations, recipes, short stories, graphic designs, manuals, avatars, reports, glitters, white papers, course plans, design tools, layout templates, books, prints, and loads of other stuff are what [it would] like to see [on its website]."

6. The new digital shoreline offers new tools for sharing content, including text and rich media of all sorts. The development of new and better copyright models has been necessitated. The most widely used of these is Creative Commons (CC) (http://creativecommons.org). Creative Commons is a nonprofit organization with a mission to encourage and expand the variety of ways individuals and companies can develop, share, and use creative works in legal and protected ways (Creative Commons, 2008). I like to think of Creative Commons as a brain trust moving humankind from necessary limitations of the economics of developing and distributing creative material to the new age where many of these restrictions are gone. To accommodate today's growing possibilities, Creative

Commons has developed several copyright licenses intended to encourage creators to communicate rights they wish to reserve and rights they waive to promote sharing and enhancement. Founder of Creative Commons, Lawrence Lessig, says these licenses will free today's creators from a dominant and increasingly restrictive permission culture that has been perpetuated by traditional content distributors in order to maintain and strengthen their monopolies on cultural products such as popular music and popular cinema, and that Creative Commons can provide alternatives to these restrictions (Lessig, 2004).

7. From the Chapter 1 discussion about Borges' Aleph representing the entirety of the Internet and its vast information resources.

8. When viewed this way, connectivism invites a comparison to social constructivism (Palincsar, 1998).

9. The following link provides hints to improve search outcomes as recommended by Google: http://www.google.com/support/websearch/bin/answer.py? answer = 13 6861

10. Recently acquired by Google.

11. Anthony Curtis provides an excellent list of Second Life sites and resources on *New Media: Great Places to Visit in Second Life*. *http://www .uncp.edu/home/acurtis/NewMedia/SecondLife/SecondLifeGreatPlaces.html*

12. The educational divide represents a persistent division between access to educational materials and opportunities of middle-class children and less privileged counterparts. It is related to social and economic status and access to technology.

13. Reprinted on the Web: http://www.irrodl.org/index.php/irrodl/article/view Article/643/1402

14. Mind maps are diagrams used to link words, ideas, tasks, objects, entities, and concepts in ways that help organize and create context. Mind maps help visualize and classify ideas and are ideal tools for documenting a network of nodes to facilitate learning from a connectivist perspective.

CHAPTER EIGHT

TAKING THE NEXT STEP
AS A TEACHER

This chapter focuses on how a teacher can move ahead despite harboring a sense that much of today's learning infrastructure is in a transitional state. Although these feelings represent valid concerns, many changes to educational methods suggested in this chapter will produce positive outcomes regardless of which technologies and products become future standards. Additionally, a fun vision of the future is provided.

Moving Forward in Changing Times:
Settling the New Shoreline

YOUNG PEOPLE ARE GENERALLY more adaptable than we teachers, who often are set in our ways. There, I said it. I keep running across professors who grumble at me and suggest we have nothing to learn from the current generation. I, as you may have surmised by this point in the book, vehemently disagree. I think we can learn much from tech-savvy millennials, but they can learn a lot from us too.

For instance, we can teach them to slow down and reflect on the incredible amount of material they encounter and sift through each day. On the other hand they can teach us to timeslice and use our time more effectively. Whether we like it or not, a new language is emerging through the use of acronyms, short-spelled words, and emoticons in online discussions. Should we study the emergence of a new language while still ensuring our charges know how to use Standard English (or French, Japanese, German, etc.) to write high-quality text? Perhaps these sorts of collaborations and mutual understanding can result in a better outcome for all of our futures. After all, isn't it a basic assumption that diversity fosters creativity and success?

Coping as a Teacher

Another huge, emerging feature of the new shoreline is the collaboration capability of educators from all walks of life. The development of educational wikis, blogs, and social networks has made it possible for ideas and classroom material, as well as lectures and live interactions, to be shared. In the not too distant past, when a faculty member attended a conference, she or he would ask a local colleague to teach their class. Now a faculty member has several choices: to teach it "live" (virtually), to teach it asynchronously via a recorded lecture, to ask a colleague from anywhere in the world to provide a virtual lecture, or to provide the lecture in any of numerous other ways. Publishing companies used to provide "middleman" services and allow faculty to share material, which generally took the form of textbooks and supplements. Now that material can be found in a variety of collaborative sharing sites. Video, audio, and other types of media provide new tools in course delivery.

This is not to say that new technologies should be used in all settings. In fact, just because all these Web 2.0 tools are emerging does not mean we should use them in all classes. In fact, the smart use of new technologies should result from the reformulation of our classes. Perhaps one of the worse approaches is to use these tools as a substitute for something that works well in its current form. One truth, however, is that Web 2.0 technologies are transforming society and the way we live and work. And this means education must change, not in a reactionary sense but as a leading force in leveraging the changes, and reinvent itself to better serve society (Tan & Koh, 2008). Here are some additional ideas for exploring and settling on the shoreline:

> *Socialization in field of study.* With the emergence of social interaction tools on the Web, it only makes sense that research-oriented universities leverage collaboration to get more students, especially undergraduate students, involved in scientific research and studies. The opportunity is there and can help bring a new sense of accomplishment and learning to the classroom. Artifacts from classroom learning and assignments can become persistent and useful to society, and our "throwaway" approach to doing class work, grading

it, and moving to the next semester can be altered to create more value from classroom experiences.

Help enable new media literacy. Educators should be looking for opportunities to incorporate new media into their classes and promote its use. After all, students will be using these tools and other ones like them in both their careers and their personal lives. Most students, in fact, already embrace new media and use it in their daily lives, and they expect to use it in their educational experiences. It is important to create course pedagogy that ensures our students will not be left behind. Students should be encouraged to develop assignments using new media (e.g., video, audio, and mixed media) as well as traditional text.

Encourage students to create mashups from educational material. Students can benefit from remixing relevant material and finding ways to improve its presentation and relevance to classroom learning objectives. Educators can use peer-to-peer sharing networks, Creative Commons material, video, audio, and other forms of new media to encourage these activities. This also provides a venue to develop discussions and learning about new forms of copyright and license agreements and fair use of material.

Create sticky learning experiences. I think that as educators we have an opportunity to create an even stickier educational experience by adding a lifelong learning partnership to our student's university experience. That means allowing students to return to the classroom as participants, teachers, and learners throughout their lives. Universities are beginning to move in this direction with open courseware and other online material that encourages interaction between current students and those who have been involved previously. Personal learning networks created in school should continue to grow and interact with the university and its resources long after a diploma is awarded.

Put play to work. Tech-savvy millennials have spent their formative years observing a different world—a world of unlimited choice and digital abundance—help guide them in putting their play to work. A lesson can be learned from kittens and puppies. Watch them play and it becomes evident that skills in play are meant to become tools of survival in adulthood. New technologies in the workplace will emerge from the games, social chat, and other interactions that our students are using in play now.

Promote self-training and learning to learn. Enable self-training on new technologies. Students don't need step-by-step instructions from educators or in the classroom. They need *know-where* to use the abundant information on the Web to self-train. Time is far better spent teaching them how to filter useless learning information and identify good information rather than provide cookbook-type instruction bound to become obsolete in the near future. Our students need to become true connectivists.

Prepare students for ubiquitous learning. Students will live in a world with abundant information. Podcasts, videos, tutorials, high-quality research papers, and incredible amounts of scientific fact and theory are all being posted online at an exponential rate. Teaching them to develop PLNs that use this information wisely will result in the capability to learn continually.

Understand how boundaries have been redefined. In today's wired world, an instructor can work 24/7 and never feel finished. Checking email, visiting discussion boards, and posting material are huge time-eaters. Instead, instructors should plan for balance and a schedule that permits time for family, friends, hobbies, and exercise. In the long run, a balanced life will become a more productive and effective career (Brabazon, 2007, p. 84).

Switch studies from passive to active learning. More than ever, higher education must be concerned with moving to active learning paradigms. In the old model of passive learning, "students are assumed to enter the course with minds like empty vessels or sponges to be filled with knowledge" (McManus, 2001, p. 424). The expert instructor presides over the class and verbalizes information while passive students take notes. Lectures are mostly verbal, and students regurgitate information on exams. In active learning, the instructor creates "a learning environment in which the student can learn to restructure the new information and their prior knowledge into new knowledge about the content and to practice using it" (McManus, 2001, p. 425). Visual aids, demonstrations, new media, and other active learning methods are used to reinforce concepts presented by the instructor. Learning methods include developing new knowledge and actively creating new content. Constructivist learning supports this approach.

Agile learning. The educational community has much to learn from the Agile software development process. The principles developed by 17 well-known software thinkers and presented in the *Manifesto for Agile Software Development* describe a better way to create software in emerging collaborative environments (Agile Manifesto, 2001). Many of these principles are well suited to modern learning. These include timeliness, cooperative development, collaboration, technical excellence, simplicity, and the use of self-organizing teams and reflection. Other principles that make sense for education are the relative importance of individuals and their interactions with processes and tools. Additionally, students need to learn to respond to changes.

Engage real problems. Students want to make a difference, and if provided with real-world problems to solve, they will become more engaged and more willing to put forth their best effort. An assignment or project that captures the imagination of a student will elicit far greater effort than one that seems meaningless or inconsequential.

Online learning. Find ways to develop and offer online courses. This is certainly one trend that will not disappear. Creating new, better, and more pedagogically sound ways of doing this will pay huge future dividends in terms of both career life and impact on students. Remember, online classes are more than putting existing methodology on a computer. Teaching this way requires rethinking the process of knowledge delivery.

Take the best of the Web. Find the best new tools, techniques, and ideas for collaboration and other relevant applications and dive in. Use your students to help you learn, and make sure you offer them opportunities to develop assignment solutions using the best new tools out there. I hear faculty members saying things like, *Well, I would use Twitter but it will probably disappear in a year and then I've learned it all for nothing.* We are in a time of transition, and every new skill makes the next skill or tool easier to understand and learn. Using too little technology shortchanges the students and fails to recognize the increasingly digital nature of their world. Too much technology risks minimizing interaction with the instructor.

Use virtual teams. If possible, using virtual teams composed of members from different cultures, time zones, countries, and schools can benefit students. Members need to use new technologies such as

Web conferencing and collaborative-authoring software to develop deliverables in their environment.

Explore virtual worlds for the classroom. Virtual worlds provide a nascent media for instruction and learning. The inherent persistence of a virtual world such as Second Life allows for complex and lasting social interactions, which can become the basis for agile, collaborative education (Berge, 2008). Teachers can create the opportunity to encourage greater student participation while carrying out tasks that are restricted in real life by cost, safety, scheduling, or geography.

Break free. In the supplementary material for the DVD of *Virtually There*, Stephen Heppell writes, "Learning is breaking out of the narrow boxes that it was trapped in during the 20th century; teachers' professionalism, reflection and ingenuity are leading learning to places that genuinely excite this new generation of connected young school students—and their teachers too. VLEs are helping to make sure that their learning is not confined to a particular building, or restricted to any single location or moment" (Heppell, 2007). The use of virtual learning environments can help move education beyond the tyrannies of time and geography. Opportunities for constructivist and connectivist learning theory are available in these venues.

Students' Roles on the New Shoreline

Will tech-savvy millennials be different in a transformed version of higher education? In many ways they will, but according to Tara Brabazon (2007), there will always be recognizable student characteristics based more on personality than the environment. The top 25 percent of the class will remain rigorous, committed future scholars. They will require little overt assistance but will operate in models of student-centered learning. Another group, the middle 50 percent, already is running late, using spell checkers rather than proofreading and using new media to find shortcuts. These students are the ones that need the most support because new technology also can facilitate laziness, sloppy scholarship, and compliant thinking.

Instead, students must be responsible to step up and become part of their own educational process. Rather than becoming simple information consumers, they must become actively engaged in debate, knowledge refinement, and new content creation. Their searches need to be more creative than using Google or Wikipedia to acquire sources. It is important to know how to use broad and shallow searches and then focus and use narrow and deep ones. Students must be prepared to learn how to learn and recognize the difference between job training and educational inquiry. The university experience is not merely a means to an end that can be replaced with simple job skills.

The Long Tail Revisited

I live in the *"Long Tail"* world enabled and promoted by the Internet. Years ago, this was called "the underground" where small enclaves of people checked out of the mainstream to enjoy music, books, movies, and other material not endorsed by the hit-making apparatus of Hollywood, the publishing world, or the music industry. The underground provided a sense of mystery and added a dimension of uniqueness to someone's persona. Some had interests that ran contrary to those of most people. Personally, I may have valued the mainstream less than others might. I didn't care about being mysterious or "in the underground." I just know what I like and am willing to dig a bit deeper for it.

Today's tech-savvy millennial no longer lives in a constrained world where the mainstream and "the underground" are clearly differentiated. In fact, on many websites it is nearly as easy to find an offbeat book or album as it is to get a best-seller. This change has allowed people to easily customize their own consumption habits in very personal ways and has led some people to comment that the *backstreets are now the main street.*

Higher Education's Long Tail

In his book *The Long Tail: How Endless Choice Is Creating Unlimited Demand,* Chris Anderson (2006) describes how digitization has affected today's retail markets. This has resulted in consumer markets being transformed from hit-centric to niche-centric. Likewise, *The Long Tail* applies to higher education and how digitization may result in a curious blend of both "hits" and "niches." The following opinions may apply:

♦ Due to the twin tyrannies of geography and time, there have never truly been tightly controlled "hits" in the world of higher education the way there have been in the entertainment industries.

Although the academic book publishing world has sought to create hits in the related area of textbooks by controlling best-selling texts and course content, by its very nature, higher education has been a business of niches.

♦ In the near future, depending on the economic climate and the state of many university endowments, online education may become viewed as a way to pay the bills and leverage university notoriety. The use of the Internet to reduce geographic and time constraints has appeal right now and may encourage some "star" universities to dramatically increase enrollment through distance learning. This could create an environment in which top universities are able to compete directly with regional ones, offering students the promise of a diploma carrying their prestige. Depending on public acceptance, this could result in regional universities' losing enrollment and, to some extent, finding themselves to be second-tier partners that simply administer exams and provide other local services.

♦ In the long term, the domination of a few universities seems unlikely because the Internet, particularly Web 2.0 applications, provides an environment more conducive to the development of niches and mass customization. This means regional universities must do several things to ensure their survival and leverage the level playing field offered by the Web. Among these are (1) ensuring they establish and maintain a strong identity; (2) developing niche research and specialty areas that are fortified by local attributes that are not available in other locations (such as Kansas State's access to the Konza Prairie for research and the NBAF research facilities on its campus); and (3) maintaining strong ties with the region (e.g., through extension services and public outreach programs).

♦ A blended world may emerge where "famous" professors provide their material in the form of streaming lectures for use in classrooms around the globe and collect a fee for providing this service. Local professors may incorporate these virtual lectures as part of their classroom instruction and conduct local discussions. This type of activity already occurs to some extent now, but it may become more popular. The Internet provides the ability for both extremes to flourish. On one hand, a long tail of niches and specializations can exist. On the other hand, a powerful venue for directly reaching world-wide audiences is available. The Internet allows local efforts to quickly go viral and snowball into international phenomena (Karp, 2006).

♦ From the other perspective, big universities may face increased competition from many small universities, community colleges, for-profit universities, and even educational firms who have low overhead costs and few aspirations for university status. The long tail provides fertile space for the obscure to establish a niche and grow to fulfill an unmet need. It also provides a filter that gives the power of choice to the students and prevents a "corporate-like" power from determining what they should do. Eventually, good solutions will emerge.

♦ Students will seek personal solutions and customized learning opportunities that blend the best offerings from a variety of universities and other institutions but will still want a local home base for the social experiences of higher education. An educational "passport" that enables students to develop custom programs for students from a consortium of accredited schools may provide this opportunity.

♦ The long tail effect may also allow small but important niche areas to flourish as a result of the ability to leverage student numbers from geographically disparate locations. This will help specializations gain prominence.

Relevance to Students

Although the long tail will ultimately affect the way institutions of higher education must conduct business, it may have the greatest impact on our students. Today's tech-savvy millennials view the world much differently than previous generations. Digitally enabled youth spend their time seeking relevant content. They use social networks, online recommendations, and search engines to explore their world of choices and customize their surroundings to form an information-based identity. For teachers, knowing how to encourage these behaviors in smart ways creates a huge challenge.

The world that lies ahead is one of nearly limitless access to information, available to everybody, created by everybody, and belonging to everybody. Facts, solutions, and data will be available whenever and wherever a person wants. The world will become one of niche jobs, niche skills, and new areas we cannot guess at right now. How do we teachers prepare students for this world? We will be forced to abandon long-held educational pedagogy and standard ways of teaching and testing students. We will have to change the way students are evaluated and eliminate rote regurgitation on meaningless exams in exchange for projects that truly enhance our students' skills.

Future Skills

Although I don't claim to have a crystal ball providing a perfect vision to the future, there are a few skills I want my students to acquire. Among these are the following:

- Less emphasis on memorization of facts and an increase in the ability to search for relevant information
- Development of knowledge about the information reliability, that is, how to validate findings and how to ensure information is trustworthy
- Literacy in new media forms, including text, audio, video, and virtual worlds, and an understanding of how to create value with these forms
- Understanding the uses and drawbacks to social networks and communication technology
- The ability to contact and leverage the expertise of those specializing in niche areas
- The ability to make sound judgments to filter unreliable content from validated information based on how important that information is to the decisions being made
- The ability to use statistics and other tools to interpret "gray areas" when evaluating information
- The ability to develop lifelong, personal learning networks drawing from a wide range of social and information-based connections

Finding the Next Big Thing in Education

Education will change, but some aspects will remain intact. For instance, we teachers will continue to interact with our students. Technology will have a hard time replacing the sight of a student's face brightening when a concept finally makes sense. Although I advocate using new ideas to our advantage, I believe that good teaching is still good teaching, no matter the manifestation. Just for fun, I'd like to provide a peek at the possible future that could emerge with existing technologies. However, keep this in mind: Generally, people tend to overestimate short-term change and underestimate long-term change. With that in mind, let's visit the future.

ROGER'S OFFICE 2020:
A Visit with Edward Deming, Quality Guru

Huh?

The uttered word broke up a line of text being transcribed to my computer screen. I had been dictating a research paper and watching my words appear as I spoke them. But for a moment, my continuity had been interrupted, and I whirled in my office chair. A shadow loomed outside the virtual door to my office. I touched an icon on my computer screen and the 8- by 3-foot plasma screen lightened, making a student visible.

"Song? Is that you?" I asked. The person standing in the doorway was glowing yellow and had eerie fangs, a wolf-like tail, and long, flowing hair. He was clearly masculine, with a finely muscled torso and large, out-of-proportion legs. He was dressed like something halfway between a Viking and a male runway model on steroids. A huge sword was slung over his shoulder.

"Hi, Professor McHaney."

The voice was clearly female and that of my student Song Yi, who had scheduled a virtual office visit for five minutes earlier.

"You're looking out of character today," I quipped.

"We were playing World of Warcraft and I ducked out to see you. Sorry I'm late. I didn't bother to switch identities. So, I am Thor at the moment."

"As long as you don't come to class that way. We don't need any battles breaking out."

"You got it!"

Song/Thor shifted around in the doorway curling his lip a little to bare his fangs. "Sorry," Song said. "I am still getting used to my avatar."

"So, what's on your mind?"

"Well, I watched your quality management lecture on Monday, and I didn't really get how Deming's quality philosophy was any different than Juran's. And you said that if we didn't understand that, we might have trouble doing the project."

"I can explain it again," I said, suddenly feeling silly looking at the giant man who spoke with the voice of an 18-year-old female. "Or . . ."

"Or we can take a trip into Second Life like you said?"

"Yeah. So far, you're the only one that's come to my virtual office hours, so let's leave a note and head out."

I pulled a virtual yellow sticky pad from my computer, said a few words that would provide a link to our Second Life destination in case someone else came to my office, and then stuck the visual/audio note to the virtual door.

"Ready?" I asked.

Song's avatar nodded its head, and I stepped onto my SL control pad and an avatar appeared next to Thor. Mine wasn't quite so outlandish. I had settled for a look that maybe took 20 years off my face, made me look fit, and tinted me slightly purple in deference to Kansas State's colors. As we walked out into the hallway, everything looked amazingly like the hallway outside my office in the "real world," except that tags floated above different doors and objects as we passed by.

"It's incredible how they've been able to render the real world into Second Life this way," Song's voice quipped.

K-State university president, Liam Allen, appeared up ahead, and we walked right through him like ghosts. A cloud of small tags floated over his head indicating his identity and information about his affiliations. He was transparent, so we knew he wasn't in-world but was actually walking down the real-world equivalent of the hallway, so his image was being fed into Second Life real time.

"Wonder why he's in my building today?" I said.

"Meeting with the dean, Dr. McHaney," President Allen's voice said.

"Guess he's wired in," Song said.

"Yeah, that guy hears everything," I said.

"Don't you forget it, McHaney," President Allen's voice said, echoing away.

We stepped outside the building. A light rain was falling, mimicking the real-world weather.

"Ready?"

"Let's go!"

Song and I rocketed through cyberspace just for a moment as we teleported to the in-world version of the American Quality Society's headquarters. We entered the front doors and walked through a crowd of businessmen and women—some were transparent versions of real-world people, and others, virtual avatars like us. A stylish man sat at the far side of the lobby. He was in the real world, but I knew he saw us in the wall-sized virtual display that formed part of the lobby.

"We're just here to visit Deming and Juran," I said. "From Kansas State."

My words brought a swirl of information to his screen, and he waved us on. "Your membership's valid for another four months. Head on in."

He picked up a pen-shaped device and began changing the color of his shirt.

We walked through a virtual doorway and suddenly appeared in a gigantic working factory recreated from 1950s photos and films taken in post–World War II Japan. Amid the clatter of machinery and busy work crews, a tall, elderly Caucasian man was explaining something to a group of what I assumed were factory workers.

"Deming," I said pointing.

Song and I walked across the factory floor, almost unable to keep our eyes off the nearly century-old technology being used to bend metal rods and stamp thin copper sheets into various shapes.

Deming turned to us and held out a hand.

"What can I tell you?" he said in his low, stilted voice. His eyes were kind but blazed with intelligence.

Song began asking questions, but I couldn't keep my eyes off a strange little dragon that was floating across the ceiling. A renegade avatar? A bot? Or just someone wanting to learn a little about the history of manufacturing?

A decade ago, who would've imagined this would all be possible? I guess I did.

Another student appeared beside me. He looked pretty much exactly as he did in the real world. It was Min Rainet. "Hey, Dr. McHaney, I got your message. I guess I need to talk with the Deming bot too."

What Next

So is this how I think the world will be? Maybe. I can't predict what may or may not happen. What I have depicted is possible, but that doesn't mean we'll get there. After all, as a boy growing up in the 1960s I thought we'd have a Mars colony by now.

What I do think is possible is the closer integration between real and virtual worlds. It will be possible to recreate large portions of the real world in virtual space and use these as a learning laboratory. New control devices and sensors will emerge to allow people to have fuller and more complete experiences. Feeds from the real world will be integrated with virtual worlds in a way that allows interaction between both worlds on a variety of levels.

A book from the 1990s by Howard Rheingold (*Virtual Reality,* 1991) provides a number of thought-provoking possibilities, and today much of the groundwork needed for his visions is being developed.

Although many barriers have to be crossed first, I do think that virtual worlds are going to be important in higher education. In the same way that the collective emergent behaviors of millions of contributors are encoding the world's vast information resources and creating repositories of knowledge like Wikipedia, the same forces will transport the real world—via tags, video, geolocation data, and other information—into a virtual representation. Live video feeds and wired people will populate both spaces. And learning will take place—in virtual field trips, experiments, and direct observation (even though it is virtual)—in ways it never has before.

Am I excited? You bet. I would like to see a Deming bot in my classroom answering quality questions or a gigantic virtual microchip running in slow motion so my student could ride the 1's and 0's on their journey to create meaning in the processor. It would be great to observe a variety of virtual worlds: Where the great pyramids of Egypt are being constructed according to the prevailing theories and I can put my class to work dragging a block up a huge ramp of sand to the top. Or where I can take students on a class trip on the *Titanic,* check them into cabins, and let them experience a recreation of it sinking in a virtual space. The list is only limited by our imaginations, and this reality will happen sooner than later!

New Age of Socratic Teaching

Higher education in the coming decades will be shaped by what we are learning today. Business models and the push to remain competitive and have a recognizable identity, coupled with the infiltration of global corporations, will push universities toward corporate practices and new funding models. Competition with for-profit universities will change the way traditional universities view the professoriate and will influence the ways money is spent and used. There is no doubt that changes in technology will continue to impact the delivery of classes and the very nature of what and how we teach. The expectations of those who have lived their entire lives playing video games and collaborating on social platforms will result in different forms of education.

The current hierarchical pattern of youths' first attending elementary schools, then high schools, then colleges and universities may need to be reevaluated and reexamined considering new collaborative environments and ubiquitous information. Learning shouldn't stop with a diploma or degree, and institutions of higher education must devise better ways to serve the new educational demands of people living in a connected world. It is almost certain that, in decades to come, our linear education systems will be replaced with nonhierarchical structures marked by self-directed, individualized, and customized learning experiences that draw on multiple resources, some of which are emerging even as you read this sentence. Personal learning networks and connectivist ideas will become the basis for lifelong learning.

Some might say that we are entering a new age of Socratic teaching, in which educators focus on providing the questions and experiences, but not necessarily the answers. We will work with our students to question goals and purposes. Together we will probe the very nature of the questions we are asking and discover problems to solve. We will inquire whether relevant information exists and focus on filtering and discovery to consider alternative understandings. We will develop and analyze key concepts and ideas. We will question assumptions and trace out consequences of our actions. And all of this can be done in a customizable and information-rich environment where teaching and learning merge until they carry the same meaning.

Conclusion

Song and I finished interrogating Deming and Juran. I was about to head back to my office and she was about to reenter the World of Warcraft portal when an idea flashed through my head.

"Want to visit one more thing before you go?" I asked. "It'll take a couple minutes."

Thor's heavy brow furrowed. "I'm getting better at emoting," Song said. "You see that brow crease."

"I did," I laughed. "I guess that means you're ready to get back to WOWing?"

"Naw, I can spare a couple more minutes."

I gave her the address and we teleported to the Virtual Tuttle Lake Second Life site.

"This used to be the location of Randolph, Kansas," I said.

Thor looked uninspired. "It's a beautiful lake," Song said. "Not much town though."

"Let me show you the way it used to be. I pressed a button at the visitor's pavilion and the lake drained. A wide main street lined with low brick buildings appeared. People and cars moved about attending to their daily routines. The temperature increased and the air was dusty and dry. "Impressive," I said. "That's how it looked back in the 1950s before the dam was constructed. What do you think?"

"Looks like a boring place to live . . . I think the lake is better." Song's voice had been replaced by Thor's deep raspy one. "See you later Dr. McHaney, I'm off to World of Warcraft."

I stayed a bit longer as Thor vaporized. Randolph *was* quaint but very different. I wondered why Song hadn't been impressed with it. But then again, it wasn't the world she grew up in . . .

REFERENCES

43 Things. (2010) *43 Things homepage.* Retrieved July 5, 2010, from http://43things.com

ActiveWorlds Inc. (2010). *ActiveWorlds homepage.* Retrieved July 5, 2010, from http://www.activeworlds.com

Agile Manifesto. (2001). *Agile software principles.* Retrieved February 2, 2009, from Agile Manifesto: http://www.agilemanifesto.org/principles.html

Alemán, A. M., & Wartman, K. L. (2008). *Online social networking on campus: Understanding what matters in student culture.* New York: Routledge.

Alexa. (2010, July 11). *Top sites.* Retrieved July 11, 2010, from http://www.alexa.com/topsites

Anderson, C. (2006). *The long tail.* New York: Hyperion.

AndroLib. (2010, July 8). *AndroLib stats.* Retrieved July 8, 2010, from http://www.androlib.com/appstats.aspx

Ann Meyers Medical Center. (2010, January 30). *Ann Meyers Medical Center.* Retrieved July 9, 2010, from http://ammc.wordpress.com

Apple, Inc. (2010a, January 5). *Apple's App Store downloads top three billion.* Retrieved July 1, 2010, from http://www.apple.com/pr/library/2010/01/05appstore.html

Apple, Inc. (2010b, June 22). *Apple sells three million iPads in 80 days.* Retrieved July 9, 2010, from http://www.apple.com/pr/library/2010/06/22ipad.html

Apple, Inc. (2010c, April 28). *iPad.* Retrieved April 28, 2010, from http://www.apple.com/ipad/

Bajarin, T. (2008, September 12). *Netbooks versus notebooks.* Retrieved July 9, 2010, from *PC Magazine*: http://www.pcmag.com/article2/0,2817,2330274,00.asp

Baker, J. (2006, April 27). *Guild wars factions.* Retrieved July 4, 2010, from GotFrag.com: http://exe.gotfrag.com/portal/story/32316/

Barker, P. (1993, August 16–26). *Electronic books and their potential for interactive learning.* Proceedings of NATO Advanced Study Institute on Basics of Man Machine Communication for the Design of Education Systems, Eindhoven, Netherlands (pp. 151–159).

Barrett, D. J. (2009). *MediaWiki.* Sebastopol, CA: O'Reilly Media.

Bennet, S., Maton, K., & Kervin, L. (2008). The "digital natives" debate: A critical review of the evidence. *British Journal of Educational Technology, 39*(5), 775–786.

Benton, S. L., Webster, R., Gross, A., & Pallette, B. (2010). *Technical report on the analysis of IDEA student ratings in traditional versus online courses: SRS 2002–2008 Data*. Manhattan, KS: The Idea Center.

Berge, Z. L. (2008, May/June). Multi-user virtual environments for education and training? A critical review of Second Life. *Educational Technology*, pp. 27–31.

Bezos, J. (2009, February 9). *Amazon home page: Letter to Amazon Kindle customers*. Retrieved February 10, 2009, from http://www.amazon.com

Bishop, T. (2004, January 26). *Microsoft Notebook: Wiki pioneer planted the seed and watched it grow*. Retrieved May 2, 2009, from Seattlepi.com: http://www.seattlepi.com/business/158020_msftnotebook26.html

Bisoux, T. (2009, June). Next-generation education. *BizEd*, pp. 24–30.

Blackall, L. (2007, August 25). *Regarding George Siemens curators*. Retrieved July 30, 2010, from Learn Online: http://learnonline.wordpress.com/2007/08/25/regarding-george-siemens-curators/

Blackboard Inc. (2010a). *Blackboard*. Retrieved July 9, 2010, from http://www.blackboard.com/Teaching-Learning/Overview.aspx

Blackboard Inc. (2010b). *Blackboard Mobile Central*. Retrieved July 15, 2010, from http://www.blackboard.com/Mobile/Mobile-Central.aspx

Blackboard Mobile Learn. (2010, July). *Blackboard Mobile Learn*. Retrieved July 14, 2010, from http://www.blackboard.com/resources/mobile/mobile_learn_splash/desktop/index.html#ipad

Blackboard Video. (2010, July). *Texas Tech Mobile Web demo*. Retrieved July 14, 2010, from http://www.blackboard.com/Videos/Mobile-Central-Demo-Texas-Tech.aspx

Bode, B. (1929). *Conflicting psychologies of learning*. New York: Heath.

Borges, J. L. (2004). *The Aleph and other stories*. New York: Penguin.

Brabazon, T. (2007). *The university of Google*. Burlington, VT: Ashgate.

Bray, D. A., & Konsynski, B. R. (2007). Virtual worlds: Multi-disciplinary research opportunities. *ACM SIGMIS Database 38*(4), 17–25.

Briggs, L. (2009, August 19). *Fostering classroom interaction, minus the clickers*. Retrieved July 7, 2010, from Campus Technology: http://campustechnology.com/Articles/2009/08/19/Fostering-Classroom-Interaction-Minus-the-Clickers.aspx?Page=1

Brynjolfsson, E. H. (2003). Consumer surplus in the digital economy: Estimating the value of increased product variety at online booksellers. *Management Science 49*(11), 1580–1596.

Business Software Alliance (BSA). (2010). *Business Software Alliance homepage*. Retrieved July 5, 2010, from http://www.bsa.org/country/Research%20and%20Statistics.aspx

Byte. (1990). The Byte Awards: GRiD System's GRiDPAD. *BYTE Magazine, 15*(1), 285.

Calore, M. (2007, February 9). *Netvibes spices up personal news.* Retrieved July 20, 2010, from Wired.com: http://www.wired.com/software/softwarereviews/news/2007/02/72673

Cassavoy, L. (2007, May 7). *In pictures: A history of cell phones.* Retrieved July 4, 2010, from PCWorld.com: http://www.pcworld.com/article/131450/in_pictures_a_history_of_cell_phones.html

Cavalli, E. (2008, December 23). *World of Warcraft hits 11.5 million users.* Retrieved July 4, 2010, from Wired.com: http://www.wired.com/gamelife/2008/12/world-of-warc-1/

Cavallo, D. (2007, June 10). *Opening keynote.* Paper presented at NUTN Conference, Philadelphia, PA.

CheatHouse. (2010). *CheatHouse homepage.* Retrieved July 3, 2010, from http://www.cheathouse.com

Chilton, M., & McHaney, R. W. (2010). Computer-mediated communication (CMC). In M. J. Bates & M. N. Maack (Eds.), *Encyclopedia of Library and Information Sciences* (3rd ed., pp. 1225–1233). New York: CRC Press.

Clarke, Arthur C. (1962). *Profiles of the future: An enquiry into the limits of the possible,* New York: Harper & Row.

Clarke, Arthur C. (1973). *Profiles of the future: An enquiry into the limits of the possible* (Rev. ed.). New York: Harper & Row.

Cohen, N. (2008, September 15). Don't buy that textbook, download it free. *New York Times* (NY Edition), p. C3.

Collins, C. (2008, September/October). Looking to the future: Higher education in the metaverse. *EDUCAUSE Review, 43*(5). Retrieved from http://www.educause.edu/EDUCAUSE + Review/EDUCAUSEReviewMagazineVolume43/LookingtotheFutureHigherEducat/163164/

Compact, C. (2001). *Annual service statistics 2000.* Providence, RI: Brown University.

Connexions. (2008). *Connexions: About us.* Retrieved October 16, 2008, from http://cnx.org/aboutus

Connexions. (2010). *Connexions home page.* Retrieved July 10, 2010, from http://cnx.org

Cook, J. (2009, December 9). *Exclusive: Wetpaint cuts staff, changes focus to publishing.* Retrieved January 5, 2010, from TechFlash: http://www.techflash.com/seattle/2009/12/exclusive_wetpaint_cuts_staff_echanges_focus_to_online_publishing.html

CourseSmart. (2008). *CourseSmart homepage.* Retrieved October 16, 2008, from http://www.coursesmart.com

Crawford, J. (2010, October 14). On the future of books. *Inside Google Books Blog.* Retrieved November 15, 2010, from http://booksearch.blogspot.com/2010/10/on-future-of-books.html

Creative Commons. (2008, October). *Creative Commons homepage.* Retrieved October 10, 2008, from http://creativecommons.org

Creeley, W. (2008, January 14). *New Facebook monitoring software raises troubling questions.* Retrieved May 22, 2009, from FIRE: http://www.thefire.org/article/8817.html

Crothers, B. (2010, July 8). *Report: iPad, tablets to cannibalize "Wintel" laptops.* Retrieved July 8, 2010, from CNet News: http://news.cnet.com/8301-13924_3-20010046-64.html

Dalrymple, J. (2010, March 22). *iPhone stealing game market share from Sony, Nintendo.* Retrieved June 10, 2010, from CNet News: http://news.cnet.com/8301-13579_3-10470102-37.html

Darrow, S. (2009). *Connectivism learning theory: Instructional tools for college courses* (master's thesis). Western Connecticut State University, Danbury.

DeMers, M. (2009, Winter). Inside the metaverse: A "Second Life" for GIS education. *ArcUser,* p. 69.

Diaz, D. P., & Bontenbal, K. F. (2000). Pedagogy-based technology training. In P. Hoffman & D. Lemke (Ed.), *Teaching and learning in a network world* (pp. 50–54). Amsterdam, Netherlands: IOS Press.

Donoghue, F. (2008). *The last professors: The corporate university and the fate of the humanities.* Bronx, NY: Fordham University Press.

Downes, S. (2008). *Places to go: Connectivism and connective knowledge. Innovate Online 5*(1). Retrieved August 1, 2010, from http://www.innovateonline.info/pdf/vol5_issue1/Places_to_Go-__Connectivism_&_Connective_Knowledge.pdf

Driver, R., Asoko, H., Leach, J., Mortimer, E., & Scott, P. (1994). Constructing scientific knowledge in the classroom. *Educational Researcher, 23*(7), 5–12.

Duffy, G. (2005, March). *Google's cookie and hacking Google print.* Retrieved June 12, 2008, from Kuro5Hin: http://www.kuro5hin.org/story/2005/3/7/95844/59875

Edgerton, D. (2007). *The shock of the old: Technology and global history since 1900.* Oxford: Oxford University Press.

ELATEWiki. (2009, March 28). *E-learning paths.* Retrieved July 10, 2010, from http://www.elatewiki.org/index.php/E-Learning_Paths

Epstein, F. (2008, August 19). *Students vs. Second Life.* Retrieved July 10, 2010, from *Metaverse Journal*: http://www.metaversejournal.com/2008/08/19/students-vs-second-life/

ERPSim. (2010, July 20). *ERPsim homepage.* Retrieved July 20, 2010, from http://www.erpsim.net

Experience Project. (2010). *Experience Project homepage.* Retrieved July 5, 2010, from http://www.experienceproject.com

Eyler, J., & Giles, D. (1999). *Where's the learning in service-learning?* San Francisco: Jossey-Bass.

Facebook. (2010, February 10). *New navigation for users and 400 million active users announcement.* Retrieved May 11, 2010, from http://www.facebook.com/

notes/facebook-ads/new-navigation-for-users-and-400-million-active-users-announcement/326050130129

Faculty Ethics on Facebook. (2010). Retrieved July 11, 2010, from http://www.facebook.com/group.php?gid = 2229343363

Feldstein, M. (2010, April 1). *A closer look at mobile app development for higher education.* Retrieved July 15, 2010, from e-Literate: http://mfeldstein.com/a-closer-look-at-mobile-app-development-for-higher-education/

Fienen, M. (2010, May 17). *Best of the mobile higher ed Web.* Retrieved July 14, 2010, from .eduGuru: http://doteduguru.com/id5154-best-of-the-mobile-higher-ed-web.html

Fini, A. (2009). The technological dimension of a massive open online course: The case of the CCK08 course tools. *The International Review of Research in Open and Distance Learning 10*(5).

Flanagan, N. (2008, March 12). *Teacher in a strange land.* Retrieved January 13, 2009, from Teacher Leaders: http://teacherleaders.typepad.com/teacher_in_a_strange_land/2008/03/luddite-lite.html

Fortt, J. (2008, December 24). *Tech's hope in 2009—or curse?* Retrieved June 20, 2010, from CNNMoney.com: http://money.cnn.com/2008/12/24/technology/fortt_netbooks.fortune/index.htm

Fosnot, C. T. (2005). *Constructivism: Theory, perspectives, and practice* (2nd ed.). New York: Teachers College Press.

Free Dictionary. (2010). *Avatar.* Retrieved July 9, 2010, from http://www.thefreedictionary.com/avatar

Frey, C. (2008, September 24). *VUE provides a rich environment for visualizing, presenting information.* Retrieved August 14, 2010, from Mind Mapping Software Blog: http://mindmappingsoftwareblog.com/vue/

Garber, K. (2008, February 28). *Q&A: Susan Jacoby: The author of "The Age of American Unreason" talks about America's infotainment culture.* Retrieved November 1, 2008, from USNews.com: http://www.usnews.com/articles/news/national/2008/02/28/qa-susan-jacoby.html

Gary, L. (2008, June 12). *The five stages of early adopter behavior.* Retrieved February 4, 2009, from http://www.louisgray.com/live/2008/06/five-stages-of-early-adopter-behavior.html

Gee, J. P. (2003). *What video games have to teach us about learning and literacy.* New York: Palgrave Macmillan.

Gibson, W. (1988). *Mona Lisa overdrive.* New York: Bantam.

Giles, J. (2005). Special report: Internet encyclopedias go head to head. *Nature, 438,* 900–901.

Girvan, C., & Savage, T. (2010). Identifying an appropriate pedagogy for virtual worlds: A communal constructivism case study. *Computers & Education 55*(1), 342–349.

Gladwell, M. (2000). *The tipping point.* Boston: Little, Brown.

GrabStats. (2010). *Video game statistics.* Retrieved July 5, 2010, from http://www
.grabstats.com/statcategorymain.asp?StatCatID = 13

Grapevine Talk. (2010, July 28). *GrapevineTalk homepage.* Retrieved July 28,
2010, from http://grapevinetalk.com/index.html

Gruener, W. (2009, July 17). *Nintendo Wii surrenders market share in weak game
console market.* Retrieved August 20, 2009, from TGDaily.com: http://www.tg
daily.com/trendwatch-features/43289-nintendo-wii-surrenders-market-share-
in-weak-game-console-market

Guess, A. (2008, June 10). *Finished with your exam? Good. Now share it.* Retrieved
February 19, 2009, from InsideHigherEd.com: http://www.insidehighered
.com/news/2008/06/10/postyourtest

Guild Wars. (2007, December 19). *Press release.* Retrieved July 10, 2010, from
http://www.guildwars.com/events/press/releases/pressrelease-2007-12-19.php

Gül, L. F., Gu, N., & Williams, A. (2008). Virtual worlds as a constructivist
learning platform: Evaluations of 3D virtual worlds on design teaching and
learning. *ITcon: Virtual and Augmented Reality in Design and Construction*
(Special Issue), 13, 578–593.

Hamilton, A. L. (2008). *IndieAuthor guide to publishing with Amazon's digital text
platform and MS Word 2003 or higher.* Independent Author Series V 1.0.

Hamilton, J. (2008, October 2). *Think you're multitasking? Think again.* Retrieved
September 18, 2010, from NPR.org: http://www.npr.org/templates/story/story
.php?storyId = 95256794

Harding-Rolls, P. (2009). *Subscription MMOGs: Life beyond World of Warcraft.*
Retrieved July 1, 2010, from Screen Digest: http://www.screendigest.com/
news/gi-270309-PHR/view.html

Hargadon, S. (2010, July 26). *World of Warcraft and learning with teens.* Retrieved
August 1, 2010, from Infinite Thinking Machine: http://blog.infinitethinking
.org/2010/07/world-of-warcraft-and-learning-with.html

Harvey, M. (2010, May 15). *Microsoft moves into "cloud" computing.* Retrieved
May 25, 2010, from Times Online: http://business.timesonline.co.uk/tol/busi
ness/industry_sectors/technology/article7124530.ece

Hayes, T. (2008). *Jump point.* New York: McGraw-Hill.

Heather. (2004, May 27). *Aiming for communal constructivism in a wiki environment.* Retrieved September 14, 2009, from Kairosnews: http://kairosnews.org/
node/3809

Heeks, R. (2008). Meet Marty Cooper—the inventor of the mobile phone. *BBC*
41(6), 26–33.

Heppell, S. (2007, May 1). Foreword. In Popat, K., *Virtually there: Learning platforms* [Print booklet accompanying motion picture DVD]. North Lincoln-
shire, UK: Yorkshire and Humber Grid for Learning Foundation.

Holland, W., Jenkins, H., & Squire, K. (2003). Theory by design. In B. Perron &
M. Wolf (Ed.), *Video game theory* (pp. 25–46). New York: Routledge.

Hughes, T. P. (2004). *Human-built world: How to think about technology and culture.* Chicago: University of Chicago.

The Innovative Educator. (2008, October 12). *5 things you can do to begin developing your personal learning network.* Retrieved June 10, 2009, from http://theinnovativeeducator.blogspot.com/2008/04/5-things-you-can-do-to-begin-developing.html

Jacoby, S. (2008). *The age of American unreason.* New York: Pantheon Books.

Jaschik, S. (2009a, May 7). *Blackboard buys Angel.* Retrieved July 5, 2010, from Inside Higher Ed: http://www.insidehighered.com/news/2009/05/07/bb

Jaschik, S. (2009b, January 8). *Online social networking on campus.* Retrieved June 5, 2010, from InsideHigherEd: http://www.insidehighered.com/news/2009/01/08/network#Comments

Jenkins, H. (2006). *Convergence culture: Where old and new media collide.* New York: New York University Press.

Johnson, G. M. (2008). *Instructionism and constructivisim: Reconciling two very good ideas.* Edmonton, AB: Grant MacEwan College.

Karp, S. (2006, July 26). *The long tail debate overlooks the snowball effect.* Retrieved January 23, 2009, from Publishing 2.0: The (r)Evolution of Media: http://publishing2.com/2006/07/26/the-long-tail-debate-overlooks-the-snowball-effect/

Kelly, K. (1994). *Out of control.* New York: Basic Books.

Kelly, K. (2006, May 14). *Scan this book!* Retrieved April 22, 2008, from New York Times Magazine: http://www.nytimes.com/2006/05/14/magazine/14publishing.html?_r = 1&oref = slogin&pagewanted = all"\o

Kerr, B. (2006, December 26). *A challenge to connectivism.* Retrieved August 2, 2010, from http://billkerr2.blogspot.com/2006/12/challenge-to-connectivism.html

Kim, T., & Axelrod, S. (2005). Direct instruction: An educators' guide and a plea for action. *The Behavior Analyst Today 6*(2), 111.

King, K. P. (2007). *Podcasting for teachers: Using a new technology to revolutionize teaching and learning* (2nd rev. ed.). Charlotte, NC: Information Age Publishing.

Kroski, E. (2005, December 7). *The hive mind: Folksonomies and user-based tagging.* Retrieved August 1, 2010, from InfoTangle: http://infotangle.blogsome.com/2005/12/07/the-hive-mind-folksonomies-and-user-based-tagging/

Kunz, P. (2004). The next generation of learning management system (LMS): Requirements from a constructivist perspective. In L. Cantoni & C. McLoughlin (Eds.), *Proceedings of World Conference on Educational Multimedia, Hypermedia and Telecommunications* (pp. 300–307). Chesapeake, VA: AACE.

Larson. (1984). [*The valley that was.*] Unpublished collection of material relating to the towns flooded by the Tuttle Dam, Hale Library 5th Floor, Kansas State University, Manhattan, KS.

Laxmisan, A., Hakimzada, F., & Sayan, O. R. (2007). The multitasking clinician: Decision-making and cognitive demand during and after team handoffs in emergency care. *International Journal of Medical Informatics 76*(11), 801–811.

Lebert, M. (2004, June 21). *Michael Hart: Changing the world through e-books.* Retrieved July 12, 2010, from Project Gutenberg: http://pge.rastko.net/about/marie_lebert

Lendino, J. (2010, June 22). *Skype 2.0 (iOS).* Retrieved July 9, 2010, from PC Magazine: http://www.pcmag.com/article2/0,2817,2365441,00.asp

Leslie, S. (2007, October 29). *Your favourite "Loosely Coupled Teaching" example?* Retrieved June 10, 2009, from EdTechPost: http://www.edtechpost.ca/word press/2007/10/29/best-loosely-coupled-teaching-examples/

Lessig, L. (2004). *Free culture.* New York: Penguin Press.

Li, S. (2010, June 4). *"Augmented Reality" on Smartphones brings teaching down to earth.* Retrieved July 10, 2010, from Chronicle of Higher Ed: http://chronicle.com/article/Augmented-Reality-on/65991/

Linden Labs. (2008). *Second Life demographics.* Retrieved November 2008 from SecondLife.com: http://secondlife.com/statistics/economy-data.php

LinkedIn. (2008). *About us.* Retrieved July 11, 2010, from http://press.linkedin.com/about

Livingstone, A. (2009). *The revolution no one noticed: Mobile phones and multi-mobile services in higher education. EDUCAUSE Quarterly 32*(1). Retrieved July 9, 2010, from http://www.educause.edu/EDUCAUSE + Quarterly/EDUCAUSE QuarterlyMagazineVolum/TheRevolutionNoOneNoticedMobil/163866

Manhattan Town Center. (2008). *Manhattan town center info.* Retrieved July 15, 2008, from http://www.manhattantowncenter.com/info/information.cfm

Mansfield, H. (2009, May). *10 Twitter tips for higher education.* Retrieved July 12, 2010, from University Business: http://www.universitybusiness.com/viewarticle.aspx?articleid = 1285

Mansfield, R. (2008). *How to do everything with Second Life.* New York: McGraw Hill.

Martyn, M. (2007). Clickers in the classroom: An active learning approach. *EDUCAUSE Quarterly, 30*(2). Retrieved from http://www.educause.edu/EDUCAUSE + Quarterly/EDUCAUSEQuarterlyMagazineVolum/ClickersintheClassroom AnActive/157458

McCarthy, C. (2010, April 15). *Andreessen-founded Ning cuts staff, free service.* Retrieved May 11, 2010, from CNet News: http://news.cnet.com/8301–13577_ 3-20002611-36.html

McHaney, R. (1991). *Computer simulation: A practical perspective.* San Diego: Academic Press.

McHaney, R. (2009a, March). *Implementation of ELATEwiki. EDUCAUSE Quarterly, 32*(4). Retrieved July 10, 2010, from http://www.educause.edu/EDU CAUSE + Quarterly/EDUCAUSEQuarterlyMagazineVolum/Implementation ofELATEwiki/192968

McHaney, R. W. (2009b). *Understanding computer simulation.* Retrieved May 3, 2010, from BookBooN: http://bookboon.com/us/textbooks/it/understanding

McManus, D. A. (2001). The two paradigms of education and the peer review of teaching. *NAGT Journal of Geoscience Education, 49*(6), 423–434.

MediaWiki. (2010, June 13). *How does MediaWiki work?* Retrieved July 12, 2010, from http://www.mediawiki.org/wiki/How_does_MediaWiki_work%3F

Messina, C. (2008). Coworking on *NPR's Marketplace* (May 22). Coworking Community Blog. Retrieved from http://blog.coworking.info/2008/05/22/co working-on-nprs-marketplace/

Microsoft. (2010, May 3). *Producer download page.* Retrieved July 28, 2010, from http://www.microsoft.com/downloads/details.aspx?FamilyID = 1B3C76D5-FC75-4F99-94BC-784919468E73&displaylang = en

Miller, A. (1949). *Death of a salesman* (Broadway play). New York: Viking Press.

MIT. (2010, August). *MIT free online courses.* Retrieved August 2, 2010, from http://ocw.mit.edu/courses

MLearning Website. (2010). *The International Association for Mobile Learning (IAMLearn).* Retrieved July 4, 2010, from http://mlearning.noe-kaleido scope.org

Moodle. (2010a). *Moodle features.* Retrieved July 8, 2010, from http://docs .moodle.org/en/Features

Moodle. (2010b). *Moodle statistics.* Retrieved July 9, 2010, from http://moodle .org/stats/

MySpace. (2010, July 10). *MySpace home page.* Retrieved July 10, 2010, from http://www.MySpace.com

Nagal, D. (2010, April 30). *Microsoft releases free classroom interaction add-on for PowerPoint.* Retrieved May 11, 2010, from The Journal: Transforming Education Through Technology: http://thejournal.com/articles/2010/04/30/micro soft-releases-free-classroom-interaction-add-on-for-powerpoint.aspx

Netvibes. (2010, July 30). *About.* Retrieved July 30, 2010, from http://about .netvibes.com

Newitz, A. (2005, March). *Adam Curry wants to make you an iPod radio star.* Retrieved December 12, 2008, from Wired.com: http://www.wired.com/ wired/archive/13.03/curry.html?tw = wn_tophead_5

Nicholas, A. J., & Lewis, J. K. (2008). Millennial attitudes toward books and e-books. *The International Journal of the Book, 5*(2), 81–92.

Nokia. (1996, September 19). *Press release: Nokia unveils world's first all-in-one communicator for the Americas.* Retrieved July 4, 2010, from http://www.nokia .com/press/press-releases/archive/archiveshowpressrelease?news id = 776253

Noor, A. K. (2009, November). *Disruption from the virtual world.* Retrieved July 10, 2010, from Mechanical Engineering Magazine: http://memagazine.asme .org/Articles/2009/November/Disruption_from_Virtual_World.cfm

Notari, M. (2006). How to use a wiki in education: "Wiki based effective constructive learning." In *Proceedings of the 2006 international symposium on Wikis* (WikiSym '06) (pp. 131–132). Odense, Denmark: ACM.

Oblinger, D. (2003). Boomers, Gen-Xers and millennials: Understanding the new students. *EDUCAUSE Review, 38*(4), 37–47.

Oblinger, D. G., & Oblinger, J. L. (2005). *Educating the net generation.* Retrieved from http://www.educause.edu/educatingthenetgen

OpenCourseWare (OCW) Consortium. (2008). *About the OCW.* Retrieved October 16, 2008, from http://ocw.itesm.mx/index.php?option = com_content& task = view&id = 4&Itemid = 5&lang = us

OpenCourseWare (OCW) Consortium. (2010, August). *About us.* Retrieved August 6, 2010, from http://www.ocwconsortium.org/aboutus

Ophir, E., Nass, C., & Wagner, A. D. (2010). Cognitive control in media multitaskers. *Proceedings of the National Academy of Sciences of the United States of America* [PDF] (pp. 15583–15587). Retrieved from http://www.pnas.org/ content/106/37/15583.full.pdf + html

Organization, S. L. (2008). *Service learning organization homepage.* Retrieved January 9, 2009, from ServiceLearning.org: http://www.servicelearning.org

Osborn, J. J. (1971). *The paper chase.* Boston: Houghton Mifflin.

Palfrey, J., & Gasser, U. (2008). *Born digital.* New York: Basic Books.

Palincsar, A. (1998). Social constructivist perspectives on teaching and learning. *Annual Review of Psychology, 49*, 345–375.

Park, J. (2010, February 23). *Flat world knowledge launches open textbook internship program.* Retrieved May 13, 2010, from Creative Commons News: http:// creativecommons.org/weblog/entry/20805

Parker, K. R., & Chao, J. T. (2007). Wiki as a teaching tool. *Interdisciplinary Journal of Knowledge and Learning Objects, 3*, 57–72.

PBWorks. (2010). *PBWorks press room.* Retrieved July 12, 2010, from http://pb works.com/content/pressroom

PCMag.com. (2010a). Amaras law. In *PCMag.com Encyclopedia.* Retrieved July 9, 2010, from http://www.pcmag.com/encyclopedia_term/0,2542,t = Amaras + law&i = 37701,00.asp

PCMag.com. (2010b). Tablet computer. In *PCMag.com Encyclopedia.* Retrieved July 9, 2010, from http://www.pcmag.com/encyclopedia_term/0,2542,t = tab let + computer&i = 52520,0.asp

Peck, A. (2010, April 21). *Will the iPad revolutionize higher education?* Retrieved July 10, 2010, from Think Magazine: http://thinksb.com/2010/04/will-the-ipad-revolutionize-higher-education

Peirano, E. (2010, May 21). *College 2.0.* Retrieved May 30, 2010, from Ning.com: http://college2.ning.com

Petzinger, T. (1999). *The new pioneers: The men and women who are transforming the workplace and marketplace.* New York: Simon & Schuster.

Pew Research Center. (2010). *Millennials portrait of generation next: Confident. Connected. Open to change.* Retrieved from http://pewsocialtrends.org/files/2010/10/millennials-confident-connected-open-to-change.pdf

Pink, D. H. (2007, August 21). *Pecha Kucha: Get to the PowerPoint in 20 slides then sit the hell down.* Retrieved July 25, 2010, from Wired.com: http://www.wired.com/techbiz/media/magazine/15-09/st_pechakucha#

Prensky, M. (2001). Digital natives, digital immigrants. *On the Horizon 9*(5). Retrieved from http://www.marcprensky.com/writing/Prensky%20-%20Digital%20Natives,%20Digital%20Immigrants%20-%20Part1.pdf

ProfCast. (2010, July 28). *ProfCast home page.* Retrieved July 28, 2010, from http://www.profcast.com/public/index.php

Qoop. (2008, October 18). *About us.* Retrieved October 18, 2008, from http://www.qoop.com/about/about.php

Rheingold, H. (1991). *Virtual reality.* New York: Simon & Schuster.

Richardson, D. C. (2008, December). *News releases.* Retrieved December 20, 2008, from Kansas State University: http://www.k-state.edu/media/newsreleases/dec08/richardsonoped122908.html

Richardson, W. (2006). *Blogs, wikis, podcasts and other power Web tools for the classroom.* Thousand Oaks, CA: Corwin Press.

Rizi, F. (2007). Rethinking educational aims in an era of globalization. In P. Hershock, M. Mason, & J. N. Hawkins, *CERC* (Ed.), *Studies in Comparative Education 20, Changing Education: Leadership, Innovation and Development in a Globalizing Asia Pacific* (pp. 63–91). Netherlands: Springer.

Rogers, E. (1995). *Diffusion of innovations (DOI).* New York: Free Press.

Ruppenthal, A. (2010, May 13). *College coaches finding ways to monitor athletes' social networking activity.* Retrieved July 11, 2010, from Missourian: http://www.columbiamissourian.com/stories/2010/05/13/college-coaches-finding-ways-monitor-athletes-social-networking-activity/

Russell, G., & Holkner, B. (2000). Virtual schools. *Futures, 32,* 887–897.

Sampson, P. (2010, July). *LectureTools homepage.* Retrieved July 7, 2010, from LectureTools: http://www.lecturetools.org

Sarno, D. (2010, January 29). *Apple confirms 3G VoIP apps on iPad, iPhone, iPod Touch; Skype is waiting.* Retrieved July 9, 2010, from Los Angeles Times Business: http://latimesblogs.latimes.com/technology/2010/01/apple-confirms-3g-voip-apps-on-ipad-iphone-ipod-touch-skype-is-waiting.html

Schrock, K. (2010). *Teacher's helpers: Digital gadgets.* Retrieved June 14, 2010, from Discovery Education: http://school.discoveryeducation.com/schrockguide/gadgets.html

Scribd. (2010, May 13). *Scribd homepage.* Retrieved May 13, 2010, from http://www.scribd.com

Dr. Sears. (2008). *Radio-Allergo-Sorbent Test.* Retrieved October 20, 2008, from http://www.askdrsears.com/html/4/T041800.asp

Second Life. (2010). *Second Life homepage.* Retrieved July 5, 2010, from http://secondlife.com

Seidensticker, B. (2006). *FutureHype: The myths of technology change.* San Francisco: Berrett-Koehler.

Seitzinger, J. (2006, July 31). Be constructive: Blogs, podcasts, and wikis as constructivist learning tools. *Learning Solutions,* 1–16.

Siemens, G. (2004, December 12). *Connectivism: A learning theory for the digital age.* Retrieved from *elearnspace:* http://www.elearnspace.org/Articles/connectivism.htm

Siemens, G. (2006). *Knowing knowledge.* Retrieved from http://www.lulu.com/product/paperback/knowing-knowledge/545031

Siemens, G. (2008, August 6). *The unique ideas in connectivism.* Retrieved July 20, 2010, from Connectivism: Networked and Social Learning: http://www.connectivism.ca/?m = 200808

Skype. (2010, August 20). *About Skype.* Retrieved August 24, 2010, from http://about.skype.com/

SL Education. (2007). *Educational uses of Second Life.* Retrieved June 19, 2008, from http://sleducation.wikispaces.com/educationaluses

Solomon, G., & Schrum, L. (2007). *Web 2.0: New tools, new schools.* Eugene, OR: International Society for Technology in Education.

Sony. (2009, August 25). *Extra, extra: Sony's daily edition rounds out new line of digital readers.* Retrieved April 24, 2010, from Sony Electronics News & Information: http://news.sel.sony.com/en/press_room/consumer/computer_peripheral/e_book/release/41492.html

Sony Online Entertainment. (2010). *EverQuest universe.* Retrieved July 5, 2010, from http://www.everquest.com

Squire, K. (2006). From content to context: Videogames as designed experience. *Educational Researcher, 35*(8), 19–29.

Stephenson, N. (1992). *Snow crash.* New York: Bantam Spectra.

Stiles, M. (2007, March). Death of the VLE? A challenge to a new orthodoxy. *Serials 20*(1), 31–36.

Stolarczyk, M. (2008). *The Long Tail—Can we find a place for it in the logistics world?* Retrieved July 4, 2010, from the Global Institute of Logistics: http://www.globeinst.org/news/news.php?id = 9091

Stone, L. (2008). *Continuous partial attention.* Retrieved October 9, 2008, from Continuous Partial Attention: http://continuouspartialattention.jot.com

Stone, L. (2009, December 5). *Why managing vulnerability and reputation is more important than ever before.* Retrieved July 7, 2010, from http://lindastone.net

Sweetman, C., & Sweetman, L. (2005). *What to eat when you can't eat anything: The complete allergy cookbook.* Toronto: Hushion House Publishing Ltd.

Tan, K. C., & Koh, T. S. (2008). The use of Web 2.0 technologies in school science. *SSR, 90*(330), 113–117.

Tashne, J., Riedl, R., & Bronack, S. (2005). *Virtual worlds: Further development of Web-based teaching.* Retrieved July 5, 2010, from Bronack.net: http://bronack.net/pubs/tashnerEtAl-2005.pdf

TeachersTeachingTeachers. (2008). *About.* Retrieved July 10, 2010, from http://teachersteachingteachers.org/?page_id=2

Techsmith. (2010, July 27). *Techsmith.com.* Retrieved July 27, 2010, from Camtasia Studio: http://www.techsmith.com/camtasia.asp

Textbook Revolution. (2010, May 13). *Textbook Revolution home page.* Retrieved May 13, 2010, from http://textbookrevolution.org/index.php/Main_Page

Thomann, A. (2006, June 9). *Skype—A Baltic success story.* Retrieved September 15, 2010, from Credit Suisse eMagazine: http://emagazine.credit-suisse.com/app/article/index.cfm?fuseaction=OpenArticle&aoid=163167&coid=7805&lang=EN

Thomas, A. (2007). *Youth online: Identity and literacy in the digital age.* New York: Peter Lang.

Tierney, W. G., & Hentschke, G. C. (2007). *New players, different game: Understanding the rise of for-profit colleges and universities.* Baltimore: The Johns Hopkins University Press.

Timpane, J. (2010, July 7). *E-readers are on the rise thanks to older readers.* Retrieved July 12, 2010, from News Tribune: http://www.thenewstribune.com/2010/07/07/1255056/e-readers-are-on-the-rise-thanks.html

Torres, C. (2008, September 10). *Working alone sucks. Stop it.* Retrieved February 5, 2009, from Digital Nomads: http://www.digitalnomads.com/2008/09/10/work-alone-sucks-stop-it

Tremblay, E. (2010). Educating the mobile generation—using personal cell phones as audience response systems in post-secondary science teaching. *Journal of Computers in Mathematics and Science Teaching, 29*(2), 217–227.

Tufts University. (2008). *About VUE.* Retrieved August 14, 2010, from http://vue.tufts.edu/about/index.cfm

Vance, A., & Richtel, M. (2009, April 1). *Light and cheap, netbooks are poised to reshape PC industry.* Retrieved May 18, 2010, from New York Times: http://www.nytimes.com/2009/04/02/technology/02netbooks.html?_r=1

Vascellaro, J. E., & Trachtenberg, J. A. (2010, May 4). *Google readies its e-book plan, bringing in a new sales approach.* Retrieved July 10, 2010, from Wall Street Journal: http://online.wsj.com/article/SB10001424052748703866704575224232417931818.html?KEYWORDS=google

Virtual Worlds Review. (2008). *What is a virtual world?* Retrieved December 28, 2008, from http://www.virtualworldsreview.com/info/whatis.shtml

VoiceThread. (2010, July 28). *About VoiceThread.* Retrieved July 28, 2010, from http://voicethread.com/about/

Wakefield, J. F. (1998, June 12–13). *A brief history of textbooks: Where have we been all these years?* Paper presented at the Meeting of the Text and Academic Authors, St. Petersburg, FL.

Ward, J. R. (2010, May 13). *History of pen computing: Annotated bibliography in on-line character recognition and pen computing.* Retrieved July 9, 2010, from Erols.com: http://users.erols.com/rwservices/pens/biblio10.html#Microsoft06i

Watson, S. (2008). *How podcasting works.* Retrieved December 8, 2008, from How Stuff Works: http://computer.howstuffworks.com/podcasting.htm

Wauters, R. (2009, April 20). *Prezi is the coolest online presentation tool I've ever seen.* Retrieved July 25, 2010, from TechCrunch: http://techcrunch.com/2009/04/20/prezi-is-the-coolest-online-presentation-tool-ive-ever-seen/

WayBackMachine. (2008). *WayBackMachine.* Retrieved July 5, 2010, from Archive.org: http://www.archive.org/web/web.php

Weimer, M. (2002). *Learner-centered teaching: Five key changes to practice.* San Francisco, CA: Jossey-Bass.

Weir, D. (2009, August). *Flat world knowledge: A disruptive business model.* Retrieved May 13, 2010, from BNET: http://industry.bnet.com/media/10003790/flat-world-knowledge-a-disruptive-business-model/

Wesch, M. (2007, January 31). *Web 2.0 . . . The machine is us/ing us.* Retrieved October 31, 2008, from YouTube.com: http://youtube.com/watch?v = 6gm P4nk0EOE

Wesch, M. (2008, January 24). *YouTube in/on/of/for the classroom.* Presented at the Instructional Design and Technology Roundtable, Kansas State University, Manhattan, KS.

Wikidot. (2009). *Wikidot in education.* Retrieved September 15, 2010, from http://www.wikidot.com/learnmore:education

Wikidot. (2010, September 15). *About Wikidot.* Retrieved September 15, 2010, from http://www.wikidot.com/about/

Wikipedia. (2008a). *Twitter.* Retrieved December 3, 2008, from http://en.wikipedia.org

Wikipedia. (2008b). *Wikipedia.* Retrieved December 3, 2008, from http://en.wikipedia.org

Wikipedia. (2010a). *ActiveWorlds.* Retrieved July 9, 2010, from http://en.wikipedia.org/wiki/Active_Worlds

Wikipedia. (2010b). *Computer multitasking.* Retrieved September 2010, from http://en.wikipedia.org/wiki/Computer_multitasking

Wikipedia. (2010c). *Deviant art.* Retrieved July 6, 2010, from http://en.wikipedia.org/wiki/DeviantArt

Wikipedia. (2010d). *Free culture movement.* Retrieved July 6, 2010, from http://en.wikipedia.org/wiki/Free_Culture_Movement

Wikipedia. (2010e). *The long tail.* Retrieved July 4, 2010, from http://en.wikipedia.org/wiki/The_Long_Tail

Wikipedia. (2010f). *Techological convergence.* Retrieved July 4, 2010, from http://en.wikipedia.org/wiki/Technological_convergence

Wildstrom, S. H. (2001, November 30). *Handspring's breakthrough hybrid.* Retrieved July 5, 2010, from Bloomberg Businessweek: http://www.businessweek.com/bwdaily/dnflash/nov2001/nf20011129_0157.htm

Wimba. (2010, July 28). *Wimba classroom.* Retrieved July 28, 2010, from http://www.wimba.com/products/wimba_classroom

World of Warcraft. (2010). *Info.* Retrieved July 10, 2010, from http://www.worldofwarcraft.com/info/basics/guide.html

Wortham, J. (2007, December). *After 10 years of blogs, the future's brighter than ever.* Retrieved November 22, 2008, from Wired.com: http://www.wired.com/entertainment/theweb/news/2007/12/blog_anniversary

WriteWork. (2010). *WriteWork.* Retrieved September 15, 2010, from http://www.writework.com

Young, J. (2008, January 28). *A professor's tips for using Twitter in the classroom.* Retrieved May 11, 2010, from Chronicle of Higher Ed: Wired Campus: http://chronicle.com/blogPost/A-Professor-s-Tips-for-Using/3643

Young, J. R. (2009, June 12). 6 lessons one campus learned about e-textbooks. *Chronicle of Higher Education, 55*(39), A18.

Young, J. (2010, March 22). *Blackboard bets on mobile future, but no iPad app yet.* Retrieved July 9, 2010, from Chronicle of Higher Education: http://chronicle.com/blogPost/Blackboard-Bets-on-Mobile/21949/

APPENDIX
Absolutes for Teaching Excellence

1) **It's not about you—it's about them!** Our success is measured by our students. We don't have to prove ourselves and demonstrate we are the smartest person in the room. Let *them* succeed.

2) **Find your voice and stick with it.** You can't teach exactly like that favorite teacher from grad school. You have your own style. Do what comes naturally and build on it. Students are forgiving. Don't take yourself too seriously when life reaches out and bites you!

3) **Insert your life into the class in small meaningful doses.** Create a sense of community and make the class safe for discussion.

4) **Remain current and add value** to the sources your students use as class reference material.

5) **Be fair and consistent.** Be respectful to everyone even those you can't stand. Be honest.

6) **Develop a method of time management**—Use virtual office hours; Create blocks of uninterrupted work time in your schedule. Set priorities in line with what you want to accomplish. Don't let email rule your days!

7) **Use technology where it makes sense.**

8) **Make *someone* a project each semester.** But sure to have a clear exit strategy before you begin. You want to integrate them into the learning process, not make them dependent on you!

INDEX

Also available from Stylus

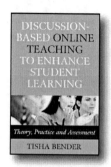

Discussion-Based Online Teaching to Enhance Student Learning
Theory, Practice and Assessment
Tisha Bender

"I . . . recommend Bender's book as an addition to the professional library of anyone hoping to implement (or improve) online discussion-based teaching and learning."—*The American Journal of Distance Education*

"Its numerous practical suggestions for creating and managing an exciting on-line learning experience make this a valuable reference for both experienced and novice educators."—*Nursing Education Perspectives*

Helping Students Learn in a Learner-Centered Environment
A Guide to Facilitating Learning in Higher Education
Terry Doyle
Foreword by John Tagg

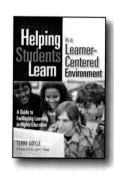

"I see this book as a great read for experienced faculty who want to figure out a new way to construct a less lecture-based classroom environment, and for new faculty who need tips on how to teach well in a learner-centered environment. I have been teaching for 20 years and have been a faculty developer for the past 10 and, even with all of that experience, I still learned several things in reading this book." —*Todd Zakrajsek, Director of the Faculty Center for Innovative Teaching at Central Michigan University*

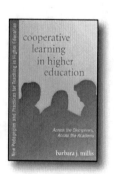

Cooperative Learning in Higher Education
Across the Disciplines, Across the Academy
Edited by Barbara Millis
Foreword by James Rhem
NEW PEDAGOGIES AND PRACTICES FOR TEACHING IN HIGHER EDUCATION SERIES

Research has identified cooperative learning as one of the ten High Impact Practices that improve student learning.

If you've been interested in cooperative learning, but wondered how it would work in your discipline, this book provides the necessary theory, and a wide range of concrete examples.

Experienced users of cooperative learning demonstrate how they use it in settings as varied as a developmental mathematics course at a community college, and graduate courses in history and the sciences, and how it works in small and large classes, as well as in hybrid and online environments. The authors describe the application of cooperative learning in biology, economics, educational psychology, financial accounting, general chemistry, and literature at remedial, introductory, and graduate levels.

22883 Quicksilver Drive
Sterling, VA 20166-2102

Subscribe to our e-mail alerts: www.Styluspub.com